Reading
Nathalie Sarraute

Dialogue and Distance

EMER O'BEIRNE

CLARENDON PRESS · OXFORD

OXFORD
UNIVERSITY PRESS

Great Clarendon Street, Oxford OX2 6DP

Oxford University Press is a department of the University of Oxford.
It furthers the University's objective of excellence in research, scholarship,
and education by publishing worldwide in

Oxford New York

Athens Auckland Bangkok Bogotá Buenos Aires Calcutta
Cape Town Chennai Dar es Salaam Delhi Florence Hong Kong Istanbul
Karachi Kuala Lumpur Madrid Melbourne Mexico City Mumbai
Nairobi Paris São Paulo Singapore Taipei Tokyo Toronto Warsaw

with associated companies in Berlin Ibadan

Oxford is a registered trade mark of Oxford University Press
in the UK and in certain other countries

Published in the United States
by Oxford University Press Inc., New York

British Library Cataloguing in Publication Data

Data available

Library of Congress Cataloging in Publication Data

Data available

ISBN 0–19–815985–4

1 3 5 7 9 10 8 6 4 2

Typeset in Baskerville
by Jayvee, Trivandrum, India
Printed in Great Britain
on acid-free paper by
Bookcraft Ltd.,
Midsomer Norton, Somerset

ACKNOWLEDGEMENTS

I owe a debt of gratitude to several people and institutions for help in the writing of this study. The D.Phil. thesis on which it is based was supervised by Ann Jefferson (New College, Oxford), for whose encouragement and critical interest I am very grateful. Nathalie Sarraute was kind enough to accord me interviews on two occasions. Jean-Yves Tadié (University of Paris IV) also provided guidance in the early stages, especially regarding my work on irony. Celia Britton and Rhiannon Goldthorpe made valuable comments on the original thesis, while Ronald Truman and the reader of the Oxford Monographs Committee gave time and energy to overseeing revisions. Malcolm Bowie generously read part of the manuscript. The editorial team at Oxford University Press handled the publication process with care and efficiency. In addition, I have received constant support and advice over the years from Barbara Wright of Trinity College Dublin, as well as from other former teachers at Trinity, most notably Eda Sagarra.

I am extremely grateful to the Pirie-Reid Fund (Oxford) which awarded me a three-year postgraduate research scholarship, and to Trinity College Dublin for previously awarding me a Hutchinson Stewart Literary Scholarship. In addition, a bursary from the Oxford-Paris Exchange Programme facilitated research in Paris, as, more recently, did a travel subsidy from Exeter University French Department.

Many thanks to Serge Cohen for kindly granting me permission to reproduce the photograph of Nathalie Sarraute on the cover of this book, and also to Gallimard for permission to reprint passages from Sarraute's works.

Friends and colleagues from Oxford, Paris, Exeter, Dublin, and elsewhere have consistently given help, encouragement, advice, and light relief. Special thanks are due to the following who read parts of the manuscript, tracked down references, photocopied inaccessible articles, or otherwise provided invaluable practical help: Keith Cameron, Stephen Colvin, Emma Kell, Kathleen Micham, Anne Mullen, Maria Sherwood-Smith, Douglas Smith, Sheila Watts, Andrea Williams.

Lastly, I wish to thank my family, and especially my mother, for all the interest, concern, and moral (as well as material) support shown over many years. Thanks too to Richard for sorting out printing problems more than once. This book is in memory of my father, with whom dialogue came to an end too quickly.

CONTENTS

ABBREVIATIONS

References to Nathalie Sarraute's works use the following abbreviations and are to the editions indicated in the Bibliography.

DI	*'disent les imbéciles'* (1976)
E	*Enfance* (1983)
ES	*L'Ère du soupçon* (1956)
EVM	*Entre la vie et la mort* (1968)
FO	*Les Fruits d'or* (1963)
Ici	*Ici* (1995)
M	*Martereau* (1953)
O	*Ouvrez* (1997)
OC	*Œuvres complètes* (1996)
P	*Le Planétarium* (1959)
PI	*Portrait d'un inconnu* (1948)
POPN	*Pour un oui ou pour un non* (1982)
T	*Tropismes* (1939)
Th.	*Théâtre* (1978)
TTP	*Tu ne t'aimes pas* (1989)
UP	*L'Usage de la parole* (1980)
VE	*Vous les entendez?* (1972)

INTRODUCTION

Few living writers can embody as well as does Nathalie Sarraute the evolution of French literature, specifically (though not solely) of the novel, across the whole of the twentieth century. Born in 1900, she is as old as the century itself and has been writing for a full two-thirds of it (she began her first collection of short prose texts, *Tropismes*, in 1932 and published her latest work, *Ouvrez*, in 1997). Between the 1940s and early 1970s her critical essays and public lectures, pursuing lines of enquiry already opened up by her novels, took issue with the relationship of fiction to reality, the ever-changing nature of that reality, and the imperative for the novelist to create new modes of representation to take account of the constant transformations in our understanding of ourselves and of the world around us. Profoundly ingrained in her writing is her response, as reader, to those Modernist writers whose novels shaped contemporary fiction, and whom of course she first read as contemporaries: above all, Proust, Joyce, and Woolf (among nineteenth-century precursors she emphasizes Dostoevsky and—to a limited extent—Flaubert). Thus the publication by Gallimard in 1996 of her *Œuvres complètes* in the renowned Pléiade series offers a unique retrospective on one prominent writer's engagements with, and contribution to, the development of fiction throughout this century. (They are of course already incomplete, for they preceded the publication of *Ouvrez* in late 1997.) Germaine Brée sums that contribution up in a recent essay:

Dans sa 'traversée du siècle', Nathalie Sarraute a confronté toutes les grandes questions qui se sont posées dans le domaine du roman: nature du 'sujet' du 'moi et de l'autre', de la narration et de sa mise en œuvre dans l'écriture; et, sans recours à une théorie, elle les a inscrites dans son œuvre, calmement, un peu ironiquement bien entendu, mais sans arrogance. (Brée 1996: 42)

These 'great questions'—the nature of the self, especially in its relations with others, and the kind of narration which can take account of it—are integral to my study, over the coming pages, of the role of dialogue in Nathalie Sarraute's prose works. Dialogue, moreover, is considered not only as it features within those works but also as it is initiated across them, with their readers.[1] Sarraute herself is a lucid and sensitive reader of everything from the most demanding Modernist prose to the most banal snippet of conversation; it is perhaps not surprising, therefore, that she should focus as intensely as she does on the anticipated reading of her own works, even in the process of writing them.

The aspect of dialogue with which I begin is its demonstration of the way meaning is constituted not through expression alone but through the response of an addressee. Viewing meaning in this way seems to offer a solution to the ironic predicament of the individual whose language, as a conventional, transindividual structure, fails to express a unique personal truth. This awareness of the expressive inadequacy of language is at the heart of Romantic irony; however, as I shall argue in Chapter 1, the German Romantic thinker Friedrich Schlegel himself stressed the way the ironic utterance's dialogic nature can overcome that inadequacy, by actively enlisting its addressee to help constitute a meaning greater than what the words alone articulate. This presentation of irony as a constructive, dialogic mode of communication may seem surprising, for it is generally portrayed as an instrument of criticism or even destruction, applied to another's discourse or to one's own. Yet thinking about dialogue and irony in terms of each other is not only valid but fruitful. On the one hand, it makes evident the nature of the power attributed to dialogue as that of transcending the (ironic) limits of language. Beyond that, a deeper understanding of the workings of dialogue, such as that offered by the readings of Nathalie Sarraute's prose writings which I propose here, will complicate but hopefully also refine our understanding of irony too, specifically as it concerns the idea of reading as transcending the limitations of the author's self-expression.

In so far as my exploration of dialogue is developed in the context of Sarraute's work, what results is neither a straightforward theory of dialogue nor a comprehensive critical analysis of her writings. Rather, the relationship between both strands of my argument could itself be described as dialogical. On the one hand, my reading of Sarraute is clearly guided by the notion of dialogue which I develop in the first chapter, and which is itself heavily influenced by

---

[1] I shall gender the reader as male throughout this study, in opposition to Sarraute as author.

Lacan's conception of the linguistic subject and its accession to truth in the psychoanalytic dialogue. Yet on the other, the ways in which Sarraute's texts—which, as Brée puts it, engage with the century's 'great questions' about self and other without subordinating them to a theory—resist assimilation to the Lacanian view of dialogue, will in fact lead to a reassessment of that view. Thus what we have is more a dialogue of theory and writing practice than the mere application of one to the other.

This interaction between both lines of my argument, while mutually enriching, also, however, illustrates what I shall argue to be an equally important but perhaps less positive feature of dialogue: the fact that it takes place across the definition by each participant of the other in his own terms. Reading Sarraute in the light of theoretical works on dialogue thus unavoidably involves some imposition of the terms of one onto the other. However, this tendency is redeemed by being reversible, as in dialogue the roles of addressor and addressee are constantly reversed. Thus dialogue, while it remains reciprocal, is more complex and even conflictual than the initial consensual conception of it might suggest.

The fact that my reading of Sarraute is guided to some extent by the notion of dialogue which her writing simultaneously helps to elucidate, means that the order in which I approach her texts is not strictly chronological, but corresponds instead to the different stages in my examination of what is involved in dialogue.[2] Thus my suggestion in Chapter 1, that the fragmentation of a monologic authorial narrative into a dialogic structure of interacting, autonomous voices within the text will none the less be unable to evacuate the 'singularity' of authorial control entirely, is developed through readings of *Enfance* (Chapter 2) and *Tu ne t'aimes pas* (Chapter 3). Both of these texts are written entirely in dialogue form, and so appear to take the subversion of narrative control to an

---

[2] This lack of chronology might seem to be a serious issue, especially since on the level of form I emphasize Sarraute's chronological development from the first-person narration of fictional author-figures, through free indirect discourse, to the total dissolution of narratorial unity in the dialogues of *Enfance* and, even more dramatically, *Tu ne t'aimes pas* or *Ouvrez*. However, despite this formal evolution, Sarraute's attitudes towards language, identity, and the relationship of writer and reader to the text which unites them, actually remain remarkably constant throughout her whole writing career. After the publication of *Enfance*, she responded to Pierre Boncenne's observation that 'pour l'essentiel, vous n'avez rien changé depuis votre premier livre', with the comment, 'D'ailleurs, si je voulais faire quelque chose d'autre, je ne le pourrais pas, parce que ça ne m'intéresse pas. Je n'arrive pas à sortir de cet univers qui est le mien' (Sarraute 1983*a*: 88).

extreme, all the more so since the various voices are all identified with the authorial subject whose monologic authority seems thereby to be definitively abolished. Yet I shall argue that, despite appearances, this authority is never entirely forfeited. Language gives rise to the subject, making one's identity a function of one's discourse; for this reason I follow my examination of the way the singular intentionality of the authorial discourse proves impossible to dissolve in *Enfance* by considering the implications of this impossibility for Sarraute's subsequent attempt, in *Tu ne t'aimes pas*, to dissolve her own singular authorial identity through that discourse.

Another point raised in the first chapter, and which is what complicates the idea of dialogue as a moment of linguistic cooperation, is the way published writing exacerbates an alienation of addressor from addressee inherent in all discourse. The impossibility of perfect communication will thus mark dialogue both between individuals and, more intensely, between the written text and its reader.[3] Chapter 4 looks at the way Sarraute represents both relations between individuals and those of a reader to an (unavoidably singular) textual subject. The text–reader relationship is dealt with most explicitly by Sarraute in *Les Fruits d'or*, *Entre la vie et la mort*, and *L'Usage de la parole*; for this reason, Chapter 4 focuses primarily on these works. The closing chapter considers, in the context of theories of reading, the possibility of a text–reader dialogue on terms other than those which Sarraute recommends. In order to relate Sarraute's ideal of aesthetic response to the range of possibilities identified by reader-response criticism, I take the narrator's response to the portrait in *Portrait d'un inconnu* as an illustration of that ideal. Its particular relevance to this discussion is due to the close echoes which its image of the relation to an artwork finds in theories of reading, most notably in those of Wolfgang Iser and Georges Poulet. Finally, the Conclusion explores an increasing trend in Sarraute's late writings (implicit in *Enfance*, explicit in *Tu ne t'aimes pas* or *Ouvrez*) in the context of *Ici*; this is the withdrawal from intersubjective dialogue altogether into the internal universe of the

---

[3] Wolfgang Iser discusses which of the 'discernible conditions that govern interaction generally [. . .] will [. . .] apply to the special text-reader relationship' (1978: 163), and identifies as common to both 'an indeterminate, constitutive blank which underlies all processes of interaction' (p. 167).

self. In *Ici*, indeed, it is not only dialogue with others but language itself which seems to compromise the serenity of the self; yet for all that the value of words is doubted, they testify, for a writer now in her nineties, to the ongoing victory of life over death. Irreducibly linguistic even in its withdrawal from language, the Sarrautean voice maintains a dialogic address to the readers of *Ici*, even if it no longer articulates any desire for an understanding reader. (In *Ouvrez*, too, the irrepressible chatter of the words which populate the private self—sealed off by a *paroi* from the more presentable words exchanged in 'censored' public conversations with others—presents the self's inner world as both a linguistic profusion where words comment on their own and others' connotations, and as a far richer and more authentic place than the space of intersubjective communication: 'Quel bousculade! On n'a jamais été plus nombreux. On dirait qu'on est tous là' (*O* 35).)

Why choose the issue of dialogue in particular as a context in which to read Sarraute? What makes her work seem particularly well suited to such a reading is the fact that the level of lived experience on which she focuses is that of instinctive reactions to other individuals; for her, the essence of human behaviour is the tropism, and the tropism exists as a form of primal reponse to others. Tropistic reality as defined by Sarraute is dramatic, a series of 'drames intérieurs faits d'attaques, de triomphes, de reculs, de défaites, de caresses, de morsures, de viols, de meurtres, d'abandons généreux ou d'humbles soumissions'; what all of these miniature dramas have in common is the fact that 'ils ne peuvent se passer de partenaire' (*ES* 99–100). This other with whom we interact is 'le catalyseur par excellence, l'excitant grâce auquel ces mouvements se déclenchent' (p. 100); engaging with him gives us access to the reality of our existence, opposed to the illusory nature of the public image we and he present. Thus it seems that for Sarraute, as for Schlegel or Lacan, the truth which transcends illusory appearances comes into being in intersubjective relations; this is why in 1956 she dreams of creating in literature a form of dialogue 'qui ne serait pas autre chose que l'aboutissement ou parfois une des phases de ces drames [. . .] tout vibrant et gonflé par ces mouvements qui le propulsent et le soustendent' (*ES* 117).

The fact that this subjective truth to which relations with others give access is located prior to a language inadequate to it, further invites one to associate Sarraute's outlook with that strand of thinking about language which sees dialogue as transcending the limitations of human beings' expressive ability (limitations of which we are ironically aware). This is a view which has gained currency in Sarraute criticism: Monique Wittig considers that Sarraute's dialogic world-view exceeds even that of Socratic irony, for in her work, 'il n'y a pas d'interlocuteur privilégié qui soutiendrait son point de vue (à la différence du *Socrate* de Platon)' (1984: 70). For Arnaud Rykner, her work manifests 'l'incapacité du langage à restituer intégralement et directement [le monde]', an inability which 'tient au caractère castrateur du mot, meurtrier du réel qu'il enferme dans des cellules bien cloisonnées, des prisons sans issues' (1991: 24). The Lacanian overtones of his analysis are echoed by Sabine Raffy, who emphasizes the importance of intersubjective relations to the 'castrated' subject of language: 'Le thème des ouvrages de Nathalie Sarraute, s'il en est, c'est celui d'un sujet en proie à l'Autre, dans ce que Lacan nomme la dialectique de l'intersubjectivité' (1988: 185). (The ironic nature of the castrated Lacanian subject, and the way dialogue allows him to transcend his condition, are discussed in detail in Chapter 1.) This perception of Sarraute's sensitivity to the 'dialectic of intersubjectivity' is of course supported by the importance she places on the act of reading, itself an enactment of the intersubjective relations on which her texts concentrate.

Yet reading Sarraute in the context of theories of intersubjectivity shows up the limits as clearly as the extent of her affinity to the view that dialogic response is what invests language with meaning. There is a striking dichotomy in her work between a perception of the inauthentic and conventional nature of the language in which people express themselves, and a belief that her own literary discourse (as well as that of her fictional representatives) can, at the price of great personal labour, escape this inauthenticity and acquire expressive power. I shall discuss in Chapter 3 the criteria according to which she distinguishes the authentic language of the true writer from that of others, and the inevitable impossibility of making that distinction absolute. Her simultaneous view of language as conventional *and* expressive will evidently have major consequences for what she conceives the addressee's role in dialogue to be, consequences evident both in her fictional representations of authentic discourse and more specifically in her own textual address to the reader.

However, it is not only the initial perception of Sarraute's texts as articulating a dialogic view of language which is modified as a result of their juxtaposition with theories of dialogue. Because dialogue involves the reciprocal transformation of *each* perspective through its engagement with the other, we can expect that the interaction set up between Sarraute's writings and the theoretical work on dialogue discussed in Chapter 1 will also lead us to a reconsideration of what is at stake in dialogue itself. Thus I shall suggest that the way Sarraute simultaneously acknowledges and denies the lack of any essential connection between language and the reality it describes, illustrates the way the conscious subject, however sensitive he may be to the conventional nature of language, is unable to relativize his own discourse completely. For that discourse is the filter through which he understands himself and the world, including what he knows about language in general. Because the subject's very identity is linguistic, he is bound to see his language as to some degree his own, and not simply as a transindividual structure which contains him. Thus the addressor in dialogue will always retain *some* faith that his intention is invested, however imperfectly, in the language he has chosen to articulate it (even the intention to articulate the meaninglessness of language implies a belief in the ability of language to express that intention).

The way Sarraute's faith in the expressivity of her own discourse affects her view of dialogue, and specifically of reading, can thus tell us something about the way participants in dialogue generally behave. In this way, I shall suggest that not only Sarraute's attempt to control her real readers by defining an ideal reader, but also the nature of what she sees to be the ideal reception of her work (affirmation without addition), merely magnify, without being qualitatively different from, attitudes all speakers bring to dialogue. Strategies for controlling an addressee's interpretation of one's words result not only from a fundamental faith in the potential of one's own discourse to mean; they simultaneously anticipate the way one's expressive intention will be alienated in the reception of the utterance. If this alienation, and its anticipation and resistance by speakers, is a phenomenon inherent in all linguistic communication, it is made especially explicit in Sarraute's work, due to her awareness of the intensely mediated nature of the text–reader dialogue which takes place across the process of publication and dissemination. Thus her work reminds us, by exaggerating it, of a factor which needs to be taken into account in any consideration of the nature of dialogue.

Finally, it is necessary to explain why, in this exploration of the dialogic dimension of Nathalie Sarraute's work, I concentrate on her prose works rather than on her plays, even though drama by definition takes to an extreme the privileging of dialogue as a formal principle. Looking at the increasingly dialogical quality of her narrative writing emphasizes the way this tendency develops in a form traditionally considered to be distinct from, if not opposed to, that of drama.[4] Thus, as Arnaud Rykner has pointed out, Sarraute's move into theatre in the 1960s underlines a dramatic quality already inherent in her novels with their 'mise en scène des voix qui se répondent, se contredisent, s'ignorent'; for these voices, 'la parole [. . .] est un enjeu vital, *dramatique* par excellence, et c'est pourquoi le théâtre s'est toujours trouvé au cœur de l'écriture sarrautienne' (1991: 110).[5] She further blurs the distinction between the genres by thematizing, in her first play, this move from narration into dialogue which was already under way in the novels: *Le Silence*, Rykner notes, opens with narration in crisis and dissolving into dialogue, as a speaker abandons his description of an idyllic landscape to let his voice become merely one of many (*Th.* 129; Rykner 1988: 56).

If I have chosen to focus on Sarraute's 'dramatic prose' rather than on her self-consciously 'post-narrational' drama, it is because I am interested not only in the way she represents dialogue within her texts, but also in the kind of dialogue she attempts to establish *through* the textual address. While drama is written to be performed before an audience, novels are generally read silently, in a private one-to-one relationship of text to reader which can be related to the kind of dialogue that takes place between individuals (indeed, as we shall see, it is in many ways paradigmatic for it). Moreover, the text–reader relationship in Sarraute is intimately linked to an

---

[4] For Jean Pierrot, Sarraute's abandonment of narrative synthesis in favour of a total 'dialogization' of the novel form means deserting the novelistic altogether: 'Après avoir traversé le roman, auquel elle doit certainement ses réussites les plus incontestables [. . .] Nathalie Sarraute a divergé sans doute définitivement vers une forme inouïe qui n'est guère définissable que par son caractère dialogué, et dans laquelle des voix anonymes, parlant depuis un endroit lui-même assez indéfinissable [. . .] continuent à développer devant nous toute une série de choses souvent passionnantes, mais qui ne constituent plus une histoire' (1990: 467).

[5] Unless otherwise indicated, all italics in quoted passages belong to the texts cited.

aspect of the dialogues within her prose works which is necessarily absent from the dialogues of drama proper. This is the unifying authorial discourse which in dialogic prose gestures towards a renunciation of its all-embracing perspective within the text, as well as appealing for the reader's perspective to complement its own from without. What I wish to do in the following pages is explore what happens to this discourse on both levels of its attempted self-relativization, and trace the way it unavoidably reasserts in both spheres the authority it tries to renounce.

IRONY, DIALOGUE, AND THE NOVEL

Nathalie Sarraute's long literary career, spanning the last two-thirds of the twentieth century and recently crowned with the publication of her collected works in the prestigious Pléiade series, is justly valued for the innovations it has brought to the novel as an aesthetic form. Her most original contribution to the evolution of fiction in the twentieth century is without doubt in the area of characterization.[1] Building on the transformations wrought on the form and scope of the novel by literary forebears like Dostoevsky, Proust, Joyce, and Woolf—transformations which enabled it to do justice to a modern conception of identity vastly more complex than nineteenth-century realist aesthetics allowed—Sarraute's fiction addresses aspects of human behaviour which lie beneath rational thought or articulate language, and which she famously calls tropisms. These she defines in *L'Ère du soupçon* as 'des mouvements indéfinissables, qui glissent très rapidement aux limites de notre conscience; ils sont à l'origine de nos gestes, de nos paroles, des sentiments que nous manifestons'; universal and innate, they are 'la source secrète de notre existence' (*ES* 8).

The universe of tropisms which Sarraute explores and articulates with remarkable dedication throughout her writing career is animated above all by one human instinct, what—quoting Katherine Mansfield—she calls the 'terrible desire to establish contact' (*ES* 37).[2] This urge is as fundamental as it is impossible to satisfy, '[un] besoin continuel et presque maniaque [. . .] d'une impossible

---

[1] In the *Notice* to *Tu ne t'aimes pas* in the *Œuvres complètes* (*OC* 1958–70), Valerie Minogue describes the half-century which separates that book's publication from the appearance of *Tropismes* in 1939 as 'cinquante années [. . .] d'un travail méticuleux autant qu'immense sur le langage et la forme, travail qui a permis à Nathalie Sarraute de se libérer—et de nous libérer—d'un réalisme de convention où régnaient des *personnages* dans un univers en trompe l'œil' (p. 1958). (Unless otherwise indicated, italics in quotations belong to the text cited.)

[2] The comment 'There is something profound and terrible in this eternal desire to establish contact', made about her friend Ida Baker, figures in a journal entry by Katherine Mansfield for Sept. 1920 entitled 'Woman and Woman' (see *Katherine Mansfield's Journal*, ed. J. Middleton Murry (London, 1927), 155; see also the note to 'L'Ère du soupçon', *OC* 1568 n. 2).

et apaisante étreinte' (p. 37). Again and again, Sarraute's writing dramatizes the attempts of human beings to relate to one another in language, and the anxieties, difficulties, and failures which inevitably attend these attempts. Interaction with others is what calls into existence the 'drames intérieurs' played out on the level of the tropism: '[Ils] ont tous ceci de commun, qu'ils ne peuvent se passer de partenaire' (pp. 99–100). Linguistic communication is beset with obstacles which speakers struggle eternally to overcome. Celia Britton (1983) notes the frequency with which characters in Sarraute's novels quote one another; this 'obsessive mental playback of quoted phrases' is the effect of 'the anxiety that they generate, and they do this because their meaning is not clear' (p. 71).

The struggle for successful communication plays such a vital part in Sarraute's conception of what it is to be human[3] that it could hardly be absent from her attitude to her own words and their reception by readers. In the landmark essay 'L'Ère du soupçon' (1950) she describes the ideal effect of a text on its reader: he should find himself 'd'un coup à l'intérieur, à la place même où l'auteur se trouve' (*ES* 76). It is a conception of reading brought to life in *Les Fruits d'or* in which, in the face of an intelligentsia whose members read only in order to enhance their position in the social hierarchy, 'un seul lecteur arrive, à la fin, à établir avec l'œuvre un contact direct, à préserver la fraîcheur intacte de sa sensation, comme s'efforce de le faire un écrivain' (Sarraute 1968: 4). The reader ideally enters into a communion with the author across the work, a communion so total that he can complete a text which the author has left unfinished in order that it may live: 'Quand le lecteur devine la fin de la phrase, ce n'est pas la peine que je la finisse. Ça donne aussi cette sorte de tremblement à la forme, qui est essentiel . . .' (Sarraute 1976a: 5)[4]

Sarraute's texts thus call out for a reader to complete them, a completion which is as precious as it is rare. The sole authentic reader of *Les Fruits d'or* can justly see himself as vital to the novel's survival: 'Je me dis souvent que c'est peut-être grâce à des gens

---

[3] As Arnaud Rykner puts it: 'L'être sarrautien est un être social qui doit affronter des subjectivités étrangères, lesquelles donnent consistance à son existence et lui permettent de se constituer à son tour en sujet' (1991: 19).

[4] A comment about painting which Sarraute attributes to Picasso, 'Les achever serait les achever', recurs throughout her essays and fiction (see Sarraute 1972a: 39; 1976b: 285; *EVM* 171). For the likely origin of this paraphrased opinion see the note to its appearance in *Entre la vie et la mort*, *OC* 732 n. 1.

comme moi, modestes et effacés, mais si opiniâtres, que ceux comme vous parviennent en fin de compte à subsister' (*FO* 157). There is none the less an ambiguity in this elevation of the reader, one which will reappear throughout this study. While the reader is vital to the text in that he completes what it does not articulate and so, by allowing it to be unfinished, allows it to live, there is also a strong sense that what he should bring to the text is something which it already anticipates, something already inscribed *en creux* in the gaps which are so characteristic of Sarraute's writing. The line is blurred between reading as a kind of expansion of the text and reading as simply reinforcing what is there.[5] As Sarraute explains in conversation with Isabelle Huppert: 'A partir du moment où je publie, c'est que je voudrais que d'autres consciences me disent: "C'est vrai". Un seul lecteur me suffirait' (Sarraute 1994: 12; cp. *EVM* 93). However, even though the response which is desired from the reader is affirmative, it only has value to the extent that it is freely made: 'Le lecteur peut interpréter comme il l'entend. Tout ce que je peux souhaiter, c'est que ce soit assez près de ce que j'ai voulu transmettre' (Sarraute 1976a: 5).

The idea that the reader contributes something essential to the text, which enhances it, makes it more intensely itself, is thus integral to Sarraute's reflections on literature (and *in* literature, for her imaginative prose is as theoretically aware as her theoretical writings are works of imagination[6]). It is enacted most dramatically (in more than one sense) in her autobiographical text *Enfance*, written as a dialogue between the remembering self and a critical counterpart whose interventions and questions figure those of the reader.[7] This emphasis on the importance of the act of reading,

[5] The extent of this blurring is evident in the abuse of the phrase 'Achever quelque chose, c'est "l'achever"' in *Entre la vie et la mort*. Here it has been hijacked by the writer's estranged double who has sold out to an inauthentic, 'dead' mode of writing, open to the reader only by default, through its own lifelessness: 'Qui a dit qu'achever quelque chose, c'est "l'achever"? Souvenez-vous de cela. Laissez donc. Ces creux sont excellents. Ne craignez rien, ils seront pleins à craquer. Chacun va s'empresser de les remplir, tout fier d'exhiber ses propres richesses' (*EVM* 171). The impossibility of a mode of reading which would complete the unfinished text without adding anything different to it is illustrated by the fate of the double in *Entre la vie et la mort*, as I shall argue in Ch. 4 (s. 2).

[6] Jean-Yves Tadié remarks that '*L'Ère du soupçon* a déjà le style des *Fruits d'or*, *Les Fruits d'or* sont aussi un ouvrage de critique littéraire' (Tadié 1984: 59). For a recent, detailed discussion of the interaction between Sarraute's critical writing and her fiction, see Ann Jefferson (1996), and her *Notice* to Sarraute's critical essays, *OC* 2034–50.

[7] For a discussion of the way this dialogic structure multiplies the 'spacings' inherent in Sarraute's prose style and so magnifies further the role of the reader in completing the text,

which runs as a leitmotif through all Sarraute's writings, is a direct literary assertion of something which critical thinking about litera-ture has been slow to acknowledge, but which gained considerable currency in the 1970s and 1980s. As Elizabeth Freund remarked in 1987: 'In the last fifteen years or so, an intense concern with the text–reader relationship, with the reading process, with our acts of understanding and interpretation, and with the subject of the "subject" has been occupying the forefront of Anglo-American critical attention' (Freund 1987: 5). In Chapter 5 I shall examine some of the most significant critical manifestations of this 'swerve to the reader' (Freund 1987: 5) in the context of Sarraute's attitude to reading (which changes over the years only to the extent that she becomes more and more sceptical about the possibility of finding her 'ideal reader' among the real reading public).

Theories of reading (whether they come under the umbrella of 'reader response' or 'reception theory'[8]) share a conception of the text as actualized in the reading process, its meaning—and by extension the meaning of all utterances—as constituted dialogically at the moment of reception. Interestingly, and perhaps unexpect-edly, this view of reading, and of linguistic communication gener-ally, is anticipated as far back as the early nineteenth century, in the work of the German Romantic thinker Friedrich Schlegel. He con-siders the act of reading in the context of Romantic irony, of which he was the first real theorist and great practitioner, and so provides a broader philosophical context in which we can explore the view of reading promoted by Sarraute. Furthermore, Schlegel's work anticipates strikingly many of the ideas of Jacques Lacan in the latter half of this century; thus the concept of irony and the idea of reading as a creative dialogue can themselves be brought into a fruitful dialogue with contemporary psychoanalytic theory. Explor-ing the nature of reading within this rather complex conceptual frame of reference necessarily means moving the spotlight away from Sarraute in the rest of this chapter. The aim of the following

---

see Gratton (1995a). He characterizes the reader of *Enfance* as 'a role-in-relation to the roles-in-relation (to one another) of narrator and protagonist' and sees the text as 'open[ing] a space [. . .] in which reading itself becomes a dialogical act' (p. 36). I shall explore the atti-tude to the reader in *Enfance* in detail in Ch. 2, looking notably at the limits it places on this dialogical activity.

[8] For a succinct outline of the differences between the two tendencies, see Holub (1984: pp. XII–XIV).

survey of critical thinking on dialogue is to provide a productive theoretical context in which to explore the idea of reading which is so
central to her works. But we should not think of this theoretical
apparatus as a diagnostic tool which might dominate the literary
text and 'explain' what is ambiguous or implicit in it (not least
because the very distinction between 'theory' and 'literature',
always problematic, is especially blurred in Sarraute's writings).
Instead, as we shall see in later chapters, the most productive relationship between them is itself one of dialogue in which power relations, while not absent, are not fixed either.[9]

1. Communication and the limits of language: irony and dialogue

For Friedrich Schlegel, writing which draws attention to the fact
that it engages in a dialogue with its reader who completes it is
ironic. And such irony is much more than just an aesthetic principle: it is the means of engaging fully with the very nature of being.[10]
Schlegel saw the novel as the ironic literary form *par excellence*, in its
ability to represent other forms within itself: it can thus offer a
reflection on literature and the limits of different literary forms, at
the same time as being itself an instance of literary expression.[11] Yet
however much it reflects on the limits of the other forms it chooses
to incorporate, it remains itself a limited artform. How can the
ironic novel transcend its *own* limits and so gain access to the
Absolute of art? For Schlegel it is the moment of critical *reading*

[9] Any juxtaposition of the writings of Sarraute and Lacan needs to acknowledge from the
start Sarraute's frequently articulated hostility to psychoanalysis (see *OC* 1581 n. 1, 2039–40).
Her scepticism ensures that there can be no easy 'mapping' of Lacan's theories onto her literary work (or vice versa).

[10] Socrates embodied for Schlegel this ideal of irony as the recognition of human ignorance, and dialogue as the dynamic process which moves the mind beyond it, towards ever
fuller knowledge. The activity of the mind is 'the alternating current of speech and counter-
speech or rather of thought and counter-thought' ('[das] wechselnd[e] Strom der Rede und
Gegenrede oder vielmehr des Denkens und Gegendenkens', Schlegel 1958: x. 353; in Behler
1972: 64), and as such is ideally represented in dialogue form. In Socrates' case 'this ever
onward-striving movement of his mind' was 'towards complete knowledge and recognition
of the Highest' ('diese[r] immer weiter strebend[e] Gang seines Geistes [war] nach vollende-
tem Wissen und Erkenntnis des Höchsten', 1958: xi. 120; in Behler 1972: 98). All translations
are mine unless otherwise indicated.

[11] Walter Benjamin, whose analysis of the concept of art criticism in German Romanticism I rely on heavily here, discusses the Romantic theory of the novel in detail (1974: 100–2).
Schlegel himself of course applied his theory in his novel *Lucinde*.

which brings this about, the moment of recognition that, like the forms it embraces and transcends, the ironic novel itself has limits of structure and language. Recognizing these limits dissolves them and thereby restores the finite work to the totality of art.[12]

Schlegel's concept of the ironic novel as making explicit its reliance on the reader to complete what it aspires to express, articulates in aesthetic terms his belief that human consciousness can transcend its finite, limited nature through interaction with another consciousness. For Schlegel, human knowledge is by definition incomplete, yet in rare moments of revelation the mind can intuit the realm of total or absolute reality which grounds it. Relations outside ourselves bring us closer to that Absolute, and language is the privileged mode of such relations. The American critic Gary Handwerk (1985), in a study of Schlegel's view of the subject which owes much to Walter Benjamin (see n. 11), has shown how this dialogical, social element of Schlegel's concept of irony is inseparable from the more familiar dimension of Romantic irony, self-reflexivity.[13]

Handwerk challenges the common perception that Romantic irony is dominated by self-reflection. Instead he emphasizes the *relative* nature of the original Romantic subject: if thought is reflective, this means that it relates—in the first instance immediately to itself, but also beyond that to a mediately accessible, infinite world of other reflective and relative consciousnesses (1985: 22–4). This infinite network of relations in which the subject is caught up constitutes absolute reality for Schlegel, and is something which we can know only indirectly, which is beyond immediate perception. The Kantian perceiving self is a false source of recognition; we can attain full subjectivity only through the mediated discovery (via reflection) of our infinite relations. For Schlegel there is no such thing as the isolated or stable subject; instead, the self exists in a constant

[12] '[Die] Kritik [löst] unwiderruflich und ernsthaft die Form [auf], um das einzelne Werk ins absolute Kunstwerk zu verwandeln, zu romantisieren' (Criticism dissolves the form, seriously and irrevocably, in order to transform the individual work into the absolute artwork, to romanticize it: Benjamin 1974: 84).

[13] In an early fragment Schlegel stresses the importance of communication over expression in literary writing: 'Man muß [etwas] wirklich mitteilen, mit [jemandem] teilen können, nicht bloß sich äußern, allein; sonst wäre es treffender, zu schweigen' (Schlegel 1958: ii. 158). (One must really communicate something, be able to share it with someone, and not just express oneself; otherwise it would be better to stay silent.)

state of relationship, inseparable from other, equally relative self-consciousnesses.[14]

Self-reflexivity and intersubjectivity thus merge for Schlegel, in his vision of a subject located in a 'medium of reflection' (Benjamin 1974: 36) where its position is always relative to that of all other subjects. This medium in which we have our being takes concrete form in *language*: the structure of language allows us to intuit the Absolute System (p. 47). Schlegel sees language as a system with its own secret internal relationships ('geheime Ordensverbindungen': 1958: ii. 364), evidenced by the fact 'that words often understand themselves better than their users do' ('daß die Worte sich selbst oft besser verstehen, als diejenigen, von denen sie gebraucht werden': p. 364). Understanding our position in the world in relation to that of other speaking subjects lets us grasp our incomplete nature in relation to the Absolute. Thus engaging in *dialogue* with our fellows offers us the closest earthly equivalent of that Absolute, the experience of intersubjectivity in the medium of language. The Romantic writer, for Schlegel, will therefore privilege the dialogic dimension of his language by foregrounding his work's reliance on the reader's response to it.

This view of the Schlegelian subject as ironically aware of being caught up in a web of relations within a linguistic order anticipates, as Handwerk points out, the much more recent and highly influential thinking on subjectivity and dialogue by psychoanalyst Jacques Lacan.[15] Lacan sees the subject as 'ce que le signifiant représente, et

---

[14] 'The response of the finite subject to an experience of transcendence [. . .] for Schlegel [. . .] necessarily leads to an awareness by that subject of its dependence on others' (Handwerk 1985: 25). There are clear connections here to the ideas of Mikhail Bakhtin, whose theory of dialogue will be discussed later in this chapter, in the context of the novel form. Though Michael Holquist opposes Bakhtin's ideas to those of Romanticism (1990: 22), he sums up his philosophy in terms which suggest close links to that of Schlegel: 'Existence is *sobytie sobytiya*, the event of co-being; it is a vast web of interconnections each and all of which are linked as participants in an event whose totality is so immense that no single one of us can ever know it' (p. 41).

[15] In fact, Romantic epistemology, especially in Benjamin's exposition of it, anticipates Lacanian psychoanalytic theory in several ways. The mystical nature of the Romantic Absolute compares to the (for consciousness) mysterious quality of the unconscious: Schlegel's representation of 'total subjectivity' in terms of a transcendent Absolute would later become internalized by Freud *within* the subject as the ubiquitous yet never wholly accessible unconscious. Lacan's interpretation of Freud in linguistic terms, his reconception of the unconscious as structured by the suprapersonal Symbolic order and like a language, emphasizes the kinship of psychoanalytic theory with Schlegelian Romanticism. While only the subject can articulate the unconscious, the fact that that unconscious both comes from

il ne saurait rien représenter que pour un autre signifiant, à quoi dès lors se réduit le sujet qui écoute' (Lacan 1966: 835). If the psychoanalyst is obliged to 'faire de son être l'axe de tant de vies', it is because of a dialectic which 'l'engage avec ces vies dans un mouvement symbolique' (p. 321). Just as for Schlegel full subjectivity involves the mediated discovery of our infinite relativity, a discovery which transcends mere self-reflexivity, Lacan's subject too must transcend the false consciousness of the ego. (The ego is the product of the mirror-stage, the developmental moment in which the child first comes to sense himself as a unitary entity, on the basis of his reflection in a mirror or of the sight of other babies: Lacan 1966: 93–100.) This means becoming conscious of the irreducible relativity of our position in the Symbolic order which mediates the Real to us.[16]

The affinity Schlegel bears to Lacan underlines the way the former's ideal of reading as co-creation of the text (an ideal Sarraute seems to embrace) fits into a much broader conception of dialogue and identity. Like Schlegel's reader, Lacan's addressee plays a central role in the creation of meaning through completion of the address (whether or not this completion is solicited by a text ironically aware of its linguistic limitations). Reading as a kind of dialogue thus becomes a specific enactment of the inherently dialogic nature of existence. Yet this is perhaps a somewhat rosy picture of reading as a consensual, cooperative activity. Sarraute's writing

without and manifests itself without (in address) means that one's articulation of it exceeds one and is transindividual (see Lacan 1966: 258). The affinity between Schlegel and Lacan is borne out by the importance both attach to the concept of *Witz* (wit/joke). For Schlegel it was the explosion of a fettered mind (1958: ii. 158) and as such the very 'principle and organ of universal philosophy', providing us with '*échappées de vue* into infinity' (p. 200). For Lacan, in a lesson he attributes to Freud, *Witz*, by surprising the subject, illustrates how 'le signifiant joue et gagne [. . .] avant que le sujet s'en avise' (1966: 840).

[16] In a late lecture, Schlegel formulates the ego–subject distinction in terms strikingly close to Lacan: 'Wo der Gedanke des Ichs nicht eins ist mit dem Begriffe der Welt, kann man sagen, daß dies reine Denken des Gedankens des Ichs nur zu einem ewigen *Sich-Selbst-Abspiegeln*, zu einer unendlichen Reihe von *Spiegelbildern* führt, die immer nur dasselbe und nichts neues enthalten' (Where the thought of the self is not one with the concept of the world, one can say that this pure thinking of the thought of the self leads only to an eternal *mirroring of the self*, to an endless series of *mirror-images* which contain nothing new but only ever the same old thing: *Philosophische Vorlesungen*, ii (1846), 38; cited in Benjamin 1974: 35; my emphasis). While references to irony are not frequent in Lacan's work, he does speak of 'l'ironie propre du langage' (1966: 258; cp. p. 521). Vaheed Ramazani sees Lacan's theory as inherently ironic: 'What is Lacan's subject if not the subject of irony itself? Subversion, misrecognition, fading: the psychoanalytic metaphor continually points to a gesture of rupture, evasion, negation—the classic gesture of irony' (1989: 555).

practice, as the following chapters will show, suggests that it is far from being the whole story, and in the process questions are raised about the consensual nature of dialogue in general. In anticipation of these questions, a closer look now at the Lacanian conception of dialogue may help to clarify both the nature and the limits of the cooperation involved in all linguistic relationships, including the act of reading.

Lacan's work in psychoanalysis is dedicated to foregrounding and developing Freud's focus on the analysand's use of language in a dialogue situation. For Lacan, Freud's work reveals how the subject constantly speaks his unconscious, but in a transindividual articulation which exceeds him: 'L'inconscient, à partir de Freud, est une chaîne de signifiants qui quelque part (sur une autre scène, écrit-il) se répète et insiste pour interférer dans les coupures que lui offre le discours effectif et la cogitation qu'il informe' (Lacan 1966: 799). In fact, Lacan sees the unconscious as governed by the same structure which informs language. He adopts Roman Jakobson's theory that language is structured along paradigmatic and syntagmatic axes, axes which find their purest manifestations in metaphor and metonymy respectively (Jakobson 1956: *passim*); and he then maps onto these key linguistic processes the psychic activities of condensation and displacement (Lacan 1966: 505–11, 689). This means that our subjectivity is linguistic in nature, but this fact is veiled from us through the primary function of language which is to signify. In other words, the individual's conscious control of his discourse to articulate a message entails the repression of his unconscious which can only be spoken 'between the lines'.

Desire is the essence of that part of us which is repressed in our unconscious. What is its connection to language and how can it be conveyed between the lines in the speech of the conscious ego? Desire in fact grounds the individual's accession to language. This happens in the Oedipus complex, which Lacan recasts in linguistic terms. The traditional Freudian moment when the father intrudes on the intimate mother–child relationship and undoes it is cast by Lacan as the inaugural moment of symbolic activity in the child. The father's intrusion simultaneously creates and represses in the child the idea of being an object of desire, for he feels himself displaced by the father from a position he had not heretofore conceptualized himself as holding. He thus attributes to the father what he now, sensing himself to have been usurped, desires to be for the mother. What he desires to be is the object of the mother's desire; Lacan calls this object the phallus, taking pains to distinguish its symbolic nature as the attribute of power from the physical penis. Yet if the discovery of a rival awakens the desire to be the phallus or object of desire, the superior authority of the Father's Law (the *nom du père*) means that this desire must immediately be repressed.

Thus in Lacan's version of the Oedipus, the Law of the Father inaugurates the unconscious by substituting one signifier (the Law) for another (the phallus). The subject is created as a split entity, conscious and unconscious, through the mechanism of metaphor (one signifier standing for another) which introduces language to the child's experience. The signifier of the Law creates and represses an original phallic signifier, so causing this repressed phallic signifier to become its signified. Naming thus begins with the repression of the desire to be the phallus in favour of the desire to have it (i.e. to have the power the father does). The subject's continued existence in language only prolongs this engagement with substitute objects.[17] Language both creates and maintains the unconscious: the subject as it exists in language is split right from its origin, with the unconscious a chain of signifiers repressed in the ego's engagement with substitutes. Like Schlegel, Lacan sees the conscious self as incomplete in a totality of language where true subjectivity is located; but here it is the very experience of language which, through repression, creates a plane of our being inaccessible to us.

Where in language is the truth of the subject (i.e. unconscious desire) located? Not in names or pronouns, the linguistic placeholders which represent us in discourse and condense to form the ego.[18] It is through the act of enunciation that the subject comes to be, and that its splitting (Freud's *Spaltung*, Lacan's *refente*) constantly recurs along the chain of discourse. The product of the *énonciation*, the *énoncé*, represents only half the truth of the subject. Thus 'la

---

[17] Jeffrey Mehlman sums up the Lacanian Oedipus as 'the assumption of a desire which is originally another's and which in its displacements, is perpetually other than itself' (Mehlman 1972b: 45 n. 11).

[18] The inadequacy of linguistic markers of the self—such as, notably, the pronoun 'je'— is a predominant concern of Nathalie Sarraute's writing (see esp. *Tu ne t'aimes pas*). She explains to Simone Benmussa: 'Dès que je dis "je", j'ai l'impression de ne jamais parler de moi, ou très rarement' (Sarraute 1987a: 82).

présence de l'inconscient, pour se situer au lieu de l'Autre, est à chercher en tout discours, en son énonciation' (Lacan 1966: 834).

This is where dialogue comes in as the means to full subjectivity. If desire manifests itself in the act of enunciation, the only way to bring the split subject of language to full self-awareness is through awareness of his enunciation which can only be perceived by a receptive addressee. Language thus has a paradoxical status: on the one hand it constitutes the *moi* of the *énoncé* by repressing desire, and so allows speech to foreground the ego at the expense of the unconscious. Yet our entire subjectivity *is* linguistic, and so language can also be the agent of full self-knowledge which is mediated through a responsive interlocutor in dialogue.

Understanding the unconscious as the space of desire and as linguistically structured explains why authentic communication can reveal it. The inseparability of language from desire is fundamental here: desire is what permits the child's inaugural repression of the phallic signifier. Desire of the mother is in fact already bound up with language even before the Oedipus complex leads the child to acknowledge (and repress) that desire and carry out the original act of metaphor which makes of him or her an agent in language. Desire is born when the mother introduces the infant to the universe of communication by responding to a cry which she interprets as a demand (for food, etc.). By interpreting the cry as a demand she inscribes the infant in the Symbolic order, subjecting him or her to the universe of her own signifiers. At this moment she is both specular other, the individual the child is relating to, and absolute Other, locus of language. This encounter with 'la mise en forme signifiante comme telle', coupled with the fact that 'c'est du lieu de l'Autre qu'est émis son message' (Lacan 1966: 690) means that the child's lived experience will henceforth be 'lesté du réseau signifiant de l'Autre' (Dor 1985: 187). This initiation into symbolic communication will culminate in the *nom du père* metaphor and the consequent mastery of articulate language.

The fact that the mother's original response was not demanded gives it a quality of *excess* of love which demand can by definition never recapture. Because this unsought love appeared prior to symbolic communication, desire of it can never be articulated; it is unnameable. Thus this excess of love is the cause and eternally displaced object of a desire the genesis and paradox of which is that it is founded and articulated *within* demand in order to capture something *beyond* that demand. Language thus speaks and constantly recreates a desire beyond itself, a desire both aroused and repressed in the very origins of that language in the subject (and of the subject in language). In other words, because the language of the subject is founded in that of the Other, and because desire, created through the imposition of language, perpetuates itself through the inadequacy of the linguistic demand the subject addresses to the Other, we can say that the desire of the subject is born and ever renewed at the level of the language of the Other.

It is because desire and the unconscious have their origin outside the subject that dialogue is the vehicle of self-understanding. As a result of the mother's original interpretation of the child's cry as a demand, self-knowledge for the subject of language entails the recognition that the ego created in language is an inherently alienated construct. One's 'own words' actually come from the other in inverted form: 'L'émetteur reçoit du récepteur son propre message sous une forme inversée' (Lacan 1966: 298). This realization in turn requires recognizing the other, one's addressee, as an

Autre absolu, visé au-delà de tout ce que vous pourrez connaître et pour qui la reconnaissance n'a justement à valoir que parce qu'il est au-delà du connu. C'est dans la reconnaissance que vous l'instituez, et non pas comme un élément pur et simple de la réalité, un pion, une marionnette, mais un absolu irréductible, de l'existence duquel comme sujet dépend la valeur même de la parole dans laquelle vous vous faites reconnaître.[19]

The ironic dimension of Lacanian subjectivity is of course that the absolute Other, embodiment of the totality of language, is also and primarily for consciousness the specular other, just as its own *moi* inevitably dominates its subjectivity. Imaginary relations (i.e. those based on a perceived similarity of other to self) persist on into the Symbolic order from the infant's identification with the mother

---

[19] Lacan 1981: 62–3. Joël Dor's summary of the dialogic principle in Lacan shows how the appeal to the addressee to establish meaning re-enacts the child's desire that the (m)other's desire be directed towards him, his 'desire of the desire of the other' ('le désir de l'homme s'aliène dans le désir de l'autre': Lacan 1966: 343): 'Le sens de la demande reste tributaire du "bon vouloir" de l'autre qui va accorder, par la nature même de sa réponse, telle signification plutôt que telle autre à la concaténation signifiante de l'appel [. . .] En effet, parce que les signifiants de la demande ouvrent à l'autre la possibilité d'un choix commutatif, le sens de la demande sera donc délivré, en dernière extrémité, par la sélection commutative des signifiants retenue, donc désirée par l'autre et dont témoignera le sens de sa réponse. L'autre *fixe* ainsi la signification de la demande en inscrivant d'une barre des signifiés sous les signifiants de l'appel du sujet' (Dor 1985: 235).

who, by conflating the positions of other and Other, founded this imbrication of the Imaginary in the Symbolic.[20] The attempt, in the analytic dialogue, to unseat the Imaginary self (the ego) through which subjects pose the question of identity at a level that avoids confrontation with its provisional nature, takes self-reflexivity into the realm of infinite relativity (as Schlegel might say). Alone, the most the subject can do is *recognize* ironically the constitution of identity by language; given the shared limitations of its language and consciousness it can never abolish through language its historically constituted ego, the persistent presence of the Imaginary in its psyche. Dialogue alone offers the possibility of transcending that Imaginary, in the addressee's reception not only of the subject's *énoncé* but also of the *énonciation*.

So far, the salutary role of dialogue seems clear.[21] Yet difficulties emerge when we begin to consider the text as an active *invitation* to dialogue. To the extent that the invitation stems from a belief in subjectivity as linguistic and dialogic, this position is held prior to and independently of the addressee's response, thus is outside the dynamic of dialogue. Lacan's own writing illustrates the problem: he argues that as a result of the 'castration' of the subject by language, truth can emerge only in dialogue; yet that argument, monologically represented by his text alone, has its own powerful truth-claim. There is a conflict—of which he is well aware—between, on the one hand, his conception of language as both unconsciously determined (thus uncontrollable) and untrue to reality in its repression of the subject's desire, and, on the other, his reliance on language to articulate this theoretical insight.

[20] Communication between subjects is always mediated by a relationship of the *moi* to a 'moi autre mais semblable': 'Fondamentalement ce sont [de vrais sujets] que je vise chaque fois que je prononce une vraie parole, mais j'atteins toujours *aa'* [the 'moi-moi autre' axis] par réflexion. Je vise toujours les vrais sujets, et il me faut me contenter des ombres. Le sujet est séparé des Autres, les vrais, par le mur du langage' (Lacan 1978: 286).

[21] Psychoanalytic theory is of course not the only contemporary discipline to privilege dialogue as constitutive of truth. Richard Kearney's 'A Note on the Hermeneutics of Dialogue' deals with the emphasis much 20th-cent. philosophy places on dialogue, and with the implications of this for the act of reading. Heidegger's pre-reflective being-in-the-world 'expresses itself primordially in the existential category of "discourse"'; involving one in 'a historical community of speakers', it reveals itself 'historically in and through language as a dialogical being-in-the-world with others' (Kearney 1984: 127). This insight is developed in the hermeneutics of Gadamer and Ricoeur: consciousness can only come to know itself via symbolic mediation; it must '*interpret* (*hermeneuein*) itself by entering into dialogue with the texts of a historical community or common tradition to which it belongs' (p. 128).

The complexity of his writing seems to be an attempt to let the unconscious articulate itself freely in his discourse and so counter-act the way language, as symbolic, ironically works to reinforce the ego and Imaginary relations. Yet the effectiveness of this strategy is bound to be compromised by the need for Lacan's text to fulfil its pedagogical function and communicate an analytical method. The problem is that there is a conscious body of knowledge to be articu-lated despite the distorting nature of that articulation. The fact that language distorts is indeed part of that body of knowledge, as is the awareness that the only way to overcome the self-ignorance pro-duced by language is in dialogue. In order for his claim that truth lies in intersubjectivity to be itself true, his writing should fulfil the conditions of truth by being an intersubjective product. Lacan's psychoanalytic *practice* is certainly dialogic, acknowledging that given the unconscious forces at work in the analyst's own interpret-ation, the performative aspect of his intervention will take priority over the informative. Yet in his writing it is clear that he has the answer to the question of the subject (the performative practice has resulted in information) before getting it through interlocution with the reader.[22]

In assimilating the performative nature of his practice, the *énonci-ation*, to an informative, pedagogic intention, Lacan compromises it, neutralizing its nature as appeal to the reader by didactically indi-cating its interpretation in advance, thus turning it into a kind of signified. Though the reader is encouraged to make his own spon-taneous associations the exact nature of which Lacan cannot fore-see, the fact that they take place at all has a certain signification, intentionally sought by his text. Rather than letting the unconscious speak in his discourse (an event which depends on an other acting as Other), Lacan's language is a *parody* of unconscious speech, a simulation of what should come into being through communication in what is only one side of a communication with the reader. Thus Malcolm Bowie can ask why, if *all* language is the metonymic

---

[22] Jacques Derrida makes a similar point in his reading of Lacan's 'Séminaire sur "La Lettre volée"'. Although 'le "style" de Lacan était fait pour déjouer longtemps tout accès à un contenu isolable, à un sens univoque, déterminable au-delà de l'écriture' (1975: 101), his writing, Derrida argues, seeks and claims to represent a *truth*: 'La requête de vérité conduit à mettre de côté la scène d'écriture' (p. 110). Both in his reading of Poe's story and in his writing, Lacan subordinates the play of the signifier (the letter) to the claim to stable mean-ing: 'Le déplacement du signifiant est [. . .] analysé comme un signifié, comme l'objet raconté dans une nouvelle' (p. 105).

displacement of desire, 'a sumptuously polyvalent language [is] to be preferred to the one-thing-at-a-time languages of logic, or conceptual analysis, or empirical description, or traditional psycho-analytic theory' (1987: 130).

At first glance it would seem that this limitation of the reader's interpretative freedom is a problem confined to 'theoretical' dis-course, which fiction can overcome. The fact that ironic fiction makes no claim to know the answer to questions about knowledge and truth which it implicitly poses certainly seems to put it at an advantage. In the novel, irony can take precedence over the fic-tional referent, thus avoiding any conflict between simultaneous claims to knowledge and ignorance, while still transcending the naïve assumption that unproblematic expression is possible in lan-guage. One of the most common techniques by which an artist can have his work solicit its own ironization without articulating such a request is *mise en abyme*, the inscription within the work of an object which reflects it (books within books, plays within plays, etc.). Indeed it is a regular feature of Nathalie Sarraute's work: *Les Fruits d'or* presents a book within a book, *Entre la vie et la mort* recounts the writing of a novel which doubles the narration and subject-matter of the real novel (cp. *EVM* 7 and 168), and *Le Mensonge* features a play within a play. This technique tacitly relativizes the whole work, encouraging the reader to consider its limitations (as Schlegel wished), letting him act as an 'Autre absolu' whose recognition of this finite linguistic entity can alone give it value. Ironic fiction can thus embody the belief that truth only emerges in dialogue without stating this in a propositional form which would necessarily be self-contradictory.

Yet while fictional discourse can renounce propositional inten-tionality, its very form betrays a certain world-view (ironic or other-wise).[23] A text which privileges devices like *mise en abyme* implicitly invites the reader to read it ironically. In soliciting its ironization by

---

[23] This complication simply emphasizes how problematic the very opposition between 'fiction' and 'theory' is. In the context of psychoanalytic theory, this point has already been well made by Shoshana Felman (1987; see esp. ch. 5). She examines the way both Freud and Lacan develop their theories around the story of Oedipus—for Freud, *Oedipus Rex* bears wit-ness to the universality of wish, wish-fulfilment, and primordial incestuous and parricidal desires. Lacan, on the other hand, reads 'beyond Oedipus' (and Freud) to see illustrated in *Oedipus at Colonus*, where Oedipus recognizes and assumes responsibility for his unknown his-tory, the vital importance to self-knowledge of the performative speech act in which the speaker takes responsibility for his 'other' (unconscious) life.

the reader, the text indicates the kind of response it desires; and by indicating the desired response, it potentially provides it. It seems then as though the reader's response to the ironic text only has the appearance of independent activity: in ironizing the text he is ultimately following instructions inscribed in its form.[24]

The question of the addressee's freedom of interpretation, of the degree to which his understanding of the utterance is shaped in advance by the speaker/writer, leads to the heart of what is at stake in dialogue. Yet it also risks oversimplifying the nature of interpretation by presenting it as a straightforward contest between addressor and addressee, fighting for 'ownership' of a text. My attempt in this book to answer that question through readings of Sarraute's prose writings may well lead to the conclusion that it is not in fact the right question to ask about the nature of reading, or of dialogue as such. But learning to distinguish between valid and invalid questions is itself a valuable step in understanding.

For now, we can say that the ironic ideal of relativizing completely one's own perspective by addressing it to another seems to be more an aspiration than an attainable reality: the ironic intention, whether articulated structurally or in propositional terms, necessarily requests of the addressee a certain interpretation, and so affects his freedom of response. The point may seem banal, but the aspiration to dialogue, however profound, cannot in itself be entirely dialogical; its request for a dialogic response will be compromised by its own—necessarily monologic—conception of what that means. Thus dialogue must struggle against even the attempt to initiate it, against the inevitable limitations of any individual conception of what dialogue is.

In terms of irony, this means that even self-relativizing irony will have its own irreducible intentionality. This, interestingly, makes it less remote than it might appear to be from the more familiar form of irony which consists in undermining a point of view (another's, or that of an ironized effigy of the self) in a discourse whose own authority is not questioned. This kind of localized irony is common both in conversations and in literature (Swift, Austen, and James are oft-cited practitioners). It is the kind in which the speaker clearly

---

[24] For a detailed discussion of strategies by which writers (specifically of 19th-cent. 'art - stories') assign a specific response to their readers by writing an ideal reading position into their fiction, see Chambers (1984: *passim*).

does not mean what he says, and which, after Dan Sperber and Deirdre Wilson who have done important work on the subject, I shall call verbal irony.[25] Reading Sarraute will show how, as the authorial invitation to dialogue is repeatedly overshadowed by a request for affirmation of a monologic outlook, the aspiration to self-relativizing, 'epistemological' irony (Handwerk 1985: 10–14) gives way to verbal irony.

The degeneration of epistemological irony into verbal irony can be seen in Lacanian terms as the difference between actually *unseating* and merely *acknowledging* the alienated nature of linguistic consciousness. Verbal irony demonstrates that signification is not the same thing as meaning (the ironist does not mean what his utterance signifies); it can thus serve to remind us that what we take to be the expression of truth is a function of linguistic convention or the Symbolic order. The ironist's feigned ignorance of the falsity of his utterance can mimic consciousness's unawareness of its alienation from the unconscious forces which determine it and its language. Yet the ironist does not *transcend* this alienation: although he gives the reader the responsibility for recognizing that the utterance is not to be taken at face value, this recognition is consciously anticipated, even required—not to see the irony is not to get the speaker's point. For such irony to work, the addressee must *adopt* the ironist's outlook, not relativize it.

To see the address to a completely 'other' reader as involving an attempt to domesticate him is not to argue that the limitations of the ironist's perspective can never be transcended. Simply, the addressee's response must exceed the terms on which the addressor invites him to respond, however dialogically motivated the invitation. If the authorial aspiration to full ironic self-relativization ends up projecting the response it desires and so approaches the structure of verbal irony, that projection will of course still fall short of a real reader's response to the text. Like any utterance, the text's language will exceed the intentions which gave rise to it; by relativizing

---

[25] Defining what the speaker *is* doing in verbal irony is anything but straightforward. Sperber and Wilson have convincingly challenged the traditional definition of this kind of irony as a trope (where the utterance has a figurative meaning which is the opposite of what is said), through their work in pragmatic linguistics. They argue that the ironist communicates by manifesting an attitude *to* his utterance rather than by means of it. In other words, he speaks to convey not a meaning but an attitude to his own words (Sperber and Wilson 1981: *passim*; 1986: 237–43).

these intentions it ironizes the limitations of even the authorial demand to be read ironically. The distinction between the text's unconscious irony and the author's irony which it exceeds is a major one and, as we shall see with Sarraute, remains valid even when the author's conscious irony appears to invite a subversive reading of the text.

2. Dialogue and the novel

Intimately connected to the kind of relationship authors set up with their readers across the fictional text is the way they represent relationships *within* the text. The way characters' dialogues are reported can make manifest, again by structural rather than propositional means, authorial and narratorial attitudes ranging from authoritative dominance (frequently illustrated in the ironization of characters' discourses) to ironic self-relativization. The rest of this chapter will look at some implications for the act of reading of the ways in which authors represent the discourses of their characters, specifically in view of the kinds of power relations which are thereby enacted (and which, according to whether they undermine the perspective of the author or his characters, can be assimilated to different modes of irony).

That authors' attitudes to their characters' words can tell us something about the kind of dialogue they envisage with their readers was argued by V. N. Voloshinov (who may or may not be Bakhtin) as long ago as 1929. In *Marxism and the Philosophy of Language* (translated into English in 1973) he claimed that the various relationships between representing and represented discourses in fiction signal the varying degrees of openness to dialogic interaction of the novels which contain them. Speech within speech is also speech about speech (Voloshinov 1973: 115): in other words, the form in which someone reports another's words inevitably tells us something about his attitude to those words. The range of forms and their implied attitudes is determined by the relationship of dominance between the two voices involved, the quoting voice and the one quoted. In indirect quotation, the narrator takes the liberty of replacing the character's discourse with his own, often summarizing, explicating, or judging the original idea as he reports it. At the opposite pole, the narrating voice makes no alteration to the quoted discourse which is reproduced directly, as originally uttered or thought. Voloshinov believes that all language forms, and especially forms of reported speech, are determined by the '*social purview* of the given time period and the given social group' (p. 21). Thus direct discourse is a 'primitive, inert' form which reflects a perception of another's utterance as 'a compact, indivisible, fixed, impenetrable whole' (p. 128). Indirect reportage, by contrast, is the product of a 'Cartesian, rationalistic period, during which an objective "authorial context", self-confident in its power of reason, had analyzed and dissected the referential structure of the speech to be reported' (p. 127).

Probably the most frequently theorized form of reported discourse lies between these poles at which one of the two voices retains total control of expression. It is the peculiar blend of both voices known as free indirect discourse and defined by Dorrit Cohn (who prefers the term 'narrated monologue') as a 'technique for rendering a character's thought in his own idiom while maintaining the third-person reference and the basic tense of narration' (1978: 100).[26] For Voloshinov it marks a 'completely *new*, positive tendency in active reception of another person's utterance, a *special direction* in which the dynamics of the interrelationship between reporting and reported speech moves' (1973: 142). It is not the mark of a drift from indirect analysis towards direct discourse; instead it indicates a much more profound change in the way the 'speaking personality', its 'ideational, ideological autonomy' and its 'verbal individuality' (p. 146) are perceived.

As a form of quotation, free indirect discourse is ideally suited to verbal irony, where a derogatory attitude is taken to another's utterance or thought.[27] It is because verbal irony is a kind of implicit quotation that full ironic self-relativization by the speaker is impossible: the very fact of quoting another discourse asserts superiority over it. Thus even where he takes himself as victim of his irony, it is an effigy, rather than the speaker himself, who suffers. The quoting and the quoted self can never fully coincide, and so the speaker's authority is never entirely undone.

---

[26] Roy Pascal (1977) gives a concise account of the controversies which followed the first full description and analysis of free indirect discourse (by Charles Bally in 1912), while later discussions of the phenomenon have been outlined and compared by Brian McHale (1978).

[27] On the relationship between irony and free indirect discourse, as well as that between parody and direct discourse, see Sperber and Wilson (1981: 311).

The same limitation characterizes free indirect discourse—while it certainly diminishes the authority of the omniscient narrator, it stops short of a fully dialogic relationship between representing and represented discourses. Indeed it is the retention of a residual narrative authority that makes free indirect discourse such a powerful tool in the evocation of characters' prelinguistic states: the welding of the voices of narrator and character allows a surreptitious attribution of narratorial language to the character's inarticulate mental processes. Directly quoted discourse, even in the form of interior monologue, suggests articulate thought with a fairly high degree of reasoning; it is restricted to the depiction of mental activity capable of being verbalized. A narrator, by contrast, is free to use imagery in order to evoke and give substance to his character's unarticulated experience, while leaving the question of whose the imagery is (his own or the character's) ambiguous.

Nathalie Sarraute's focus on the border between articulate language and preverbal sensation accounts for the frequency of free indirect discourse in her early novels.[28] Indeed Dorrit Cohn comments on the profusion of narratorial imagery in Sarraute's *Le Planétarium*, and points out how the use of the present tense as the tense of narration lets the imagery which conveys subverbal mental activity blend more smoothly into its free indirect context (Cohn 1978: 45). For Cohn an authoritative narratorial element is indispensable to any attempt to represent the deeper levels of the mind (an ambition which drives Sarraute's whole literary project):

The novelist who wishes to portray the least conscious strata of psychic life is forced to do so by way of the most indirect and the most traditional of the available modes. The correlation drawn by critics of the stream of consciousness novel between the relative depth of the levels of consciousness portrayed and the relative directness of the techniques used to portray them is therefore entirely erroneous. (p. 56)

Yet Sarraute's novels show an unmistakable progression away from free indirect discourse and towards direct dialogue, culminating in the dramatic composition of *Enfance*, *Tu ne t'aimes pas*, and

---

[28] In the essay 'Conversation et sous-conversation', she describes 'ce qui se dissimule derrière le monologue intérieur: un foisonnement innombrable de sensations, d'images, de sentiments, de souvenirs, d'impulsions, de petits actes larvés qu'aucun langage intérieur n'exprime, qui se bousculent aux portes de la conscience, s'assemblent en groupes compacts et surgissent tout à coup, se défont aussitôt, se combinent autrement et réapparaissent sous une nouvelle forme, tandis que continue à se dérouler en nous, pareil au ruban qui s'échappe en crépitant de la fente d'un téléscripteur, le flot ininterrompu de mots' (*ES* 97–8).

Ouvrez which are made up purely of internal dialogues.[29] What might be the attraction of a more thoroughly dialogic form over the evocative power of free indirect discourse whose imagistic potential Sarraute had previously exploited so successfully? It can hardly be a belief in the greater mimetic accuracy of the direct utterance, for Sarraute had very early rejected interior monologue as inadequate to the prelinguistic psychological depths she wished to explore (see n. 28). If it is not for the descriptive accuracy of the spoken word, then, the attraction of dialogue as a form seems likely to be more a function of its structure. Divorcing the blended perspectives in free indirect discourse, it on the one hand restores the straightforward utterance, in itself 'monologic', while simultaneously introducing one or more opposing voices, each with a separate single perspective of its own.

The dissolution of all remaining narrative authority in favour of a multiplicity of independent perspectives can be seen as an authorial refusal to take (or give to an omniscient narrator) expressive responsibility for the thoughts and words of others. Historically, the decline, in the twentieth century, of the authoritative third-person narrator and thus also of free indirect discourse which 'prospers only in his atmosphere' (Pascal 1977: 140) coincides with the demise of the Cartesian notion of the autonomous individual in control of his destiny. This dissolution of the subject's autonomy is chiefly associated with Freud's analysis of the unconscious and its influence on conscious behaviour.[30] Free indirect discourse depends on the narrator being considered as still ultimately in control of the world he describes; this is in part what makes it 'so characteristic of the nineteenth century' (Pascal 1977: 134) and unsuited to the postmodern vision of an irreducibly chaotic world. Thus problems arise when the technique is used by contemporary writers whose aim is to

---

[29] This evolution will be discussed in more detail in the next chapter in the context of a reading of *Enfance*. The gradual dissolution of an all-embracing narrative perspective (first- or third-person) in favour of the characters' discourses was noticed already in 1976 by A. S. Newman. Celia Britton (1983: 72) has discussed the way *sous-conversation*, the preverbal 'tropistic' activity which in the earlier novels gives rise to a profusion of imagery (as noted by Cohn), 'tends more and more to be presented textually as speech' by Sarraute.

[30] Paul Ricoeur (1965: 40) lists Marx and Nietzsche along with Freud as 'masters' of the 'school of suspicion' (and so worthy initiators of Sarraute's 'age of suspicion'); what they have in common is 'la décision de considérer d'abord la conscience dans son ensemble comme conscience "fausse"', to go beyond Descartes by doubting not only the objects of consciousness but consciousness itself (p. 41).

usurp narratorial credibility. In texts where the narrator has no
more, and indeed often less knowledge than the characters in his
story, free indirect discourse becomes 'an inner contradiction'
(p. 140) in so far as it still implies some power to penetrate
characters' minds and interpret their unspoken mental processes.
What comes after the era of free indirect discourse (for Bernard
Cerquiglini 'une des plus belles réussites du dix-neuvième siècle.
Lequel s'achève [. . .] à la fin des années 1960': 1984: 14)? Sarraute's
novels in the 1960s and 1970s pursue ever more intensely
'l'effacement de la voix narrative au profit de celles des personnages' (Newman 1976: 196). Characters are given their own voices,
not only to express themselves aloud but also to make perceptible
for the reader the emotions and sensations, the *sous-conversation*
which underlies what they say to others and others to them.[31]
Such communication with the *reader* predominates increasingly in
Sarraute's later work, as Chapters 4 and 5 will show. In *L'Usage de la
parole* or *Enfance*, the discursive floor is no longer shared between a
vestigial narratorial presence and the (real and imagined) voices of
its characters; now the authorial voice speaks openly, acknowledging and seeking to include the reader's perspective on the text.[32]
    Sarraute is not alone in the evolution towards an ever more rad-
ically dialogic prose form—Brian McHale identifies a particular

[31] See n. 29. Hans Rudolf Picard points out that *sous-conversation*, especially that represented through direct speech, though it is not part of a dialogue in that it is not openly
addressed to the fictional interlocutor, does communicate the character's feelings directly to
the *reader*, and in this way 'wird [. . .] zu einer Konversation, zu einem Mitteilungsversuch
zwischen Autor und Leser' (becomes a conversation, an attempt at communication between
author and reader: 1982: 139). Of course everything in the text is ultimately directed towards
the reader, but being the real addressee of a character's pseudo-address draws us into the text
in a particularly emphatic way.

[32] This evolution from a narrative where the *narrating* voice is relativized by those of the
characters, to the self-relativization of the *authorial* voice as it solicits the reader's perspective,
can be seen in the two engagements with the phrase 'Si tu continues, Armand, ton père va
préférer ta sœur' in *Entre la vie et la mort* and *L'Usage de la parole*:

Ils s'écartent les uns des autres pour mieux se voir, les lunettes des vieillards descendent sur
leur nez . . . 'Ton père va préférer ta sœur . . . C'est ça [. . .] je dois avouer que ce sont des mots
que moi aussi, je dois faire mon mea culpa . . . Elle frappe comiquement sa poitrine avec son
poing . . . C'est ma faute, c'est ma très grande faute [. . .]'
Ils s'agitent, les fils télégraphiques invisibles qui les relient les uns aux autres bourdonnent,
des messages qu'il reconnaît sont envoyés, captés . . . Moi je m'en suis toujours méfié . . . Il me
met mal a l'aise [. . .] (*EVM* 56–7)

'Si tu continues, Armand, ton père va préférer ta sœur.'
    Écoutez-les, ces paroles . . . elles en valent la peine, je vous assure . . . Je vous les avais déjà
signalées, j'avais déjà attiré sur elles votre attention. Mais vous n'aviez pas voulu m'entendre

emphasis on dialogue and plurality of discourses ('polyphony' in the term of Mikhail Bakhtin, whose work will be considered in the next section) to convey a world of radically fragmented perspectives as a characteristic of postmodernist fiction generally: 'Bakhtin has shown us how dialogue among discourses is a staple of all polyphonic novels. Postmodernist fiction, by heightening the polyphonic structure and sharpening the dialogue in various ways, foregrounds the ontological dimension of the confrontation among discourses, thus achieving a polyphony of *worlds*' (1987: 166). The fact that writers like Sarraute, writing largely since the Second World War, have tended to privilege a dialogic prose form which is democratic in its juxtaposition of voices rather than the 'annexation' of one by another, seems to endorse Voloshinov's argument that language forms are directly related to social configurations.[33] A dialogic form implies a recognition of the lack of authority of any discourse over the discourses (and lives) of others. And when dialogism is taken to its formal extreme, as in the dialogues which make up the whole of *Enfance* or *Tu ne t'aimes pas*, the renunciation of a transcendent, all-embracing perspective in favour of a diversity of voices of equal status (and which acknowledge the reader's perspective too) seems complete.

Voloshinov himself recognizes that free indirect discourse cannot establish a fully dialogic relationship between quoting and quoted languages. It can only capture one phase of dialogue, the reception of another person's speech; it fails to embody the *reciprocal* nature of the addressor–addressee relationship, where that reception gives rise to a response which is responded to in turn as a new address. Yet this reciprocity shapes our very consciousness which for Voloshinov (as later for Lacan) is linguistically constituted through contact with others: 'Consciousness becomes consciousness only once it has been filled with ideological (semiotic) content, consequently, only in the process of social interaction' (Voloshinov 1973: 11). Understanding is 'a response to a sign with signs', part of a proto-Lacanian

. . . il n'est pires sourds . . . Non, pas vous? Vous vous les rappelez? J'avoue que c'est là pour moi une vraie surprise [. . .] (*UP* 49)

Enfance (1983) of course goes even further by assigning the reader a voice within the text, as the author's *alter ego*.

[33] 'In the forms by which language registers the impressions of received speech and of the speaker, the history of the changing types of socioideological communication stands out in particularly bold relief' (Voloshinov 1973: 123).

'chain of ideological creativity and understanding' which links sign to sign and consciousness to consciousness (p. 11).

This means that every utterance (including the literary text), as well as calling for a response, is also itself a response to previous performances (p. 95). Its double nature as simultaneously response, and address inviting response, is a result of the fact that every word is '*a two-sided act* [. . .] determined equally by *whose* word it is and *for whom* it is meant. As word, it is precisely *the product of the reciprocal relationship between speaker and listener, addressor and addressee*' (p. 86). Free indirect discourse, because it remains within a syntactically unified narrative, is incapable of enacting this reciprocity; its active relation of one message to another is restricted to the incorporation of the utterances of others 'into a bound monologic context' (p. 112). In dialogue, on the other hand, 'the lines of the individual participants are grammatically disconnected; they are not integrated into one unified context [. . .] *There are no syntactic forms with which to build a unity of dialogue*' (p. 116). It would seem that as long as narrative unity is maintained, the full implications of language as dialogue cannot be enacted in literature.

The particular way in which Sarraute uses dialogue in her later works in fact points to a double abdication of narrative authority. Whereas her earlier novels created an ever more structurally anarchic world of competing discourses which drowned out any narrative voice, her subsequent dissolution of authorial discourse into an *internal* dialogue in *Enfance* and, even more strikingly, *Tu ne t'aimes pas* (or indeed *Ouvrez*, where the internal dialogue is not among the mind's multiple perspectives but among its *words*) seems to suggest that the conscious self, no longer, as Freud put it, master in his own house, is not master of his own discourse either. *Tu ne t'aimes pas* illustrates the disintegration of monological authorial control particularly spectacularly through the dialogue which composes it and in which the countless voices are so many exploded fragments of the authorial self. Dialogue, for Sarraute, thus becomes the medium for the treatment not only of intersubjective relations but also of the subject's lack of internal authority, which is what gives rise to the need for dialogue in the first place.[34]

---

[34] This dual function of dialogue initially appears unproblematic; yet it contains a latent tension between, on the one hand, dialogue seen as a request for otherness, and, on the other, the desire for a response whose perspective would be identical to the addressor's (coming

In the context of narration, then, dialogue can be seen as aiming for the full structural realization of that demolition of speaker-authority towards which free indirect discourse gestures but which its relation of domination and submission, of quoter and quoted, keeps it from attaining. Dialogue goes beyond free indirect discourse not only in completing the abdication of narrative authority, but also in the way it offers a solution to the predicament of the subject in language. Recognizing the value of response as a complement to the speaker's perspective, it is an act of faith in the power of intersubjective relations (including those between text and reader) to transcend the ironic plight of the linguistic subject.

If, as Voloshinov argues, the treatment of discourses in the text represents in microcosm the text's own degree of dialogic openness, then we can expect writing like Sarraute's to be intensely open to the reader's absolutely other perspective and the total ironic relativization of the text it promises. However, I have suggested that the invitation to dialogue is not necessarily so unconditional, for the nature of the invitation itself will indicate the kind of response desired. To close this discussion of dialogic writing and the reading process, I want now to consider more closely what exactly happens to the authorial voice in the dialogic text, and consequently what kind of relationship is established across that text between author and reader.

3. Narration into dialogue

If dialogue as a compositional principle rejects narrative authority, what does this imply for the act of narration? Prose fiction without narrative content seems inconceivable; how then is that content affected by the absence of narrative authority? Moreover, what are the implications of the rejection of a monologic narrative voice in favour of a multiplicity of discourses for the way the reader relates to the text as the work of an individual author? In other words, if an author, by privileging dialogue within his or her work, emphasizes that writing is part of a dialogue to which the reader actively contributes, with whom is the reader's dialogue? The many voices of

from another of the self's voices), and would thus in fact *reinforce* the addressor's identity. This conflict is of great significance for dialogue in Sarraute, both within the novels and on the level of their address to the reader, and will be a major factor in my discussion of her work.

the text or the organizing principle which orchestrates them and which can have its source only in the author?

The first of these issues—the relationship of dialogue to narration—comes into play in a very concrete way in the psychoanalytic process. Analyst Roy Schafer has explored its implications in the context of approaches to biography in psychoanalytic discourse. Criticizing the sequential life history usually established by psychoanalysts as no more than 'a second-order retelling' of the analytic procedure, he suggests a form 'methodologically more adequate to the psychoanalytic occasion': the history of the analytic dialogue (1981: 48). This first-order history is true to the nature of psychoanalytic reality in beginning 'in the middle', the present, and constitutes more a set of histories told from multiple perspectives than one seamless narrative. It starts not, as traditional biographical case histories do, at the chronological beginning ('Freud's wish-fulfilling hallucination of the absent breast': p. 49), but with 'a narrative account of the psychoanalyst's retelling of something told by an analysand and the analysand's response to that narrative transformation' (p. 49). The dynamics of dialogue are the proper focus of a narration concerned to establish the truth of the subject. The analytical nature of the psychoanalytic narrative of course demands that it contain a propositional argument; the way this unfolds, however, will be dictated by the shape of the dialogue: 'The account of the origins and transformations of the life being studied is shaped, extended, and limited by what it is narratively necessary to emphasize and to assume in order to explain the turns in this dialogue' (p. 49).

In so far as the analyst, in Schafer's view, possesses the professional authority to establish an analytical history on the basis of the dialogue, his commentary will retain narrative authority (during the dialogue itself, in contrast, the analyst does forgo this authority, being frequently unreliable as a narrator of the analysand's experiences). Schafer thus ultimately stops short of calling for a dialogic psychoanalytic writing (his straightforwardly monologic exposition contrasts sharply with the obliquities of Lacan's style). Yet he does make dialogue the origin and guide of the psychoanalytic narrative, and he calls for changes in the focus of that narrative in consequence: emphasis on the dialogue as a present event, subordination of the commenting narration to the 'turns' in the dialogue, and, importantly, the commentary's awareness of its own status as a narrative structure chosen at the level of the analyst's precritical assumptions for its efficacy in *constituting* its data (pp. 26–7).

Fictional discourse, as we saw earlier, is in a position to capitalize on dialogue's capacity to explore and reveal truths about the constitution of identity. Having a much less strongly propositional nature than didactic psychoanalytic discourse,[35] it is not obliged to betray the notion of dialogic truth by asserting an illusory authority. Instead it can remain within the structure of the dialogue of which any narrative would be an arbitrarily chosen interpretation at one remove, and tell less directly, in an uncommented dialogic representation, the 'several histories' (Schafer 1981: 49) of the individual. This seems to be exactly what is going on in Nathalie Sarraute's *Enfance* which, though autobiographical, has the inherent 'fictionality' Barbara Herrnstein Smith attributes to all literary discourse (see n. 35). Valerie Minogue has described its narration-in-dialogue of the writer's past as 'always ironically aware of the perils inherent in narrative, and always reaching out to the reader, inviting participation, challenge, verification or dissent' (1988: 221). Whereas the narrative structures adopted by psychoanalysts to construct an authoritative account of the analysand's history 'control the telling of the events of the analysis, including the many tellings and retellings of the analysand's life history', a literary dialogue like that of *Enfance* seems better able to address that history while enacting the truth that 'the time is always present. The event is always an ongoing dialogue' (Schafer 1981: 49). However, as Chapter 2 will show, the dynamics of the dialogue of *Enfance* are not quite so straightforward, and show up complexities and pressures which abstract discussions of dialogue can overlook.

If the truest construction of the analysand's life history is from the perspective of the present dialogue which explores and constitutes it, this does not mean that the subject's narration disappears; it merely becomes subordinated to the dialogic structure which contains it. The analytic dialogue is an 'interweaving of texts' (the analysand's stories about himself and the analyst's retellings of those stories), and their gradual transformation into 'a radically new, jointly authored work or way of working', a 'cluster of more or less

---

[35] The notion of fiction as propositionally indeterminate has been argued by Barbara Herrnstein Smith (1978: chs. 2–3) who sees all literature as designed to be experienced as the representation of an utterance, and therefore as inherently fictive.

coordinated new narrations' (p. 32). This tension of narration and dialogue corresponds to Schafer's view that 'the self is a telling' (p. 31), that the telling of stories about oneself and about others constitutes these entities; thus, telling 'others' about 'ourselves' is doubly narrative (p. 31).

Similarly, in literary writing, the framing of narration within a dialogic structure does not leave narration behind entirely, but critically weakens its power to convince, to create a plausible fiction. A text entirely in dialogue can draw attention to the act of narration through the constant interruption and contradiction of different narratives by one another, displaying for the reader the doubtful validity of any given narration, the inherent bias and concealed motives in the way we relate events. Where the dialogue to which the many different narratives belong takes place within a single mind, as in *Tu ne t'aimes pas*, it becomes possible to emphasize particularly clearly the simultaneous existence of a multiplicity of possible 'histories of self' (and so to compromise their individual persuasiveness). In this case, the diversity of internal voices will compare to the range of roles Schafer sees the analysand play in free association: 'Each of these parts [hero, victim, dodger, stranger] is one of the regulative narrative structures that one person, the analysand, has adopted and used simultaneously with the others, whether in combination, opposition, or apparent incoherence' (p. 40).[36]

Having concentrated so far on the place of dialogue *within* the literary text, we should turn now to the second issue raised at the beginning of this section, namely the relationship of the *reader* to the dialogic text. How are the intratextual and the text–reader dialogues linked? While the exact nature of the relationship between textual dialogism and the dialogue of text and reader is not easy to define, some connection between the two can be assumed. The limited perspectives represented in the dialogic text reflect after all its own limitations as the work of an individual author, limitations which the reader may acknowledge and so transcend. It seems

[36] It should be underlined that while such diversity represents what dialogue as a form is capable of, its use in practice may not realize this potential. Texts which are structurally dialogic can still end up for one reason or another limiting, or even counteracting entirely, the potential for polyphony their choice of form provides (without, of course, ever entirely evacuating the multiplicity of registers inherent in language use). In fact, as Chs. 2 and 3 will show, both *Enfance* and *Tu ne t'aimes pas* ultimately resist the total dissolution of the singular authorial voice even as their structures gesture towards it.

reasonable that a text which rejects the falsity of narrative authority
in favour of a democracy of voices none of which is all-knowing and
where knowledge is a function of address and response, will encourage (in an ironic gesture) its own reader to assume an active role in
the constitution of its meaning.[37]

In dialogic writing which is designed to engage the reader, what
happens to the author's voice? And what kind of dialogue can the
reader engage in with a polyphonic text? The place of the author in
such writing has been considered by Mikhail Bakhtin, whose
concept of dialogism is important for this whole discussion and so
warrants an outline here. Like Schlegel and Lacan, Bakhtin sees
truth as intersubjective, dialogic. For him Dostoevsky is the master
of the polyphonic novel, taking up the thread of a dialogic form
existent since Socrates in the way he grants independent voices
priority over plot. If we think of the polyphonic novel as a microcosm of the world and its multiplicity of independent and clashing
voices, we can see its affinity to Lacan's Symbolic order or Schlegel's
Absolute System, both of which defy the attempts of the consciousnesses they contain to embrace their (linguistic) totality. The monologic viewpoint which the Dostoevskyan chaos exceeds is thus the
aesthetic equivalent of the restricted viewpoint of consciousness in
the face of the always already symbolized Real.

For Bakhtin, as for Lacan or Schlegel, dialogue is the means to
full self-knowledge.[38] He sees the 'depths of the human soul' as

---

[37] In philosophical discourse, Richard Kearney sees the written dialogue as extending to
include the reader: 'The written dialogue is in itself an open invitation to the reader to fill in
the gaps between the original speakers' words. It summons the reader to recreate and
reinterpret the authors' original meanings according to his or her own hermeneutic and
experiential presuppositions. In this sense, we might say that once the reader has entered the
dialogue, it becomes a dialogue that never ends' (1984: 129). Rolf Kloepfer (1980) also discusses the relationship between the text's internal dialogism and its relations with the reader.
And, as Ann Jefferson points out in the *Notice* to Nathalie Sarraute's critical writings,
Sarraute's use of dialogue, by locating the action of the text in the present moment of its reading, also works to include the reader: 'L'originalité fondamentale de Nathalie Sarraute réside
dans cet autre aspect technique de ses romans qu'est la manière dont elle travaille la forme
du dialogue [. . .] La distance qui d'une part sépare l'auteur du texte, d'autre part permet au
lecteur de se tenir à l'écart, est abolie; le dialogue empêche l'auteur d'agir en meneur du jeu,
en maître, en même temps qu'il exige la participation sans réserve du lecteur' (*OC* 2041).
Jefferson concludes that 'toute la réflexion menée par Nathalie Sarraute sur les procédés
romanesques repose sur un principe fondamental: l'implication de l'auteur et du lecteur dans
les drames psychiques mis en scène dans les romans' (p. 2042).

[38] Bakhtin's description of Dostoevsky's works as 'a word about a word addressed to a
word' (1984a: 266) anticipates strikingly Lacan's claim that the subject, 'c'est ce que le signifiant représente, et il ne saurait rien représenter que pour un autre signifiant, à quoi dès lors se

revealed for Dostoevsky only in 'an intense act of address'; only in interaction can the 'inner man' be revealed, for in dialogue a person 'not only shows himself outwardly but he becomes for the first time that which he is [. . .] To be means to communicate dialogically' (1984*a*: 251–2). It should be noted that the truths which Bakhtin sees Dostoevskyan dialogue as establishing pertain as much to moral questions as to identity—Dostoevsky, according to Bakhtin, sees the two as inseparable, the individual being conscious of everything about himself (p. 48). This in fact leads Bakhtin to discuss polyphony in terms of the ideological content of the dialogues as much as of their structure,[39] despite his criticism of the way critics of Dostoevsky tend to focus on ideological problems to the neglect of 'the deeper and more permanent structural elements in his mode of artistic visualization' (1984*a*: 3–4). This perception of dialogism in ideological as opposed to purely structural terms has significant implications, as we shall see; the distinction is particularly pertinent to Sarraute.

Bakhtinian dialogism exists at all levels of a text, from the individual word or utterance which bears the several accents of the contexts in which different voices have spoken it (this is 'microdialogue'), to the compositional dialogues that take place among characters, right up to the 'great dialogue' constituted by the novel as a whole (1984*a*: 40). The phenomenon of microdialogue makes language the arena for a double assault on the autonomous individual, both on the opinions he expresses and on his very autonomy as a speaker. The several accents words acquire when attributed to different characters who give them different, often conflicting meanings, result in the infiltration of each point of view by those of others. Because Dostoevsky focuses on the individual's

---

réduit le sujet qui écoute' (Lacan 1966: 835). Although the knowledge Bakhtin sees as resulting from dialogue is generally ideological or moral (see n. 39 below), and as such is far removed from the irrational desiring self revealed by the Lacanian dialogue, dialogues like those of Ivan Karamazov and Smerdyakov operate along more Lacanian lines. In these, Ivan's will is properly unconscious, 'hidden even from himself', and is recognized by him, 'dimly and ambiguously at first and then clearly and distinctly [. . .] in another person' (Bakhtin 1984*a*: 259).

[39] What takes shape in dialogic interaction is the idea: 'Human thought becomes genuine thought, that is, an idea, only under conditions of living contact with another and alien thought, a thought embodied in someone else's voice, that is, in someone else's consciousness expressed in discourse [. . .] The idea is inter-individual and intersubjective—the realm of its existence is not individual consciousness but dialogic communion *between* consciousnesses. The idea is a *live event*, played out at the point of dialogic meeting between two or several consciousnesses' (Bakhtin 1984*a*: 88).

consciousness and shows the world through it, all that can be juxta-posed to it are other consciousnesses: 'To the all-devouring con-sciousness of the hero the author can juxtapose only a single objective world—a world of other consciousnesses with rights equal to those of the hero' (pp. 49–50). For Bakhtin, the dialogic universe this creates extends to include the author, whose position relative to his hero is 'a *fully realized and thoroughly consistent dialogic position*, one that affirms the independence, internal freedom, unfinalizability, and indeterminacy of the hero. For the author the hero is not "he" and not "I" but a fully valid "thou"' (p. 63).

This, then, is what happens to the authorial voice in dialogic fiction as Bakhtin sees it: the intratextual dialogue extends to include its creator; the author speaks *with* his characters rather than about them. Yet the parties in this interaction can be considered as equal only as long as it is seen purely as a confrontation of *ideas* independent of their representation. Once the text's nature as rep-resentation is considered, the idea of an author–character dialogue becomes impossible. The author's existence is of a completely different order from that of his characters who are rhetorical con-structs created by him. The supposedly autonomous discourses of independent textual voices are an illusion, the product of a single authorial perspective which remains concealed but in control.[40] Necessarily elevated above what he represents by having created it, an author who attempts to conduct a dialogue with his characters, the objects of his creation, will remain in control of it, making such a dialogue a rather one-sided affair.

What do this godlike power of the author over his text as creator of its fictional world, and his resulting inability to engage in a fully equal dialogue with his characters, imply for the relationship between author and reader in the space of the text? That the inter-nally dialogic text also works to include the reader's perspective in its dialogic dynamic is commonly assumed (see n. 37). David Shepherd (1989) points out that while 'there is no theory of reading or the reader to be plucked ready-formed from the diverse Bakhtinian legacy' (p. 91), the reader does have a place in Bakhtin's concept of

---

[40] Paul Ricoeur makes a similar point in relation to the ostensibly unrepresented status of dramatic dialogue, but where the author as 'reporter' is always behind the scenes: 'La dimen-sion théâtrale consiste en cela: oublier la situation de citation que produit la représentation. Le spectateur croit entendre de vraies personnes. Mais que le rideau retombe, et l'illusion aussitôt s'envole, la pièce entière retourne à son statut de fiction rapportée' (1991: 43).

dialogism. The fact that dialogism is not merely 'a description of the immanent characteristics of [. . .] the novel' but 'insistently gestures to a world outside it' brings the reader into the picture: 'As the intra-textual gives way to the intertextual, it is possible to glimpse a reader no longer threatened by [. . .] redundancy' (p. 94).

One critic who argues explicitly, in the tradition of Voloshinov (Bakhtin?), that the more dialogic the text, the more freedom the reader will enjoy, is Susan Yell. She echoes Voloshinov's view that polyphonic texts allow for more dialogic relationships between character, narrator, text, and reader than do monologic ones (1990: 143); in the latter, the narrator's control of his characters' discourses 'allows for the text to construct a relationship of control with the reader, by constraining in different ways the reading positions which can be taken up' (145). Yet Yell tempers the potentially utopian view of the dialogic text as the space of consensus, freedom, and equality, by making the very useful point that participants in dialogues necessarily engage in power relations—power is asserted through strategies like consistently initiating dialogue, being the provider of information and so in a position of cognitive superiority, giving non-compliant responses to an interlocutor's questions, etc. (p. 142). This introduction of the issue of power to the discussion of dialogue is timely and of considerable importance, for it acts as a counterweight to the notions of cooperation and complementarity in terms of which dialogue is often characterized. In the context of reading, it affirms that, while the totally dialogic text may be struc-turally best placed to engage the reader dialogically, fictional dialogues can accommodate a hierarchy of knowledge and power which is monologic in spirit and which will be reproduced in the way they engage the reader.

All participants in dialogue, then, are not necessarily equal, and inequities within fictional dialogue will surely have consequences for the ways in which that fiction is read. Dialogue like that extolled in Dostoevsky by Bakhtin, where the creating author attempts to mingle his own voice with those of his created characters, takes such inequity to an extreme, given the different planes on which the different voices exist; this dialogic gesture cannot get around the ontological differences between author and character, and the relations of power these differences imply. Assuming that the in-ternal dynamics of the polyphonic text influence its approach to the reader, will the author's irreducible power over the voices which speak within even the most dialogic fiction extend into the text's relationship with its readers? I would argue that while it ultimately cannot, it can affect the kind of dialogue that the author attempts to initiate with those readers. To close this chapter I wish to consider how the author's inability to retain, in his dialogue with the readers of his text, the kind of power he enjoys within the fictional dialogue can leave its mark on that text.

The fact that the reader is other to the author in a way his characters can never be, is of course what makes reading an authentically dialogic act: for Lacan, Schlegel, and indeed Bakhtin too, it is the encounter with a perspective completely outside our own which gives meaning to our words and inscribes us in an order which transcends the finitude of our consciousness. But this 'otherness' which gives dialogue its importance and power makes communication an infinitely complex phenomenon, and all the more so when it takes place across a written and published text, remote from its author and open to an infinite range of readers. Every interlocutor, no matter how well known to us, is capable of interpreting our words in unforeseen ways, or of saying something which we have difficulty interpreting; the anonymity and alienation involved in reading a published work whose author is not only absent (as with all writing) but not addressing us personally only increase the likelihood of divergence between intention and interpretation.

Jacques Derrida has written at length about the alienation involved in writing, and the way this alienation is paradigmatic for speech too. Utterances, spoken as well as written, have a structural permanence which allows them to exist and produce meaning independently of both their source and their original addressee: 'L'absence de l'émetteur, du destinateur, à la marque qu'il abandonne, qui se coupe de lui et continue de produire des effets au-delà de sa présence et de l'actualité présente de son vouloir-dire, voire au-delà de sa vie même [. . .] appartient [. . .] à la structure de toute écriture—et [. . .] de tout langage en général' (Derrida 1972: 372). This absence of the utterer from his utterance is obvious in the case of written language, yet Derrida argues that it also governs spoken communication. The presence of a speaker in his words is illusory: the mark of that presence, the speaker's 'oral signature', must, like any signature, be repeatable in order to be identifiable as his. This very repeatability means that it becomes detached from the person it represents and from his intention in supplying it on a specific occasion (pp. 391–2). Any authorial gesture of control, of ownership of one's words, itself becomes uncontrollable, readable independently of the intention behind it. This 'absence essentielle de l'intention à l'actualité de l'énoncé' (p. 389) is what makes all communication, spoken or written, *écriture*. And,

En tant qu'écriture, la communication, si l'on tient à garder ce mot, n'est pas le moyen de transport du sens, l'échange des intentions et des vouloir-dire, le discours et la 'communication des consciences' [. . .] L'écriture se lit, elle ne donne pas lieu, 'en dernière instance', à un déchiffrement herméneutique, au décryptage d'un sens ou d'une vérité. (p. 392)

Of course this means that even what we may identify as an authorial signature or gesture of control in texts we read is the product of our interpretation rather than an absolute mark of the author's claim to jurisdiction over the text, transmitted intact to us. My reading of Sarraute in the following chapters is obviously subject to this fact whose implications for that reading, and for dialogue more generally, will be discussed at the end of Chapter 4.

That the concept of *écriture* has important implications for dialogue is clear from Derrida's criticism of Lacan: he accuses him of repressing the problems which *écriture* poses for the idea of presence in language. The problem is Lacan's belief in the 'parole présente, vivante, authentique' as the bearer of truth: 'C'est l'effet de parole vivante et présente qui garantit, en dernière instance, la singularité indestructible et inoubliable de la lettre, l'avoir-lieu d'un signifiant qui ne se perd, ne s'égare, ne se divise jamais' (Derrida 1975: 127). But, Derrida points out, writing (and so speech) exists in a situation of mutual *absence* of author and reader (or speaker and listener). This fact is bound to complicate the kind of dialogue in which these can participate through the text. The inherently solitary nature of writing, the absence of the addressee from the situation of address, his total anonymity as an unknown member of the reading public, are aspects of the text's existence which we need to address. And by exploring the evident alienation of author from reader in the writing and reading of the published text we can better understand the mutual absence which spoken dialogue, in so far as it too is governed by *écriture*, must also involve.[41]

---

[41] For Lacan, according to Derrida, 'la voix [. . .] a les caractères phénoménaux de la spontanéité, de la présence à soi, du retour circulaire à soi'. But 'il en irait tout autrement si

How might the solitude of the author (the dominant theme of Sarraute's *Entre la vie et la mort*) and the concomitant lack of control over the text's interpretation (the subject of *Les Fruits d'or*) influence the act of writing? I would suggest that the attempt to achieve a similar kind of control to that possessed over his characters marks to some degree even the most dialogic author's relationship, through the text, to a reader whose interpretation of the text may differ greatly from what it is intended to convey. Even dialogic fiction, I have claimed, has an intentional agenda, an ironic world-view which it desires to have understood: through its way of reporting speech it demonstrates the belief that truth is dialogic and requires the independent response of an interlocutor. Like any implicit ideology this is ultimately a monologic position, one which paradoxically demands that the independent respondent it desires should first assent to its world-view. Thus Umberto Eco can argue that the most ostensibly 'open' texts are the most defining of the reader's role: 'An open text outlines a "closed" project of its Model Reader as a component of its structural strategy' (Eco 1979: 8). Such texts, to ensure the 'correct' response which they need to survive, are forced to try to influence and limit possible interpretations, so diminishing the equality of their desired dialogue with the reader who finds his response to the text guided in certain ways.[42]

Paul Ricoeur, in a series of lectures on interpretation theory (1976), specifically addressed the problems which writing poses for the aspiration to a dialogue of author and reader in the text. The author's mental intention becomes divorced from the reader's experience of the text because in writing the quality of discourse as 'event', a quality evident in the spoken utterance, is diminished; this, for Ricoeur, is what gives the reader freedom of interpretation.[43] This situation has important consequences for the notion of reading as a dialogue with the text: while discourse is of its nature dialogic, always both addressing someone and pointing

l'on se rendait attentif à l'écriture dans la voix, c'est-à-dire avant la lettre [. . .] L'instance de la lettre lacanienne est la relève de l'écriture dans le système de la parole' (1975: 126).

[42] Barbara Herrnstein Smith too notes that literature doesn't simply provoke interpretative activity but also shapes it: 'Even as certain possibilities of interpretation are opened, they are also directed, lured, and redirected by the poet through the verbal structure he has designed' (1978: 145).

[43] There is obviously some common ground between Ricoeur and Derrida here, though Ricoeur's emphasis on the 'event' quality of speech contrasts with the absolutism of Derrida's assimilation of speech to writing.

self-referentially back to the speaker through marks of his meaning in the event of interlocution (1976: 12–15), the fact that this dialogic quality is a feature of discourse as an *event* means that it is diminished in the written text (pp. 25–8). Ricoeur, like Derrida, sees full self-presence as impossible in spoken discourse too. Yet the fact that the speaker belongs to the situation of dialogue generally allows speaker-meaning and utterance-meaning to be harmonized—the speaker witnesses the addressee's interpretation and can respond to it. In writing, no such adjustment of the text's interpreted meaning to the authorial intention takes place (p. 29).

However, if the written text normally excludes reference back to its originator for clarification, it does, for Ricoeur, retain some evidence of the event of its enunciation. This dialectical link with its source is more emphatic than Derrida's notion of the authorial 'signature' which, while it marks the text, is devoid of the illocutionary force the moment of signing wished to embed in it. Seeing the question of authorial input to the text in dialectical terms as Ricoeur does makes of it a more complex issue than is allowed by the simple alternative between on the one hand the traditional 'intentional fallacy' (of seeing literature as authorial self-expression) denounced by the 'New Critics' in the 1950s in favour of a view of the text as aesthetic object, and on the other the poststructuralist authorless text. Instead, Ricoeur sees authorial meaning as inseparable from the text (hence the possibility of discerning a non-propositional authorial intention in formal features): 'The authorial meaning is the dialectical counterpart of the verbal meaning, and they have to be construed in terms of each other' (p. 30).

The attenuation of authorial control in written discourse is complemented for Ricoeur by the increased responsibility given to the reader over the addressee of spoken dialogue. To the textual dialectic of event and meaning corresponds the interpretative dialectic of understanding and explanation (p. 71; these should be thought of as simultaneous rather than consecutive). The loss of situational reference, which in oral communication is grounded in the dialogic event, requires the reader to create a *new* event of enunciation—this new event is created from the text in which the original event was objectified. In this way the written text emphasizes the fact that all expression is a dialectic of event and meaning, presence and absence, in contrast to the way speech conflates the two by making speaker-meaning and utterance-meaning appear to coincide.

Looking at the other pole of the textual encounter, the reader's dialectical interpretation and creative input is the full development of an attitude dissimulated in the interpretative activity involved in spoken conversation.

Ricoeur judges the absence of situational reference in the written text to be a good thing: it reveals that the nature of discourse is to project a world, by making the reader do just that, free of the constraints of face-to-face exchanges. Writing, and specifically for Ricoeur literature, entails an abstraction from the surrounding world, and this lets the reader 'imaginatively actualize the potential non-ostensive references of the text in a new situation' (p. 81). This is how the text points towards a possible world which is disclosed in front of it rather than being concealed behind it in some relation to the situation of writing.

How much is the discovery of the text's 'possible world' determined in advance and how much does the reader's interpretative activity supply in constituting it? Ricoeur's dialectical view of reading shows that the attribution of responsibility cannot be such a simple 'either–or' affair—indeed, the development of an alternative conception of the nature of reading to those grounded in this opposition will be an important aspect of my reading of Sarraute. None the less, Ricoeur does affirm that 'it is the response of the audience which makes the text [. . .] significant' (p. 31); thus 'a specific kind of onesidedness is implied in the act of reading' (p. 78). And as interpretation begins with a subjective guess as to the nature of the text and is then validated according to a logic of probability rather than of truth or falsity, as many interpretations are possible as there are reading perspectives. Added to this is the fact, already mentioned, that while the speaker knows his addressee (though, we might feel, never completely) as 'a "thou" whose identification precedes discourse', written discourse is open to a potentially universal audience: 'The meaning of a text is open to anyone who can read' (p. 93). It is easy to see how the interpretative authority given to the reader can lead to a divergence from the author's ideas on how his text should be interpreted.

The text's semantic autonomy thus creates considerable tension between the author's claim to authority and the reader's rights of interpretation. The reader's relationship to the text, as Ricoeur sees it, is anything but collaborative: 'The right of the reader and the right of the text converge in an important struggle that generates the whole dynamic of interpretation' (p. 32). Given that authors of texts are themselves readers of texts,[44] and as such are aware of the liberties readers may take with the texts they read, it is only to be expected that they will try to arm their texts in anticipation of a battle for control of their interpretation. One very obvious way of attempting to influence the reader's perspective and values in advance is by embodying 'good' and 'bad' readers within the text. It is a strategy, as we shall see in the next chapter and again in Chapter 4, that Nathalie Sarraute makes great use of in works like *Les Fruits d'or*, *Entre la vie et la mort*, and *Enfance*. In the context of Bakhtin's author–character dialogue, we can see this strategy, which at first seems to acknowledge the importance of the reader as 'other', as in fact turning him from the representation's *addressee* into a character and so into an *object* of representation (see Ch. 5 n. 14). In this way, all the implications of authorial godliness in the earlier relationship of control are now projected into the relationship with the reader too. I shall examine the reader's options, faced with such a challenge to his freedom of response, in the final chapter, in the context of an interrogation of the whole adversarial notion of reading which gives rise to such strategies of control.

If speech as well as writing is marked by the mutual absence (more radical for Derrida than for Ricoeur) which gives rise, in some of Sarraute's prose works, to the attempt to shape the reader's response by defining an ideal reading in advance, then such a strategy cannot be specific to writing. The solitary situation of the writer simply exacerbates the solitary nature of any act of expression, including—despite the physical presence of an interlocutor—speaking. The limited perspective of the speaking subject means that, like the author, he can never know his addressee in all his otherness, but only from his own standpoint. It thus seems likely that, just as the author does, he too will project onto his interlocutor an interpretative stance to which the other should conform. In other words, Sarraute's creation of model readers may well be only an extreme manifestation of the linguistic subject's inherent inability to engage with his interlocutor's radical otherness in its reality, an inability masked by the projection of an illusory sameness to which

---

[44] Writing, as Antoine Compagnon has pointed out, is always a rewriting of what one has already read: 'Toute l'écriture est collage et glose' (Compagnon 1979: 32).

the other is expected to conform. For Lacan, this inability and this imposition of a specular image on the other are intrinsic to language use: 'Fondamentalement, ce sont [de vrais sujets] que je vise chaque fois que je prononce une vraie parole, mais j'atteins toujours aa^1 [the 'moi-moi autre' axis] par réflexion [. . .] Le sujet est séparé des Autres, les vrais, par le mur du langage' (Lacan 1978: 286).

The alienation of both writer and speaker from the reception of their address thus produces an attempt to control interpretation, a struggle for power not acknowledged in a view of dialogue which sees it simply as a consensual meeting of minds in the service of truth. In the light of this chapter's exploration of dialogue as it relates to narrative and the act of reading I now wish to move on to the main subject of this book, the role of dialogue and the representation of reading in Nathalie Sarraute's prose writings. I shall begin with her two most fully dialogical texts, *Enfance* and *Tu ne t'aimes pas*, both highly unusual in being constructed entirely as dialogues, with no governing narrative voice.[45] My main concern in the next two chapters will be to see what happens to the narratorial discourse in these works, and to what extent an authorial monologism persists through the fragmentation of the narrative into a dialogue which appears to be opening up the text to the reader. In relation to *Tu ne t'aimes pas*, I shall discuss the tension between the ironization of linguistic convention and the discourse in which this is operated. The kind of response Sarraute attempts to project onto the reader of her work, and his options as he reads that work, will be the subject of the two final chapters.

---

[45] *Ouvrez*, which appeared too recently to receive extended attention in this study, is of course also entirely structured in dialogue. Unlike *Enfance* or *Tu ne t'aimes pas*, though, the dialogue here is not between the inner voices of the subject, but between words—those used or, more often, those purposely kept out of conversations with others (conversations in which, therefore, the self is never fully engaged).

2

THE WRITING SELF: IRONY AND AUTHORITY

We saw in the last chapter that dialogic fiction has much in common with irony. Not only do both involve the representation of discourses, but both also make evident the limitations of the discourses they represent. The diversity of discourses in a dialogic text emphasizes the limits of each monologic perspective but also shows how these limits are transcended through dialogic interaction. And while verbal irony—the rhetorical device in which the speaker seems to express a certain point of view while tacitly deriding it—treats the discourse it represents as an object to which a derogatory attitude is adopted, epistemological irony acknowledges the intrinsically flawed nature of all language and its inadequacy to the speaking subject even as he attempts to articulate this insight. Here, too, transcendence of the limits of expression is a function of the dialogic reception of the ironic text.

That irony permeates all of Nathalie Sarraute's work has been noted in passing by several critics and explored in some detail by a few (Racevskis 1977; Minogue 1987a). Generally, the focus has been on local instances of verbal irony and their possible motivations, rather than on ways in which the text might try to undermine the authority of its own discourse. Thus for Karlis Racevskis, Sarraute's irony is a vehicle of social criticism, specifically of the 'cultural establishment' (1977: 37) which includes both the represented readers and writers of her novels, and their real readers in so far as these reflect their fictional counterparts. Valerie Minogue, on the other hand, sees Sarraute's use of irony as inseparable from the project of articulating the prelinguistic tropism, for 'l'utilité de l'ironie c'est [. . .] de suggérer sans définir' (1987a: 8).

The aspect of irony which concerns me in relation to Nathalie Sarraute's work is how, beyond simply illustrating the expressive inadequacy of conventional language (whether another's or the ironist's own), it simultaneously indicates that dialogue can overcome that inadequacy. Irony, whether verbal or epistemological, actively acknowledges the interlocutor's importance, for its critical thrust is complemented by a strong cooperative dimension. Verbal irony, by managing to convey something at odds with the utterance's lexical signification, emphasizes the way all communication depends on inference by the addressee for its success. Epistemological irony, more radically, sees the involvement of the addressee in the constitution of meaning as supplying a (provisional and ever to be renegotiated) validation of language which offers a momentary transcendence of the linguistic subject's fallen state.

Nathalie Sarraute's writing clearly has much in common with the ironic view of the subject as trapped in a web of symbols and trying within it to articulate a truthful utterance in interaction with another subject. Her work has from the first concentrated on the disparity between sensation and expression, the intensity of tropistic experience contrasting ironically with the banality of the words which translate it into conversation. Successful dialogue is always the goal of her characters as they seek full mutual understanding with an interlocutor who will share their sensitivity to the reality of the tropism. While interpersonal relations generally remain unsatisfactory in her work, she presents the text–reader relationship as potentially providing such a successful dialogue, and thus as compensating for the inadequacies of relations between individuals.

However, given the conclusions of the last chapter regarding the alienated character of written communication (and, less obviously, of speech), an alienation even more marked in published work with an unknown readership, Sarraute's 'ideal' dialogue with the reader is likely to have its own imperfections. The dialogic writer, unable to enact a dialogue with a reader who is not yet present, can only anticipate the dialogue he or she desires. But by anticipating it, he or she indicates how the text is to be read, in a gesture of control not dissimilar from those which repeatedly cause relations among Sarraute's fictional characters to fail. Yet the very ways in which the relationship Sarraute offers her readers falls short of full dialogic equality will be instructive to note, as by pointing up the limitations of her commitment to dialogue they illustrate the predicament of all subjects in language.

Dialogic openness to the reader is, as we saw in the last chapter, closely linked to a dialogic narrative structure, the foregrounding of the discourses of characters at the expense of narratorial authority. This chapter will concentrate on such textual dialogism in Sarraute, specifically on the way in *Enfance* the authoritative narrative discourse we would expect to find in an autobiographical text is replaced by the dialogue of a plurality of authorial voices. Before embarking on a study of *Enfance* in section 2, it will be useful to review the way the representation of discourses in her preceding prose works becomes ever more dialogic, constituting an ever stronger structural attack on narrative monologism. This attack will culminate in the fragmented discourse of *Enfance* (and, even more emphatically, *Tu ne t'aimes pas*). We can then consider how Sarraute's own comments on writing promote the view of her work which this formal evolution suggests, that of an anti-authoritarian and dialogic engagement with the dilemma of the linguistic subject in the search for truth. However, they also reveal considerable limitations in that view, limitations which, I shall argue, reappear in *Enfance* despite its apparently radical dialogism, and ultimately reinforce in her writings the obstacles to dialogue inherent in the written text.

1. Narration and irony in Sarraute

The disintegration of an overarching narrative perspective in Sarraute's novels up to *Vous les entendez?* has been closely and comprehensively analysed by Anthony Newman (1976). Rather than cover the same territory again, I shall briefly summarize his observations before outlining the way her more recent work continues the trend he identified.

Newman follows Émile Benveniste (1970: 18) in seeing the novel as an enunciation on two levels, the utterances of the fictional characters taking place within the global enunciation of the writer (Newman 1976: 1–2, 11). His examination of the status of reported discourse in Sarraute's novels starts out from Cranaki and Belaval's observation that 'de plus en plus le dialogue devient le centre de gravité de ses romans' (Cranaki and Belaval 1965: 113; Newman 1976: 23), a comment which contradicts Sarraute's own impression of a reduction in dialogue from *Les Fruits d'or* to *Entre la vie et la mort* (Sarraute 1967*b*: 285; Newman 1976: 23). The conflict of views is explained by the fact that reported discourses are not always announced as such, but instead are indicated contextually, so perhaps dissimulating 'la presque omniprésence de l' "oral" dans les œuvres de Sarraute' (Newman 1976: 32–3).

Newman observes how, from *Le Planétarium* on, the speaker himself becomes the narrator of his utterances; that novel's abandonment of the unifying first-person narrator of *Portrait d'un inconnu* and
Martereau is 'un grand pas vers l'effacement de toute conscience
centrale et organisatrice (l'auteur omniscient)' (p. 61). This effacing
of monologic authority through the juxtaposition of different perspectives will, in *Enfance* and *Tu ne t'aimes pas*, be pursued within the
authorial voice itself as it fragments into independent voices. (The
dialogic multiplicity of *Ouvrez* undoes the authorial self's authority
in a somewhat different, and indeed even more dramatic way: here
the many voices are attributed to autonomous words rather than to
a multi-dimensional 'self'.)

Moving from the level of discourse as *énoncé*, Newman bases his
'paralinguistic' study of characters' *énonciation* on a reading of *Entre
la vie et la mort*, the opening sequence of which enacts the lesson that
narration always originates in a particular point of view. The
reader's discovery that the narrator of the first paragraph is a participant in the action creates a 'personnalisation radicale du texte et
de l'expérience qu'il évoque' (p. 92). While this 'je' disappears
immediately into the group, to become a 'chaînon anonyme' (*EVM*
10), its initial identification affirms a 'présence affective, diffuse dans
le "nous" de la suite' (Newman 1976: 92) and, in a dialectic of objectivity and subjectivity, of the 'il' and the 'je', which for Newman is the
essence of Sarraute's fiction, reminds the reader that every 'il' is a
potential 'je', every character a subject (p. 92).

Such character-narrators still require the intervention of the
authorial voice to articulate their prelinguistic experiences in a
'discours *pour* le personnage' (p. 95). Newman, like Dorrit Cohn (see
Ch. 1, p. 29), notes that 'c'est toute la périlleuse entreprise des
romans de Sarraute que ce prêt de sa voix à ce qui n'en a pas chez le
personnage, que ce discours *pour* les tropismes' (p. 96). This
accounts for the way free indirect discourse (as Cohn also points
out), 'de procédé syntaxique [. . .] est devenu principe d'écriture,
lieu privilégié de l'écriture de Nathalie Sarraute' (p. 99). However,
Newman discerns in Sarraute's 'style libre relâché' (p. 106) a drive
to occlude the author as far as is possible given her task of articulating the unexpressed. He notes the increasing use of dialogue to
represent *sous-conversation*, and sees it as a way of linking the outside,
tangible world of conversation (where characters do not need an
authorial voice to speak on their behalf) to the inner world of

tropisms which does not have such linguistic autonomy (p. 102). It thus seems likely that Sarraute's attraction, even at this early stage, to dialogue as a vehicle for representing the tropism, is part of an attempt to minimize the status of the authorial voice.[1]

These novels governed by free indirect discourse and devoted to denouncing the artifice of social interaction are ideal terrain for verbal irony. Interestingly, this ironic unmasking of the tropistic reality behind superficial conversations frequently takes the form of self-irony in which the victim is a figure close to Sarraute's aesthetic position. This suggests an openness to having that position relativized and taken issue with by a critical reader, anticipating the formal enactment of just such an encounter in *Enfance*. Yet it must be acknowledged that in many of the cases of self-irony where typically Sarrautean literary values are held up to ridicule, the effect is in fact to reinforce rather than subvert those values. Thus when one voice rejoices because in the fictional 'Fruits d'Or' 'on [ne] trouve pas de "profondeurs"'. Pas de grouillements de larves, de pataugeages dans je ne sais quels fonds bourbeux qui dégagent des miasmes asphyxiants, dans je ne sais quelles vases putrides où l'on s'enlise' (p. 42), the irony of such words—virtual quotations of Sarraute's own unique imagery, articulated here in a clearly derogatory tone—ultimately rebounds on the speaker, for the authorial discourse which in turn quotes his words takes its own eloquent distance from them through its style which promotes what they mock.

Sarraute's self-mockery appears less obviously recuperable in a scene later in the same novel, when one of the fictional voices parodies a female apologist for a 'new reality':

Il fallait l'entendre, la brave dame, elle était toute rouge, toutes ses plumes hérissées: 'Mais Monsieur, moi je trouve Les Fruits d'Or factice . . . c'est trop littéraire . . . ce n'est pas ça, la réalité [. . .] Les sentiments, c'est tellement plus complexe . . . Il pépie . . . on nous a appris . . . à l'heure actuelle nous savons' [. . .] La pauvre était

---

[1] Celia Britton has also drawn attention to this tendency: 'An examination of the novels in chronological sequence shows that *sous-conversation* tends more and more to be represented textually as speech' (1983: 72). She, however, sees the invasion by reported speech of the theoretically prelinguistic, tropistic realm of *sous-conversation* as symptomatic of a thematic paradox, namely 'Sarraute's representation of communication as *both* predictable, inevitably intelligible [. . .] and, on the other hand, elusive and treacherous' (p. 78). This relates to the conflict which I shall discuss in terms of Sarraute's attitude to the reader, one between the desire for immediate contact with and total knowledge of the other, and the fundamental alienation which makes it impossible.

hors d'elle: 'Ce que nous appelons la réalité aujourd'hui—c'est bien autre chose
. . . Depuis un demi-siècle, toutes ces découvertes [. . .]' (p. 79)

So familiar are these phrases from Sarraute's critical writings that
we might be hearing snatches from essays like 'Nouveau Roman et
réalité' (1963) or 'Les Deux Réalités' (1964). At the same time, the
qualities described in these snippets are abstract enough not to
point uniquely to Sarraute's particular literary style in the way the
evocations of her imagery did (while *Les Fruits d'or* does indeed present a more complex vision of reality than much traditional fiction
does, this is a sufficiently general characteristic to seem, while
eminently relevant, not uniquely applicable to her writing). For this
reason the speaker's scorn is perhaps not so directly undermined by
its context as in the previous example, the authorial self-irony not so
obviously overcome. Yet the limits of the capacity of verbal irony to
subvert one's own discourse remain visible: the very fact that the
author's values must be embodied in a fictional character, however
close that character is to the self, illustrates how in verbal irony the
self being mocked is never entirely coextensive with the self doing
the mocking. Mediating self-irony through a fictional representative, as Sarraute does here, simply magnifies the way it always
ultimately spares the speaker by targeting an image he or she creates. A barrier remains which keeps self-directed verbal irony,
where the author's status is reinforced rather than undermined by
his ability to create an amusing effigy of himself, from the total self-
subversion by the speaking voice which is the aim of what I have
called epistemological irony.

What scope is there for a more radical ironization of the authorial
perspective than such local instances of author-directed irony allow?
It seems that as long as a superior narrative vantage-point is retained
which embraces and transcends the discourses it represents, however much irony these direct at the text or the authorial project, they
will ultimately be defeated by the authority of the discourse which
frames them. In this light, the fragmentation, in *Enfance* and *Tu ne
t'aimes pas*, of the authorial point of view into first two and then
several voices, suggests itself as a solution—through dissolution—to
the limits which narrative authority imposes on an ironic attitude to
one's own language. The dialogue among the exploded elements of
the authorial discourse not only exploits the spontaneity of conversation to give these works the air of events in progress, free of the textual order a unified narrative discourse imposes. In addition, this

diversity of voices presents itself as the ideal way to subvert any attempt by a single narrative thread to prevail.

Both the structure of opposing voices and the idea of the text as an event in progress (a feature I shall return to in Chapter 4) had been explored by Sarraute in works written since Newman's study: *'disent les imbéciles'* continued the tendency towards representing *sous-conversation* as dialogue, and *L'Usage de la parole* incited the reader to cooperate in the task of revealing tropistic reality, and so help write the text. *Enfance* and *Tu ne t'aimes pas* thus appear as further explorations in a mode of writing which aims to erode narrative authority by privileging the diversity and unpredictable actuality of a dialogue in whose development the reader is actively involved. Yet we have already seen that the nature of writing as deferred communication with an unknown other poses complications for the authorial attempt to initiate a dialogue with the reader (these complications will be addressed in the context of Sarraute's work in Chapters 4 and 5). In sections 2 and 3 of this chapter I want to look at the problems which arise already in the structural project of dissolving narrative authority and discursive unity into a fully dialogic text, in this case the autobiographical *récit Enfance*. That *Enfance* illustrates these problems in a particularly striking way seems to me to be connected to a distinction Sarraute makes between everyday language and artistic expression. It is a distinction which affects her entire conception of dialogue, especially of dialogue with the reader, and which we need to examine before turning to the literary dialogue of *Enfance*.

Sarraute's view of the writer, as outlined frequently in interviews and essays, is clearly situated in the Romantic tradition of the poet as seer, one who intimates a reality beyond everyday appearances and who strives to capture this reality in the work of art:

Cet invisible que l'art rend visible, qu'est-ce que c'est? C'est quelque chose de très difficile à définir, quelque chose qui est fait d'éléments épars, que nous devinons, que nous pressentons très vaguement, d'éléments amorphes qui gisent privés d'existence, perdus dans la masse infinie des possibilités, des virtualités, fondus en un magma, recouverts par la gangue du visible, du déjà connu, du déjà exprimé. Ces éléments l'artiste les dégage, les réunit, les construit en un modèle qui est l'œuvre même. (Sarraute 1964: 72)

Like the Romantic artist, the Sarrautean writer's perception of a truth concealed behind the conventional terms in which we see the world isolates him: 'Devant cette réalité inconnue que l'écrivain a l'impression d'être le premier à voir, il se trouve seul [. . .] Il est seul juge des formes qu'il lui sera nécessaire de créer pour rendre compte de cette réalité qui est la sienne' (p. 73).

In many respects, the web of conventions which Sarraute sees as enclosing us remains within the tradition we have seen, where the conscious individual is held to have only a limited understanding of his full subjectivity, being unable to grasp alone the chaos which contains him.[2] For Sarraute as for Schlegel, Freud, and Lacan, our blindness in this respect is related to our use of language: she equates the 'déjà connu' with the 'déjà exprimé', and our ignorance is attributed largely to those texts which inform our view of reality. 'La réalité banale, celle du lecteur et de l'auteur, c'est une image du monde donnée par toutes nos connaissances, notre culture, par toutes les œuvres qui constituent l'expérience littéraire, philosophique, artistique de chacun' (1963: 433).

The affinity of Sarraute's ideas on the problems of literary creation with the analyses of language and identity outlined in the last chapter becomes even more apparent when she discusses what she considers to be the epitome of conventionality in fictional writing, the fictional character or *personnage*. Just as in life, as psychoanalysis teaches us, the *moi* is a mask held up over the chaos of the self, so the character in a novel, 'cette pure convention romanesque', is no more than 'le support, fragile et mouvant, de la matière nouvelle qui le déborde de toutes parts . . . une matière devenue si complexe que les contours bien définis, épais et rigides, du héros de roman traditionnel ne peuvent plus la contenir' (436). If the Freudian critique of the concept of identity relates so closely to this critique of the traditional novel, it is because, for Sarraute, literature has informed our perception of reality: we see others and ourselves in the terms in which fiction has taught us to see them, and so we judge new literary characters in turn according to a false standard of human verisimilitude acquired from nineteenth-century novels. Thus the dismantling of characters in the novel, and that of the fictional *moi* we construct daily above the vastness of the self, are inseparable processes. Sarraute, like Bakhtin, singles out Dostoevsky as a pioneer in the attack on the unitary fictional character: 'Chez

---

[2] We live in a 'monde en trompe-l'œil', surrounded by 'tout un ensemble de notions à travers lequel chacun de nous voit la réalité' (Sarraute 1963: 433).

Dostoievski [. . .] des traits de caractère tout à fait opposés s'affront-ent constamment dans le même personnage' (1967b: 288).

Like Lacan or Bakhtin, Sarraute privileges the role of dialogue in constituting a more authentic selfhood founded in intersubjectivity. Beneath the false sense of singularity and autonomy which language gives to the subject is the 'fond commun' of prelinguistic experience which Sarraute famously calls tropisms. Because this level of experience is universal, it provides a founding inter-subjectivity from which language as a conceptual medium alienates the self, and to which all our efforts at communication aim to be adequate: 'Quand je parle de "fond commun" c'est tout simple-ment que je pense que ces tropismes, ces mouvements, existent absolument chez tous [. . .] C'est eux qui créent certains rapports entre les gens, qui forment les sympathies, les antipathies, qui déter-minent les conduites que nous avons les uns à l'égard des autres' (p. 289). But if language causes the isolation of the individual, it is also seen by him as his one way out of it, potentially providing access to the secular human Absolute of a fully realized intersubjectivity: 'Je crois que s'il y a un absolu que mes personnages recherchent c'est toujours le besoin de fusion et de contact avec autrui. Le silence de quelqu'un rompt le contact. Et de même le mensonge: c'est une rupture. Il s'agit chaque fois d'une rupture qu'on essaye de réparer' (pp. 293–4).

Sarraute's characters are not alone in struggling to overcome lin-guistic isolation through address to an interlocutor; the writer too must battle against the 'action asséchante et pétrifiante' of language (1972a: 32) to communicate her vision to the reader. While her earl-ier work opted for imagery as a way of overcoming the opacity of language, and thereby required of the reader a less active role,[3] the dialogical structure of her more recent writing with its fragmented authorial discourse explicitly acknowledges the importance of the reader's input. The Sarrautean character's search for a responsive interlocutor is mirrored in the way the more recent works present themselves as coming into being through negotiation with their

---

[3] For Sarraute in the 1960s, images seemed able to overcome the materiality of the lan-guage which composed them, evoking 'ces tropismes [qui] *ne sont pas exprimables par des mots*' (1967b: 289; my emphasis). This faith in the power of the image to transcend language con-fined the reader's role in establishing successful communication to simply recognizing the image: 'Je suis obligée de choisir des images très simples pour que le lecteur n'ait pas à se creuser la tête, pour qu'elles lui soient transmises directement'.

reader (as in the invitation at the start of *L'Usage de la parole*: 'Ne nous hâtons pas, allons au plus près d'abord': p. 11).

In 1978, between '*disent les imbéciles*' and *L'Usage de la parole*, Sarraute spelt out to Lucette Finas the role she saw dialogue play in self-definition. She began by accepting Finas's definition of 'l'essentiel de votre œuvre' as 'la hantise et le refus d'une certaine forme de *résistance* [. . .] la résistance qu'opposent, à celui qui tient la parole, ses interlocuteurs réels ou imaginaires' (Sarraute 1978: 4). Thus dialogue in her work has the status of an ideal, menaced by the other's indifference to a speaker who not only, for Sarraute, 'tient la parole' but also 'tient *à* la parole'. This speaker in search of dialogue stands apart from the conversational power struggles so often represented in her fiction: '[Il] n'a pas en vue la soumission de la personne de son interlocuteur. Il souhaite la soumission de sa parole à un ordre qui les dépasse tous deux et auquel il se soumet lui-même'. This transcendent order, with its clear affinities to Lacan's Symbolic or Schlegel's concept of the infinite relativity of existence in language, is the order of dialogue, Sarraute affirms, concurring emphatically with Finas's view that 'le postulat implicite de vos textes est que la rectitude du dialogue se porte garante de la bonne marche du monde'.

Yet alongside these similarities to the ideas of identity as intersubjective and linguistic which I discussed in Chapter 1 (her description of the dialogue-seeker's words as 'pleins' seems to echo Lacan's 'parole pleine'), there persists undeniably in her work a belief in language as individual expression rather than intersubjective creation. Sarraute's 'mots pleins' are in fact the embodiment of an idea which the speaker holds prior to dialogue; their value thus pre-exists their address to the other. Her 'chevaliers', representatives of values dear to her, aim to transmit these to an interlocutor ('Que faire d'une valeur reconnue d'un seul? Alors, ils communiquent [. . .]'), but more often than not the fate of the idea is, as in *Elle est là*, to be 'happée au passage . . . enfermée là-bas, livrée sans défense, étranglée en silence' (*Th.* 14). If dialogue fails more often than it succeeds in Sarraute's work, it is because it is a collision between two already constituted *values* embodied in the speakers, and each of which can only survive at the cost of the other's annihilation.[4] The struggle

---

[4] While this may recall Bakhtin's concept of dialogue as ideological, there remains the all-important difference that, for him, the idea itself is a product of intersubjectivity (see Ch. 1 n. 39).

which the Sarrautean dialogue enacts is thus ideological rather than epistemological: it is not to *establish* a value for language but to *impose* a value and the spontaneous, living language in which, with much difficulty, it is articulated. Dialogue is motivated not by the creation of a transindividual truth, but by 'la recherche de l'assentiment' (1978: 5).

Sarraute in fact never goes more than halfway toward seeing language as limiting our ability to grasp reality, and this ambivalence is visible in her account of her own writing practice: 'Quelquefois la sensation vous fait partir à la découverte du mot, mais quelquefois un mot surgit et ce mot à son tour produit une nouvelle sensation' (1976*b*: 285). The ultimate expressibility of sensation, of the *sous-conversation* normally described as unnameable, is clearly demonstrated by the fact that it surfaces into the spoken dialogue of Sarraute's dramas. While the uncanny character of these dialogues is often emphasized,[5] their strangeness lies not in any lexical or syntactic distortion of spoken language but simply in the way they articulate feelings not normally considered suitable for conversation: 'Les gens parlent d'une manière qui paraît tout à fait naturelle, mais en réalité ils disent des choses qu'on ne dit jamais, ils expriment ce qui se passe en eux [. . .] Le dialogue est irréel parce qu'il contient le pré-dialogue: ce que d'ordinaire on ne dit pas' (1976*b*: 288). That the would-be *indicible* is thoroughly compatible with ordinary language is clear from the fact that, as Sarraute complains to Lucette Finas, readers of her drama are capable of not even noticing the unreal nature of its dialogues (1978: 4).

If Sarraute's characters ultimately become able to articulate their prelinguistic mental processes in a dramatic dialogue, this suggests that what she sees the subject of language as lacking is not so much a lexicon adequate to experience as a social sanction. Similarly, if the writer must struggle in order to articulate a perception of reality, it is not because language is held to be *inherently* insufficient to that reality but because large areas of it have become devitalized through everyday use. They have become so marked by overuse that their referent has been occluded behind the veneer of convention. This enduring faith in the expressive potential of language for those who can seek out spaces not yet conventionalized into cliché is made very clear in something Sarraute says about Flaubert in her

---

[5] Including by Sarraute herself, in the essay 'Le Gant retourné' (1975).

address to the 1972 colloquium on the *nouveau roman* at Cérisy-la-Salle. She is incredulous at his admission that 'à chaque ligne, à chaque mot, la langue me manque et l'insuffisance du vocabulaire est telle que je suis forcé à changer les détails très souvent', and sees it as running entirely counter to Modernism. In her view, 'c'est précisément vers ce qui ne se laisse pas nommer, vers ce qui échappe à toute définition, à toute qualification pétrifiante, que se portent tous les efforts des modernes'.[6] For Sarraute, the perception of what is unnameable is only the starting-point for the modern writer whose goal must be, beyond indicating its existence, to make it nameable: 'Toute écriture vivante doit mettre au jour quelque chose qui n'a pas encore été pris dans l'écriture' (1984*b*: 41).

Thus the apparent ambivalence in Sarraute's attitude to the status of language is explained by the fact that she sees it as a two-tiered structure. Language at its most familiar is certainly limited and limiting, a web of convention in which the speaking subject is unable to articulate anything truly his own, and which cuts him off from any possibility of understanding his position in the world. But where she differs from much contemporary critical thought is in seeing this web of convention as only partial, concealing behind it not just reality but in the first instance a purer language in direct contact with that reality. This view, by considering expression to be problematic yet ultimately achievable, simultaneously suggests that our mental activity is limited by the language we use, and creates a space for literature as a way of overcoming those limitations within language.[7] Sarraute makes clear in a 1981 interview that literature, as writing, far from epitomizing a lack of self-presence true of all language use, can express what speech cannot; she agrees strongly

---

[6] 1972*a*: 33. In the discussion following her talk, Jean Ricardou defended Flaubert's 'considération du langage comme matière signifiante dont il faut respecter les lois' as on the contrary 'une prise de conscience tout à fait moderne' (p. 42).

[7] Ann Jefferson elucidates Sarraute's attitude to linguistic representation in terms of Gérard Genette's notion of 'secondary cratylism', where cratylism denotes the belief in language's organic and necessary relation to what it names, and secondary cratylism sees language, though imperfect, as none the less 'perfectible dans le sens d'une plus grande mimésis' (Genette 1972*a*: 394; cited in Jefferson 1978: 524). She discusses how Sarraute's imagery works toward this second-level mimesis by 'deconstruct[ing] both the more traditional realist reading whereby the language of the text behaves as if it were a copy, and the more radical anti-representational reading implied by pure scriptural activity, in order to produce as much meaning as possible' (p. 524). This combination of the subversion of conventional representational discourse with an insistence on their own realist motivation puts Sarraute's texts 'on the conservative side of that fundamental division between representation on the one hand, and pure scriptural activity on the other'.

with its definition as 'un autre discours [. . .] la tentative d'exprimer de manière plus subtile et moins limitée cette complexité de choses que le discours parlé n'atteint pas' (1985*b*: 306–7). If Germaine Lemaire in *Le Planétarium* feels Flaubertian anguish at the banality of her writing, it is only because 'cet écrivain n'était pas un véritable écrivain; c'était un écrivain académique' (p. 307); Alain Guimier is the real writer, for 'il patauge dans une matière trouble; il n'a pas encore trouvé le langage à travers lequel il pourra faire passer une sensation encore intacte'. Hence the Romantic isolation of the Sarrautean artist: just as her speakers only engage in dialogue *after* they have established certain values, and purely to get confirmation of these, the writer's search for truth is also solitary. He finds a true language not in dialogue but in a private struggle to name 'ce qu'il est seul à voir [. . .] ce qui exige pour se révéler, qui ne peut se révéler que par un nouveau mode d'expression, par de nouvelles formes' (1963: 432; cp. 1972*a*: 32).[8]

This differentiation between authentic and conventional language explains how Sarraute can claim that the writer creates new forms *ex nihilo*, transporting himself outside 'ces régions déjà en tous points occupées où le langage littéraire dress[e] ses modèles admirables et écrasants' (1972*a*: 35), while remaining able to write.[9] Positing a mode of expression which has a direct, organic relationship to experience (to write in this register is to 'laisser circuler le plus librement possible à travers le langage la sève qui monte de ces régions inconnues où il plonge ses racines': p. 34) allows Sarraute to blur the boundary between the domain of sensation and the status of the writer as a linguistic subject. Authentic writing recreates the

---

[8] The problems which attend the concept of expression for modern critical thinking were evidently not an issue for Sarraute in 1963. We can contrast her lively reaction, some years later, when asked by Alain Robbe-Grillet whether the world she writes about exists for her before the writing or is produced by it: 'Je n'ai pas employé le mot "expression", que Dieu m'en préserve! Je sais parfaitement dans quel piège vous essayez de me faire tomber' (Sarraute 1972*a*: 50). She goes on to assert that the fictional world doesn't pre-exist the text but that 'ce qui existe, ce sont des sensations vagues . . . qui ont besoin du langage, qui vont à sa recherche'.

[9] The idea that one can remove oneself entirely from literary language when writing in a received literary form and acknowledging Dostoevsky, Kafka, Proust, and Joyce as forebears is clearly problematic. The confidence it displays in the separability of one's own artistic creation from the context the genre provides is perhaps comparable to Sarraute's belief that the tropism as a mental creation develops, and can be represented, independently of the specific social or mental context in which it occurs, 'à l'état pur' and in a 'porteur anonyme, à peine visible, un simple support de hasard' (1972*a*: 35).

sensation by hovering between invention and representation: 'Ce que j'ai cherché, c'est de *faire exister* quelque chose *d'encore inconnu* et qui *exigeait une nouvelle forme*' (p. 49; my emphasis). Inauthentic writing instead names the sensation, and so remains within the realm of abstract definition: 'Je ne les [les choses informes] ai jamais nommées. Vous ne trouverez pas une seule fois une définition d'un de ces états dans un de mes livres' (p. 48). The whole stake of Sarraute's writing is to articulate the 'innommable' without naming it—ultimately an expressive project, despite her protestations (see n. 8). It is this fragile distinction which lets her simultaneously aspire to 'investir dans du langage une part, si infime fût-elle, d'innommé', and claim that tropisms attracted her because 'ils ne portaient et ne pouvaient porter aucun nom' (p. 34).[10]

Given this view of language in which, despite the elevation of the concept of dialogue, the role of the writer as solitary seeker after truth remains, what can we expect the reader's place in Sarraute's literary universe to be? The two-tier view of language, which combines a belief in words as inadequate conventions with a simultaneous belief in truth as expressible, seems finally to generate an aesthetic less close to epistemological than to verbal irony, where dialogue is only partial: the inadequacy of language has already been overcome by the ironist, and that victory requires simply to be endorsed by a more or less passive interlocutor. If the Sarrautean writer can break free of the bonds of convention and cliché, escaping the mystified state of the Lacanian subject of language, the reader has no such insight, for he personifies convention and so is dependent on the writer for enlightenment. Sarraute is in no doubt that left to his own devices, the reader's unfailing response to a text's dismantling of convention will be to restore it, to 'ramener l'inconnu au connu le plus banal' (1972*a*: 38) by abandoning that text's revelation of reality for the world of appearances.[11] The

---

[10]   Celia Britton has discussed the ambivalence in Sarraute between writing seen as *creation* and as *expression*, and summed it up as follows: '[The unnamed] is on the one hand the only reality worth *expressing*, and on the other hand the modality of its existence is so fragile and elusive that it can also be said not to exist until the writer *creates* it in a text' (1992: 127). The stylistic means by which Sarraute evokes the movement of the tropism are the subject of a monograph by Françoise Asso (1995).

[11]   Like most of Sarraute's views, this opinion of the reader remains remarkably constant over the years. In 1981 she outlined to Carmen Licari a view of the reader's role in her work which is in fact highly undialogical: 'Beaucoup d'auteurs modernes renvoient à du non-dit; et cet énorme non-dit, où le lecteur est libre de mettre ce qu'il veut, il l'emplit souvent de

appearance dismantled by the text 'se reconstruit fatalement dès qu'on se détache du texte et qu'on le reprend dans un autre langage, un langage banal déjà rempli de définitions, de catégories' (pp. 52–3). Whatever Sarraute sees the reader as contributing to the text (see Ch. 1, pp. 11–13), it is certainly not his own inevitably conventional language.

How then should we read Sarraute? It seems that to read her writing on her terms means to deprive oneself of any metalanguage and simply assent to its address, for any conceptualization of the text beyond a direct and unselfconscious engagement with it (like that extolled in *Les Fruits d'or* for example) is condemned as convention-bound in its recourse to abstract language. Bernard Pingaud elaborates on this aspect of reading Sarraute:

Il est quasi impossible d'exprimer la saveur d'une lecture sans poser sur l'œuvre un nouveau masque, sans la reconstituer en objet, bref sans en faire encore, toujours, un personnage [. . .] Si je cherche à me tenir au plus près de l'œuvre, à 'l'amadouer', je ne pourrai que la paraphraser. Si je m'en écarte, pour la considérer avec le recul de 'l'esprit critique', je lui imposerai cette figure qu'elle ne veut pas avoir, je la classerai, la définirai, l'étiquetterai, la nommerai, elle deviendra *mon* œuvre, et par là même une image qui m'échappera aussitôt. (1963: 34)

Sarraute puts it more bluntly: 'Les critiques prennent l'apparence pour la réalité' (1987*b*: 123).

I shall look more closely in Chapter 4 at the way Sarraute's views on language hamstring the reader by condemning critical discourse as intrinsically contrary to the spirit of her writing. In this way she promotes as the only valid approach to the text an engagement with it as a present event (the desire for control of interpretation which lies behind the emphasis on the text as event was explored in the last chapter): 'Il est certain que le lecteur dès qu'il quitte le texte, retrouve l'apparence. Ces mouvements se révèlent par le texte, existent en lui, disparaissent hors de lui' (1972*a*: 45). The question of the reader's ability, or even obligation, to read Sarraute's texts on terms other than those inscribed in them will be the subject of the final

---

sentiments d'une grande banalité, comme ceux qu'on lui a appris à connaître. Cette sorte de collaboration-là avec le lecteur chez moi n'existe pas: rien n'est sous-entendu, c'est là, on est allé aussi loin qu'on le pouvait [. . .] Mon langage emplit les trous, je ne laisse pas ces vides dans lesquels on peut s'ébattre à son aise' (Sarraute 1985*c*: 13). Thus when the double of *Entre la vie et la mort* approves the gaps in the writer's text, it is a sign that he has sold out to conventional public opinion: 'Ces creux sont excellents [. . .] Chacun va s'empresser de les remplir, tout fier d'exhiber ses propres richesses' (*EVM* 171).

chapter. Now, however, having considered some of Sarraute's views on dialogue as it relates to expression in speech or writing, it is time to turn to the way dialogue actually functions in her writing. I shall focus on *Enfance*, the text which with its opposing authorial perspectives seems to embody most dramatically the overthrow of the singular, authoritative narrative voice and the establishment instead of the truth of the subject through dialogue.

2. Enfance: *The fragmentation and restoration of the self* [12]

Many critics writing on *Enfance* have discussed the way its fragmentation of narration into two voices, one largely narratorial and one critical and doubting, problematizes the conventions of autobiographical discourse, in terms of both the accuracy of recollection (especially when the focus is a childhood long past) and the influence of the narrative act on how remembered events are recreated. For Bruno Vercier, 'l'interrogation en forme de dialogue permet à Nathalie Sarraute de déjouer tous les pièges que pose l'écriture autobiographique' (1985: 164), while Sabine Raffy sees 'cette conscience surmoïque qui travaille le texte d'un questionnement très attentif' as giving rise to 'un mouvement de glissement qui déstabilise la narration et rappelle sans cesse au lecteur que "la vérité" n'existe pas, et que sous chaque phrase, chaque mot, des pièges sont tendus' (1988: 238).[13] Aside from the fact that the very presence of another voice opposed to the dominant voice of narration relativizes it and so exposes it to critical attention, the characters of the voices in *Enfance* emphasize respectively the problems of recollection and representation as these are encountered in

---

[12] The use of the word 'self' here is on one level due simply to the autobiographical nature of this linguistic subject's enterprise (it is talking or writing about and to it*self*). However, there is also a more difficult terminological issue involved in the choice between the words 'self' and 'subject' when talking about Sarraute's representation of identity, one which has to do with the limits of her affinity to the Lacanian view of identity and language. For Sarraute, having access to language (being a subject of language) ultimately does not cut the individual off from the truth of his (incommensurable, undefined) self, as the descriptions of that self in *Tu ne t'aimes pas* or *Ici* make clear. For further discussion of this distinction, see Ch. 3 n. 3.

[13] In a similar vein, Raylene O'Callaghan sees the dialogic movement of *Enfance* in Derridean terms as a metaphor for 'the "différance" that the writing (symbolic) process introduces into the "real" of unmediated feeling' (1988: 92). Elsewhere she praises Sarraute's 'meta-textual deconstruction of a Western logocentric psychology and system of thought that is limited, limiting' (1989: 457).

the narration of childhood. Valerie Minogue says of them, 'the one is that of the burrower, who delves into and tries to merge with the recollected sensation: the other that of the critical sifter who challenges, warns of self-indulgence, exaggeration, falsification, and points to the gap between the sensation of *then* and the words and images of *now*' (1986: 72). Thus the two voices by their separate emphases keep in the foreground 'the flaws of memory and the processes of composition involved in this "roman de la mémoire"'.

This description of *Enfance* as a 'roman de la mémoire' raises the question of its relation, as (however problematized) autobiography, to Sarraute's fiction. Sarraute herself has constantly stressed that her novels too have their origin in her lived experience (something borne out by the 'real' events described in *Enfance* which had already featured in her fiction[14]). In 1980 she spoke to Carmen Licari of her project to 'écrire des textes où je retrouverais, dans mes propres souvenirs d'enfance, la même substance que celle qui se trouve dans mes livres' (Sarraute 1985c: 4). Aside from supporting the truth-claim of her fiction (see Jefferson 1990), *Enfance* of course also raises questions about the truth of autobiography: for François-Olivier Rousseau (from whom Minogue takes the description 'roman de la mémoire'), 'les deux voix feutrées, hésitantes, qui se répondent tout au long d'*Enfance*' tell us principally that 'la mémoire [n'est] qu'une longue invention' (1983: 26). The imbrication in *Enfance* of the problems of self-definition, fiction, and narration, strongly recalls Roy Schafer's analysis, discussed in Chapter 1, of how the psychoanalytic dialogue constructs the analysand's biography. It also, in my opinion, justifies reading this 'roman de la mémoire' in the same way as the novels proper: as neither wholly fictional nor wholly autobiographical.

Enfance is, however, first and foremost the story of a child up to the end of primary school, and it is in the framework of this story that general questions regarding identity are posed. It is thus at the same time the particular account of one child's maturation and the more universal story of the maturation of the subject in literature (as character, as writer, and as reader); this broader concern is not only with the way the self becomes a problematic concept but also with the

---

[14] Some of these—the children's laughter which is central to *Vous les entendez?*, her father's mimicry which recalls *Le Planétarium*, etc.—will be discussed later in this chapter. Françoise Asso identifies as a kind of 'primal trauma' in *Enfance* a scene which originally appeared in *Martereau*, where the mother chooses for the servants the worst cuts of meat (Asso 1995: 14–15).

consequences for the way we represent it. The limits of the auto-biographical enterprise correspond to the limits of the child's per-spective on life, one marked, thanks at least in part to the primary school system, by a faith in the knowability of the world.[15] Setting the child's unitary point of view within the divided voice of the adult recalling it, emphasizes the way the child's unproblematic percep-tion of the world and of others collapses when it enters the *lycée* (an event significantly just outside the bounds of autobiographical recollection, even one relativized by outside voices). It further evokes the way the twentieth century lost faith in the narration of identity when it reached the age of suspicion and recognized the lack of a stable self either as subject or as object of language.

Yet if *Enfance* raises major questions regarding memory, identity, and the consequences of the subject's inconsistency both for the kind of self it represents and for the act of narration, it seems to me ultimately to resist the destructive implications these questions have for narrative; indeed, we shall see that it ends up using the issues it raises to restore all the more powerfully its own narrative authority. The second voice may seem designed to shake the reader's confi-dence both in the memory of the autobiographical narrator and in the authority of a narrating voice to recount other lives (including the past life of childhood). Yet as the coming pages will show, as the dialogue of *Enfance* develops, the capacity of this 'critical sifter' (Minogue 1986: 72) to challenge narration is diminished, to the point where it ends up collaborating in the reaffirmation of memo-rative and narrative authority. The unequal status of the two voices, which is what allows this relapse into monologism, is itself, I shall argue, simply the manifestation within the dialogue of a false oppos-ition at its origin.

---

[15] This faith is described when the narrator recalls Natacha's reaction to her mother's offer to have her return to live in Russia, after the child had joined the *école communale* in Paris:

— Quelque chose s'élève encore, toujours aussi réel, une masse immense . . . l'impossibilité de me dégager de ce qui me tient si fort, je m'y suis encastrée, cela me redresse, me soutient, me durcit, me fait prendre forme . . . Cela me donne chaque jour la sensation de grimper jusqu'à un point culminant de moi-même, où l'air est pur, vivifiant . . . un sommet d'où si je parviens à l'atteindre, à m'y maintenir je verrai s'étendre devant moi le monde entier . . . rien ne pourra m'échapper, il n'y aura rien que je ne parviendrai pas à connaître . . .
— Il est curieux que tu aies éprouvé précisément le sentiment que l'enseignement primaire cherchait à donner [. . .] Et quelle perte d'équilibre, quel désarroi après, au lycée, quand tu t'es aperçue que ce monde bien clos, entièrement accessible, s'ouvrait de toutes parts, se défaisait, se perdait . . . (*E* 173–4)

The challenge to narrative authority in *Enfance* is not restricted to the intrusions by the second, questioning voice; the narrating voice itself appears to reject the authority over others' discourses which its position as narrator offers, generally choosing to represent the words of others as direct speech. Thus not only on the basis of the work's form as internal dialogue, but also on that of how discourse is represented within the first voice's narration, *Enfance* certainly seems to be striving for a dissolution of narrative monologism.

The critical voice, however, is clearly the most extreme embodiment of textual dialogism. Its autonomy is asserted from the start: it opens the dialogue which forms this autobiographical *récit* by ironizing the narrator's project to 'évoquer [s]es souvenirs d'enfance' (*E*7). Thus it establishes its relationship to the other voice in terms of the verbal ironist's superiority over an interlocutor who is also the target of the irony: 'Comme ces mots te gênent, tu ne les aimes pas. Mais reconnais que ce sont les seuls mots qui conviennent. Tu veux "évoquer tes souvenirs" . . . il n'y a pas à tortiller, c'est bien ça' (p. 7). The narrating voice is at a disadvantage from the start, with doubt cast on the value of its narration before it even begins. (We should note however that, despite this confident start, the critical voice will open only two other sections: pp. 27, 162.)

Having introduced the narrative project, the critical voice is also responsible for the direction it takes, initially at least. In fact, the entire narration is seen as a response to its initial words, not just in terms of being a challenge to its opposition, but also by picking up on its actual language. Its opening sceptical 'Alors, tu vas vraiment faire ça?' (p. 7) arouses the memory of similar words spoken long ago, by a German-speaking governess to the child Natacha: ' "Nein, das tust du nicht" . . . "Non, tu ne feras pas ça" ' (p. 10). The similarity of the phrases, with their varying degrees of disapproval ranging from scepticism to interdiction, bridges the years between their enunciation, the years which separate the act of narration from the first of the periods of time recalled. As with almost all the recollections which will follow, the past is here remembered initially as language, an utterance around which a whole experience will be recreated before the critical interlocutor.

The founding role of the critical voice's question is emphasized by the nature of the childhood memory it resuscitates, an event which is clearly an allegory of the act of writing as Sarraute envisages it.[16] All the features of the writer's activity are represented in the child's transgressive desire to tear away the silk covering of the sofa and reveal the formless matter beneath. As an image of the autobiographical project, and of all Sarraute's writing as an attempt to articulate experienced sensations, it evokes the isolation of the misunderstood and unjustly criticized writer whose writing is an attempt to make contact ('vous laisser le temps de m'en empêcher, de me retenir': p. 12). It also suggests the nature of writing as the revelation of an amorphous reality behind the superficial solidity of appearance; the struggle of the seeker after truth to formulate something for which she has no ready terms and thus working in a 'foreign' language;[17] and of course the writer's persistence in her lonely task despite the hostility of the literary 'authorities'. The allegorical memory fuses with its narration at the end of this opening sequence, through the double reference of the 'je' which designates the adult narrator as well as the remembered self to whom it lends its voice. In this way the text to come is both equated with the exposure of truth just evoked, and also presented as an event about to take place: 'Voilà, je me libère, l'excitation, l'exalt-ation tend mon bras, j'enfonce la pointe des ciseaux de toutes mes forces, la soie cède, se déchire, je fends le dossier de haut en bas et je regarde ce qui en sort . . . quelque chose de mou, de grisâtre s'échappe par la fente' (p. 13).

Thus, at the very start of this dialogical text, we have what appears to be a striking example of the emergence of the truth of the subject in dialogue, that Socratic ideal we have seen echoed in Schlegel and Lacan, as well as in Roy Schafer's study of the rela-tionship between biography and the psychoanalytic dialogue.[18] In an exchange reminiscent of the Lacanian dialogue, the words of the

[16] See Minogue (1986: 79–80) on the paradigmatic function of this opening scene.

[17] Here German, as in 'Ich sterbe' where Chekhov announces his death in the foreign doctor's language which paradoxically alone allows him to 'opérer . . . ne suis-je pas médecin aussi? . . . la mise en mots' of that for which he has no language: 'L'indicible sera dit. L'impensable sera pensé. Ce qui est insensé sera ramené à la raison. Ich sterbe' (*UP* 13). Bruno Vercier compares the opening of *Enfance* to that of Tolstoy's *Enfance et adolescence*, where the first memory described is also of words spoken in German (1985: 170 n. 7).

[18] Arnaud Rykner certainly reads *Enfance* in this light, and extends its dialogic lesson to the act of reading: for him, Sarraute 'postule l'existence d'une complicité entre l'auteur et son lecteur, complicité qu'emblématise l' "autobiographie" constituée par *Enfance*. Tout ce dernier texte avance, de fait, selon un mouvement dialogique, où le narrateur confronté à son double cherche à entraîner celui-ci sur la voie d'une révélation totale de soi et de l'autre, à travers une exploration de l'univers tropismique' (1991: 16).

critical (analytical) voice reverberate in the totality of language which makes up the writing subject's unconscious, and recall from a forgotten past an utterance which echoes them. The recalled incident is further clearly intended to be read as emblematic of the writer's identity, not only as remembered child but also as remembering adult, the present explorer of the amorphous matter of subjectivity as well as the past little girl with her transgressive urge.[19] But there are limits to the Lacanian overtones of this opening dialogue, limits to which I shall return and which herald an increasing pull towards authoritative monologic narration in *Enfance*, as it resists from within its own dialogic enterprise.

The second voice's subversive role as critic of memory is manifested in situations ranging from the most trivial (as when it counters the narrator's mention of a 'devoir de français' with 'N'est-ce pas plutôt rédaction qu'on disait à l'école communale?': p. 207), to more considerable corrections. In these it restrains the adult narrator from lapsing into a present interpretation of past events rather than maintaining its effort simply to recreate them.[20] Examples are generally linked to literary topics, as if to emphasize that the difficulty of narrating the past without reflecting the present—of telling without interpreting—is at the centre of this particular literary enterprise. The reminder 'Il n'est pas possible que tu l'aies perçu ainsi sur le moment' (p. 86) refers to the criticism by a family friend of the poor spelling in Natacha's first novel. Similarly, when the narrator recalls Véra telling her as a child that she had been 'dumped', her typically Sarrautean musings on the various pejorative connotations of the Russian phrase 'Tiebia podbrossili' ('un rejet brutal en même temps que sournois') are interrupted by the second voice which objects: 'Tu ne t'es sûrement pas occupée à ce moment-là à découvrir toutes les richesses que ce mot recèle' (p. 183).

---

[19] It is possible to hear Véra's later catchphrase 'Ça ne se fait pas' (p. 191) as another indirect echo of 'Tu ne feras pas ça'. This would link both mother-figures to the theme of transgression through writing which this passage exemplifies, (the silk of the sofa, as Valerie Minogue has pointed out (1986: 80), is associated with the mother). As both women embody non-communication (Maman's words with their air of final judgement render Natacha 'muette, comme pétrifiée' (p. 104, cp. p. 95), while ' "Ça ne se fait pas" arrête tout examen, rend inutile toute discussion' (p. 191)), the new kind of revelatory writing which transgresses their law seems designed to be a reaction to monologue as much as a tearing away of the smooth surface of the already written.

[20] i.e. to 'faire surgir quelques moments, quelques mouvements qui me semblent encore intacts, assez forts pour se dégager de cette couche protectrice qui les conserve, de ces épaisseurs blanchâtres, molles, ouatées qui se défont, qui disparaissent avec l'enfance . . .' (p. 277).

It must be pointed out, however, that this kind of incursion by the second voice is relatively rare, for it is generally the first, narrating voice which is obliged to remind the second to respect the limitations of the child's point of view on events. Furthermore, even in the situations just mentioned, the first voice's responses to the other's objections emphasize its own commitment to rediscovering the past ('ce qui est resté là, enfoui': p. 86), unsullied by the adult mind recalling it, and even deny the accusation of *ex post facto* analysis. Regarding its response to Véra's words, it insists: 'Je n'en étais pas émerveillée comme je le suis maintenant, mais ce qui est certain, c'est que je n'ai pas perdu une parcelle . . . quel enfant la perdrait? . . . de tout ce que ce verbe et le "tu" qui le précédait "tiebia podbrossili", me portaient . . .' (p. 183).

Occasionally, however, the second voice does seem to make a real difference to the way memories are recreated in narration. At points where the memory is not already firmly established in the mind of the first voice, and where the other's interventions are neither confined to providing minor details nor dismissed immediately, we do get the impression of a narration emerging out of a dialogue which works backward and forward, simultaneously narrating, exploring, and revising its narration. Not surprisingly, the principal instance of this is highly evocative of a psychoanalytic dialogue. Here the recalled occasion centres on Natacha's intervention in a playful struggle between her mother and Kolia, her mother's second husband. Her mother rejected the child's attempt to defend her, saying 'Laisse donc . . . femme et mari sont un même parti' (p. 74). The memory of this scene emerges as a result of the second voice's distrust of the narrator's claim that as a child Natacha always benefited from the warmth of her mother's and Kolia's relationship. The narrator initially resists but ultimately gives in to the doubt cast by the other on its version of the past; in good analytical fashion this doubt is not accompanied by an alternative interpretation but simply jogs the narrator's recall:

— Une fois pourtant . . . tu te rappelles . . .
— Mais c'est ce que j'ai senti longtemps après . . . tu sais bien que sur le moment . . .
— Oh, même sur le moment . . . et la preuve en est que ces mots sont restés en toi pour toujours, des mots entendus cette unique fois . . . un petit dicton. (pp. 73–4)

The first voice then follows the prompt and tells of the incident and the mother's words. Yet its resistance to the second voice's probings continues, as it clings for a time, despite a doubting 'Crois-tu vraiment?' (p. 74) from its interlocutor, to an initial, benevolent interpretation of the meaning behind the mother's phrase: 'Il m'a semblé sur le moment que maman avait pensé que je voulais pour de bon la défendre, que je la croyais menacée, et elle a voulu me rassurer . . . Laisse . . . ne crains rien, il ne peut rien m'arriver . . . "Femme et mari sont un même parti" ' (pp. 74-5). Questioned again on the accuracy of this version, it hears the other renarrate the incident, in the present tense this time, and with the suggestion that the mother seemed 'un peu agacé[e]' (p. 75). The clear echo of its own narration in the other awakens the truth of its feeling at the time, and the 'analyst's' suggested interpretation is accepted as true: 'C'est vrai . . . je dérangeais leur jeu'. With more exhortation (but no more suggested interpretations) it arrives at the end of the analysis, having worked through the past experience to a full recognition of how these words affected it when it first heard them: 'J'étais un corps étranger . . . qui gênait . . .' (p. 75).

Yet even here, the apparent success of the second voice is qualified towards the end, when it risks the logical conclusion that to feel oneself to be a foreign body implies the expectation of expulsion. But, 'Non, cela, je ne l'ai pas pensé [. . .] Non, tu vas trop loin . . .' (p. 76). This suggestion by the dialogue that the truth of what the subject has experienced can never be fully established, evokes the interminable nature of analysis, where even the analyst's interpretation is ultimately only that, and is itself open to further analysis.[21] An interpretation is chosen on the basis of an instinctive recognition of personal truth, and neither partner in dialogue holds a monopoly on that truth. The sequence ends unresolved, with the last word given, unusually, to the analytical voice:

— Non, tu vas trop loin . . .
— Si. Je reste tout près, tu le sais bien. (p. 76)

---

[21] The second voice again takes on the role of analyst, but much more briefly, when it interprets Natacha's complicity in her humiliation by the 'uncle' who criticized the spelling in her first novel: 'On dirait même qu'on le désire, que c'est cela qu'on cherche . . .' Here too the narrator agrees: 'Oui, ça vous tire . . . une drôle d'attraction . . .' (p. 84). Yet for the reader as for the voices, there is no security of interpretation, for the very next page warns against facile psychoanalysing, when the conversation moves from recollection to remind us of Sarraute's writing career and so of our own role as readers. The narrating voice, on the other's prompting, acknowledges having spoken publicly about this incident which it used as a convenient but false explanation for having begun to write rather late: 'C'était si commode, on

It should be noted, though, that this acknowledgement of the impossibility of separating the 'moments intacts' (see n. 20) of the past from their present representation is not taken any further. Moreover, sequences like this one, where the disagreement between the voices centres on the actual truth of the child's feelings during the recalled incident rather than simply on the deforming power of the discourse used to narrate a solidly established memory,[22] are rare in *Enfance*.

There is, however, an obvious problem with interpreting passages like the 'Femme et mari . . .' sequence or the opening section where the memory of a former interdiction was triggered by a similarly worded question, as enacting the constitution of truth through dialogue. The problem lies in the relationship of the voices to each other, and an inconsistency which occurs in the 'Tu vas vraiment faire ça?' sequence will point up the way it manifests itself and the important way it qualifies the comparisons with contemporary theories of subjectivity, dialogue, and the constitution of (auto)biography, which the text seems otherwise to invite. On the surface, the opening exchange evokes as much as does the later one the dynamics of the (Lacanian) psychoanalytic dialogue where full self-knowledge depends on the speaker's coming to awareness of his utterance's enunciation beyond its lexical signification as *énoncé*. This awareness, we recall, is mediated through the analysand's interlocutor who represents language as a whole (the Other), including the chain of repressed signifiers which is the linguistic unconscious of the speaker; thus the speaker ultimately comes to realize his identity as subject of desire through the echoes of his utterance in an addressee who stands for the whole Symbolic order. In psychoanalytic terms, then, the question 'Tu vas vraiment faire ça?', beyond its lexical signification, allows through its articulation

pouvait difficilement trouver quelque chose de plus probant: un de ces magnifiques "traumatismes de l'enfance" [. . .] Tout de même, j'y croyais . . . par conformisme. Par paresse' (p. 85).

[22] As with: 'Ne te fâche pas, mais ne crois-tu pas que là, avec ces roucoulements, ces pépiements, tu n'as pas pu t'empêcher de placer un petit morceau de préfabriqué [. . .] un joli petit raccord, tout à fait en accord . . .' (pp. 20–1). Yet while some of the description's excesses are recognized and disowned, the essence of the narrated memory is defended: 'Bon, tu as raison . . . mais pour ce qui est des clochettes, des sonnettes, ça non, je les entends . . . et aussi des bruits de crécelle, le crépitement des fleurs de celluloïd rouges, mauves, tournant au vent . . .' (p. 21). Thus this interruption, close to the beginning of the text, in fact allows the first voice to highlight its concern for authenticity and its general reliability.

in dialogue the revival of an unconscious memory which, we have seen, has exemplary value in terms of articulating the writer's personal truth.

At odds with the dynamics of the psychoanalytic dialogue, however, is of course the fact that in this exchange the voice which enunciates the question and the voice which experiences the involuntary memory are not the same. If this seems to pose a problem (for the question becomes a 'parole pleine' not for the one who utters it but for another), it is resolved by the fact that both voices do ultimately belong to the same linguistic subject, the adult self from whom all the recalled scenes depart and to whom they return. Thus the long-forgotten utterance ('Das tust du nicht') can be seen as unconsciously influencing, and, once remembered, elucidating the subject's own discourse ('Tu vas vraiment faire ça?'). But this sameness poses another, more serious problem, for to acknowledge that the same subject is at the origin of both sides of the interlocution is to throw into question the whole status of the dialogue. The invitation which the text extends in passages like the opening one, to interpret its dialogic structure in terms of the concept of intersubjective truth associated with dialogue, shows itself to rest on a false foundation by revealing the lack of any real difference in terms of subjectivity between the two voices, the lack of any 'otherness' which would provide a genuine possibility of self-discovery. The echo of 'Das tust du nicht' in 'Tu vas vraiment faire ça?' is based on an artifice, specifically on the subject's address to itself as 'tu'. The dialogic basis for the elaboration of an intersubjective truth is skewed by the fact that both sides of the dialogue unavoidably originate in the same consciousness and so within the same linguistic limits.

This singular origin may seem such a self-evident feature of invented dialogue as to be hardly worth delaying on, but it has two major consequences for the text of *Enfance* which need to be spelt out. First, it necessarily reduces, if not eliminates altogether, the possibility of any real engagement by the narrating voice with the 'Other' of its language, that area of language which is specifically *outside* its consciousness. The artifice revealed by the first sequence's elimination of difference between the two voices must also be present in the later analytic dialogue around 'Femme et mari . . .', which is also located within a single consciousness and so within a single discourse in the totality of language. The analyst and the analysand are ultimately the same, the speaker not only displays the symptoms but is her own diagnostician.[23] This gives rise to the possibility of one voice (the critic, in this case) being constantly subordinated to the authority of the other (the narrator), for the same consciousness controls both, 'tire les ficelles', in the words of Philippe Lejeune (1990: 32). For him, *Enfance* presents 'des voix fabriquées qui prêchent le naturel' (p. 33). He sees this fabrication as a ruse to conceal *authorial* control by focusing on the question of *narration* alone: 'En exhibant ses soupçons sur le travail de la voix narratrice, la voix critique détourne l'attention du lecteur du véritable objet à soupçonner: le travail de l'écrivain qui a inventé les deux voix et mis en scène minutieusement leur recherche "spontanée"' (p. 34). While the rest of this chapter will look at ways in which the textual dialogue of *Enfance* betrays evidence of the controlling consciousness behind it, Chapter 3 will go beyond this to consider, in relation to *Tu ne t'aimes pas*, how the text itself invariably exceeds any such assertion of monologic authorial control.

The second consequence of the absence of otherness in this dialogue has to do with the act of reading the text as a whole. As the critical voice's role is to listen to (ever less critically, as it turns out) and interpret the other's narrative, it clearly figures the activity of reading (its dual status as both the writing subject's externalized self and its model reader identifies it with the writer's double, who was also his first and closest reader, in the earlier novel *Entre la vie et la mort*). Modelling the text–reader interaction on a relationship where difference is only simulated works to resist the introduction of a really other voice into the text, that of the ever unknowable real reader. If the other in the dialogue is not beyond the limits of the speaker's perspective, his recognition is both guaranteed yet also redundant, for his understanding of the speaker is coextensive with the speaker's own rather than being that of an external embodiment of the totality of language which would give intersubjective value to what the individual says by inferring a meaning from it. Thus the way *Enfance* marks out the role of the real reading

---

[23] This scene has been discussed by Michael Sheringham (1993) who similarly compares the roles of the two voices to 'that of the analyst in relation to the analysand in the psychoanalytical encounter' (p. 163). While he too questions the potential of *Enfance*'s internal dialogue for real self-exploration and self-discovery ('Is it not precisely by virtue of being a controlled demonstration, a simulation of dialogical openness, that *Enfance* effectively fails to do more than ape the dynamics of exchange and transference?': p. 163), he does not see its second voice as disenfranchising the real reader, for as readers 'we must understudy all the roles in the mobile dialogue between the voices' (p. 164).

other, given that this role must necessarily remain within the sphere of what the author herself can know, runs entirely counter to what Lacan sees as the aim of dialogue, namely the awareness of the presence of the Other in one's own discourse as its origin and what makes it meaningful.[24] To project the reader explicitly as an *alter ego*, as Sarraute does here, makes particularly graphic the way any projected ideal reader (or interlocutor) will reflect its creator's own values.

How does the apparent dialogue between the two voices of *Enfance* end up at once reaffirming the narrative perspective of the first voice and proposing a reading position of acceptance rather than critical questioning? There are (at least) two aspects to this: first, the narrating voice reveals itself throughout the text to be more or less equivalent to the writer of *Enfance*. Consequently, the critical interventions of the second voice which is not thus identified stand in much the same relation of subordination to the first voice as they do to the writing consciousness behind the whole text.

The imbalance in authority between the two voices of *Enfance* is manifested in the way the very dimensions of the text are dictated by the first voice. It is the one which undertakes the project of recollecting childhood, a project to which the opening words of its double are simply a response. Similarly, the decision to stop is taken by the narrating 'je', in a comment which indicates the dominant role it has held in the whole enterprise: 'Rassure-toi, j'ai fini, je ne t'entraînerai pas plus loin . . .' (p. 276). From the symbolic sofa-tearing scene of the opening sequence onwards, the act of writing will always be associated with the first voice rather than with the second.

I have mentioned how in that scene the use of the historic present tense conflates the past trivial transgression with the present one of writing, while mapping the 'je' of the child onto that of the adult rememberer underlines that the narrator too is an agent of transgression. Thus the bulk of the *récit* which follows this anecdote is presented as a revelation of hidden reality on the plane now of memory rather than upholstery. This conflation of represented event and narration encourages in the reader the impression given earlier by the first voice, that all is still unwritten: 'Quelque chose

---

[24] Michael Sheringham comments on the ambivalence of the dialogic structure of *Enfance* as it concerns the reader: 'Initially it seems quite liberating, to open up the process of autobiography, to involve the reader more. But often it seems to do—and to be designed to do—precisely the opposite: to forestall the reader's response, to shut us out of the action, to protect the writer from us' (1989: 30).

d'encore informe se propose [. . .] Aucun mot écrit, aucune parole ne l'ont encore touché' (p. 9). In this way, the reader is invited to consider the text as an unfolding event rather than as a product of writing; this illusion of course presents the text–reader dialogue in the guise of spoken interaction, so dissimulating its highly mediated nature, as well as the 'donné d'avance' status of the response it will seek from the reader. It is telling but in retrospect perhaps not so surprising that already in this anecdote which acts as a paradigm for the rest of the *récit*, the second voice is almost entirely silent, leaving the narrative floor to the first. (Its one intervention in the narration of the anecdote, to question how Natacha could have understood the German phrase as a child, although it is often cited as undermining the authority of the narrator, is in fact not taken up at all; and the claim that the child *did* utter 'Ich werde es zerreissen' is repeated twice afterwards, emphasizing its truth if not to the letter—though even this is not conceded—then at least to the spirit of the event narrated.)

The first voice's authority is perhaps most decisively established when it is referred to as the author of *'disent les imbéciles'* by the second. When the narrating voice comments that Véra's mother 'n'a pourtant pas grand-chose dans son aspect de ce qui rend exquises les grand-mères décrites dans les livres', the critic interjects: 'Pas grand-chose de commun avec celle que tu as montrée plus tard dans l'un des tiens . . .' (p. 226). This overt reference to Sarraute's work, and the consequent identification of the first voice with the author of *Enfance* as of *'disent les imbéciles'* (the fact that the novel is 'un des tiens', not 'des nôtres', implies that the critical voice does not have the right to be considered a co-author of either of the works), seals the narrator's authority. It openly acknowledges within the dialogue what we saw to invalidate that dialogue as an instance of intersubjective communication of the kind privileged by Lacan. For if the first voice is coextensive with the consciousness in which the whole text originates, then it must also embrace any point the second voice might make, and the discourse in which it might make it. Once again, the second voice's ability to make a difference reveals itself as illusory.[25]

[25] The second voice seems to be in much the same position of powerlessness as the servant Françoise in *A la Recherche du temps perdu* when Tante Léonie imagines her dishonesty and invents dialogues in which she confronts her: 'Habituée, quand elle faisait seule des parties de cartes, à jouer à la fois son jeu et le jeu de son adversaire, elle se prononçait à elle-même les

3. Memory, language, authority

To acknowledge the imbalance which is intrinsic to the dialogue of *Enfance* is obviously not to detract from its power as a literary work. Indeed the predominance of the first voice is necessary if the child's perspective is to emerge intact from memory. This is the ambition of *Enfance*, and it is because it is an ultimately monologic ambition, based on the belief that the child's view of events can be recovered without being deformed by the context in which it is recalled, that the second voice, situated within the adult present of the dialogue and referring only rarely to the past, can frequently seem superfluous. Its suggested interpretations of past events, and with them all the unknown interpretations of the readers it represents, are repeatedly sidelined. Far from being valuable for what it contributes to the narrating process, the second voice seems more and more to figure the *irrelevance* of the kind of assumptions and inferences made by readers.[26]

The predominance of the child's perspective over that of the adult is illustrated in the way scenes which in Sarraute's earlier works had been explored in depth and their apparent innocuousness exploded, are here presented in a childlike manner which determinedly overlooks their 'tropistic' potential. Thus a reference to Natacha's father's tendency to mock any acquaintance he doesn't like, to 's'emparer de lui et [. . .] en faire un personnage si inquiétant, si compliqué et si comique que tous l'écoutent comme fascinés' (p. 197), mentions only in passing the vague unease this mockery causes in his listeners, Natacha and Ivanov. Natacha's recreated voice simply claims 'J'ai un peu mal, un peu peur', and

---

excuses embarrassées de Françoise et y répondait avec tant de feu et d'indignation que l'un de nous, entrant à ces moments-là, la trouvait en nage, les yeux étincelants, ses faux cheveux déplacés laissant voir son front chauve' (Proust 1987: 223). In both cases, one of the interlocutors has the advantage of being the author of the dialogue as well as a participant.

[26] The adult interventions of the second voice are constantly dismissed as irrelevant to the recreation of the child's version of events. When it contradicts the family myth that Natacha's father fell ill with grief at the death of his first daughter (in fact he caught scarlet fever from her), it is answered: 'Je le sais maintenant, mais ce n'est pas ce qu'on m'avait dit et que je croyais encore' (p. 119). Occasionally it is simply ignored, the narrating voice picking up exactly where it had left off before the intervention of an adult analysis. Thus the narrator's comment that 'Lili [n']avait pas peur [de Véra]' gives rise to the other's analysis of Véra's passionate love for Lili and its motivation; yet the narration resumes exactly where it had been interrupted with 'Quant à moi, je n'avais pas peur non plus de Véra' (p. 145; cp. p. 157).

Ivanov's reaction is not guessed at beyond the physical symptoms which throughout Sarraute's previous fictional writings served to introduce the tropism: 'Tout à coup on dirait que son sourire se fige un peu, dans ses yeux passe comme un mouvement, il me semble que quelque chose en lui se contracte' (p. 197). We can contrast the development of an almost identical situation in *Le Planétarium* when Alain ridicules his aunt for the amusement of his listeners; there the tropistic reactions of his interlocutors, which their outward appearance barely suggests, are described in great detail (*P* 24–33). Similarly, the whole text of *Vous les entendez?* comes to the mind of the reader familiar with it when Natacha mentions the obligation and the inability of the children playing at the Péréverzev house to suppress their uncontrollable laughing fits, for the parents working next door must not be disturbed:

Dans la chambre des enfants les objets, les jouets cassés, les meubles défoncés ont un air de liberté, d'insouciance [. . .] Ces fous rires auxquels [Boris] s'abandonnait, qu'il nous communiquait, que l'interdiction de faire du bruit entretenait et fortifiait, qu'interrompaient des silences pleins à craquer, prometteurs de dangereuses, de voluptueuses explosions [. . .] (*E* 124)

In *Vous les entendez?* we have an identical situation told from the point of view of the adult in whom the absence of signification of laughter, and the resulting inadequacy of any rational explanation he can provide for it, produce profound uncertainty and anguish. Here, however, Sarraute's narrator is allied instead with the laughing children, and so confined to the simplicity of the child's view of events. It is equally this simple view which leads Natacha to take the Florimond couple (pp. 269–70), clones of Martereau and his wife, at face value; unlike her creator, the child believes that nothing in her parents' world could be the subject of literary interest (here literature is, admittedly, equated with works like *Rocambole*: pp. 265–7).

The reader familiar with Sarraute's work (and for whom the second voice's reference to *'disent les imbéciles'* is a model) is likely, and probably expected, to recognize in the ingenuous descriptions of *Enfance* the outlines of the much deeper explorations of similar moments contained in her earlier novels. While such passing allusions in *Enfance* may invite us to expand them with material from elsewhere in her writing, filling gaps in the narrative is elsewhere actively discouraged. In a passage which is often cited as articulating Sarraute's awareness of the limited access an autobiographical narrator has to the truth of the (frequently distant) events he or she narrates, but which also serves to warn the reader against unauthorized elaboration on the facts narrated, we hear how the child Natacha returns to play in the Jardin du Luxembourg after a snack:

— Pour faire quoi?

— Ah, n'essaie pas de me tendre un piège . . . Pour faire n'importe quoi, ce que font tous les enfants qui jouent, courent, poussent leurs bateaux, leurs cerceaux, sautent à la corde, s'arrêtent soudain et l'œil fixe observent les autres enfants, les gens assis sur les bancs de pierre, sur les chaises . . . ils restent plantés devant eux bouche bée . . .

— Peut-être le faisais-tu plus que d'autres, peut-être autrement . . .

— Non, je ne dirai pas ça . . . je le faisais comme le font beaucoup d'enfants . . . et avec probablement des constatations et des réflexions du même ordre . . . en tout cas rien ne m'en est resté et ce n'est tout de même pas toi, qui vas me pousser à chercher à combler ce trou par un replâtrage. (pp. 23–4; cp. also pp. 71–2 and n. 11 above)

This careful control of interpretation belies the impression *Enfance* gives even on the visual level of being a loose weave of spontaneously interacting voices, with the blank spaces between the utterances creating a sense of openness, even unfinishedness (see Gratton 1995a: 37–8)—what the reader should bring to the text is in fact kept within clear limits. Seeing *Enfance* as a construct where the gaps to be filled by the reader are a conscious part of its design emphasizes its aesthetic kinship with the portrait described in Sarraute's first novel, *Portrait d'un inconnu*, and which embodies the narrator's (strongly Sarrautean) view of reality and of art. I shall return in Chapter 5 to this model of the ideal work of art as in appearance open to interpretative completion while in fact strongly directing the way it is received; it finds a clear echo, as we shall see, in one branch of contemporary reader-oriented theory, that associated with Wolfgang Iser and his questionable claim to give the reader power over the text.

The project to restore the child's perspective, aside from privileging the first voice which has access to it, and correspondingly minimizing the second voice's role (and that of the reader it represents), also has major implications for Sarraute's view of the relationship of language to reality. This, I have argued, is a somewhat clouded issue, for she tends to blur the distinction between language as representing or as creating reality.[27] The ability of language to revive past sensation is perhaps most openly questioned in *Enfance* in the narration of Natacha's epiphany in the Jardin du Luxembourg, yet even here its power seems ultimately to be endorsed. Despite the doubt cast on the very point of trying to narrate this experience— 'Pourquoi vouloir faire revivre cela, sans mots qui puissent parvenir à capter, à retenir ne serait-ce qu'encore quelques instants ce qui m'est arrivé' (p. 66)—a description of the 'sensation d'une telle violence' and a series of inadequate definitions ('bonheur', 'félicité', 'exaltation', etc.: p. 67) follow. Yet while these terms are rejected as soon as they are uttered, the fact that something of the experience is mediated to us suggests that the description somehow succeeds despite the limitations of language.

In fact, the successful communication of this particular experience seems to result from *exploiting* those very limitations: by using negation as a stylistic technique, Sarraute manages to identify or at least gesture toward the nature of the sensation in question. This is because negative description actually evokes the experience in its effect on Natacha as a subject of language, for the absence of a language in which to define the epiphany is a symptom of the loss of identity which takes place in this experience of '[la] vie à l'état pur, aucune menace sur elle, aucun mélange' (p. 67). Life in its pure state is finally that of everything but herself: 'Je suis en eux [walls, blossoms, grass, air] sans rien de plus, rien qui ne soit à eux, rien à moi', not least her language.

Thus language, despite the denials of its user here, does succeed in representing, albeit negatively, the sensation in question; but this negativity is perfectly suited to the representation of the absence of self-consciousness and of the language through which that self-consciousness operates. The very inadequacy of language is harnessed here (as often) by Sarraute to articulate the unnameability of life beyond or prior to language. What is important here is the fact that, despite the text's dialogic form, dialogue is not actually exploited as a means to overcome the inadequacy of language; the principle of composition remains firmly representational. In this light, the fact that the 'epiphany' sequence is a monologue with no

---

[27] This ambiguity is reflected in some Sarraute criticism also: Valerie Minogue, for example, remarks that it is 'with words that Sarraute the mature writer attacks glittering verbal surfaces to *uncover and create* the real' (1986: 73; my emphasis).

intervention at all by the second voice is telling: the problems of expression are overcome by the first voice alone, in a narration which only it may problematize. The redundancy of the second, adult voice in the face of a narrator with access to both adult's and child's perspectives is nowhere clearer than here.[28]

Sarraute's distinction between authentic and conventional language, discussed earlier in this chapter, is central to *Enfance* where, as we might expect, convention, characterized by abstraction, is associated with the second voice. Even if what Natacha's father feels for her mother can be defined as 'de la rancune, de la réprobation . . . osons le dire . . . du mépris', the first voice (the voice of authenticity) finds these terms inadequate, for as a child 'je n'appelle pas cela ainsi. Je ne donne à cela aucun nom, je sens confusément que c'est là, en lui, enfoui, comprimé . . .' (p. 127). The analytical adult's abstract language is thus a reflection of its loss of an immediate link to the reality of events, the implication being that the return to a child's view of the world such as the first voice seems able to effect will restore an authentic relationship of language to reality, necessary if its narration, and by extension the *récit* as a whole, is to be a work of art.

Ultimately this accessibility of the child's experience, and the rejection of adult labels as a feature of the critical voice alone, all imply that the adult mind is not limited by its own discourse in establishing a perspective on the world. Rather, the availability of past sensation to the narrator suggests a Proustian faith in a sensory memory which preserves sensations intact over time and outside language. The fact that the sensations recalled in *Enfance* are responses to words does blur the role language plays in the recollection of the past, but it remains true that these words act simply as stimuli to emotions which, for Sarraute as for Proust, can be rediscovered without first passing into symbolic form. Thus the narrator can experience street names in terms of their present associations ('des noms [. . .] charmants quand tu les entends maintenant': p. 123) but can equally well relive the earlier gloomy atmosphere they aroused: 'Mais quand je les retrouve tels qu'ils étaient en ce

---

[28] That the problems of expression *do* seem to be overcome illustrates that the dialogic nature of communication is more—or other—than what a staged dialogue from an ultimately monologic authorial perspective can offer the reader. I shall return to the question of what the dialogue between text and reader might actually entail at the end of Ch. 3.

temps-là, ces noms, Lunain, Loing, Marguerin, ils reprennent aussitôt, comme ces petites rues, leur aspect étriqué, mesquin' (p. 123).

This Proustian ability to find the past again exactly as it was experienced is a commonplace of *Enfance*, and even when that past is rendered through the metaphors of the adult rather than in the child's terms, it is not occluded by them: 'Tu n'as pas besoin de me répéter que je n'étais pas capable d'évoquer ces images . . . ce qui est certain, c'est qu'elles rendent exactement la sensation que me donnait mon pitoyable état' (pp. 98–9).[29] Seen in this light, the way the second voice breaks into the historic present of the narrative to remind us of the actual present of narration seems designed less to challenge any illusion created by that narration than to emphasize the way these memories have survived intact over several decades. It may well be reminding us that the narration is a reconstruction, but Sarraute's faith in the ability of that reconstruction to make the memory present without deforming it, means that this reminder is not of an illusion but of the power of metaphoric language to revive past sensations.

The principal implication of a belief in language as expressive and able to represent, if only negatively, even what is inherently irreducible to it, is that narration can be authoritative and dialogue thus dispensable as a means to truth. The superfluity of the second voice as regards the recollection of the truth of the past, its primary usefulness as a foil to the integrity of the narrator's reconstruction of the child's perspective, are symptoms of the way *Enfance* disables its own dialogue from within and returns increasingly to monologic narration, forgoing the search for a new truth in favour of the representation for a listener/reader of one already established. The dialogue of *Enfance* in fact becomes an *elimination* of difference on several levels: the first voice refutes the interventions of the second, and within the first voice the intention is to restore the child's perspective at the expense of the adult's. As the fact that the narration takes place through the adult's perspective and language is not considered an insurmountable obstacle to reviving the past, there are ultimately no limitations of perspective that need to be overcome dialogically.

---

[29] Expression through imagery, with its ideal of leaving as little as possible to the reader (see n. 3 above), thus always remains viable for Sarraute even within a dialogic structure.

It seems, then, that despite initial impressions, dialogue in *Enfance* does not actually operate according to the intersubjective principle of epistemological irony where truth is not stated by one interlocutor to the other but emerges through the dynamics of response to an address. In fact, the kind of intersubjectivity *Enfance* manifests has more in common with that of verbal irony, bearing out my conclusions earlier in this chapter regarding Sarraute's stated views on writing and reading. The second voice almost always remains under the control of the first (indeed, even when it plays the role of ironist in the opening scene, the validity of the other's project is reaffirmed and so the irony is defeated). On the rare occasions where it takes the initiative in the dialogue, it is still under the control of the author whom, as we have seen, the first voice figures. The meanings it is capable of inferring from the words of the narrating voice are always either known to and intended by that voice already, as is the case in verbal irony, or, if not, are still choreographed by the author. In this case, the fact that they exceed what the first voice anticipates is compensated for in terms of ironic control by the fact that they prescribe a response from the reader whom the second voice figures, thus enacting similar control by the author on the level of *her* dialogue, through the text, with the reader. Where the interjections of the second voice bring no new insight to the first, they can be a way of airing certain opinions without these being attributable to the authorial consciousness represented by the first voice who neither confirms nor denies them. This principle of letting the interlocutor infer something without claiming responsibility for that inference is of course basic to verbal irony and is occasionally used in *Enfance* where the second voice's unsanctioned interpretation informs the reader. Thus when Véra's passion and ambition for Lili are analysed by the second voice (p. 145), or when it gives us the background to Natacha's mother's contempt for formal education (pp. 251–2), information is conveyed without the intention to convey it being ascribable either to the first voice or, by extension, to the author it represents.

Given this tendency of *Enfance* to enact the power structure of verbal rather than epistemological irony, with the tone of the exchange one of assertion and assent rather than of ignorance (not feigned but real) and cooperative discovery, it is not surprising to find that within the first voice's ever more authoritative narration, its own representation of other discourses becomes ever less dialogical, that is, ever more indirect. The increasing slide into indirect discourse towards the end of the *récit* is all the more striking as it is accompanied by more retrospective narration by the first voice. This stands in sharp contrast to the otherwise determinedly 'eye-witness' approach we have seen to the recreation of the child's perspective, where the refusal to analyse involves both adhering to the historic present tense and reporting the words of others as they were experienced, directly. (For example, in the discussion of Véra's subjugation to Lili, the first voice limits itself to venturing only: 'Elle avait dû se borner à me dire "Ne la touche pas, je t'en prie. Laisse-la." Et j'avais dû répondre "Mais je la laisse" ': p. 147.) It is as though the first voice's consolidation of its authority in the course of the text entitles it, towards the end, to assume the position of a traditional narrator, all-powerful in relation to the other lives and discourses it recounts:

Adèle m'emmenait parfois à l'église de Montrouge où je faisais les mêmes gestes qu'elle [. . .] Avec grand-mère à l'église russe de la rue Daru, je me prosternais front contre terre auprès d'elle, je faisais le signe de croix [. . .] Mon père me laissait aller dans toutes les églises où l'on m'emmenait [. . .] Mais plus tard, chaque fois qu'était soulevée cette question, j'ai toujours vu mon père déclarer aussitôt, crier sur les toits qu'il était juif. Il pensait que c'était vil, que c'était stupide d'en être honteux. (pp. 234–6)

The reassertion of narrative authority by the first voice is perhaps most explicit in the sequence relating Véra's decision to hire English *au pair* girls in order to teach Lili English. Continuing the increasing trend to retrospective narration,[30] the first voice here narrates the three-page account of the English girls' effect on the household almost entirely in the past tense (where the past tense was used earlier, it was for commentary rather than narration), lapsing into 'eye-witness' mode only midway through the last paragraph. The words of others are quoted indirectly, with free indirect discourse used for ironic effect:

Peu de temps après le départ de grand-mère, Véra a décidé que le moment était venu où Lili devrait absolument avoir une gouvernante anglaise. Si l'on attendait davantage, Lili n'aurait plus le bon accent.

---

[30] The previous sequence (pp. 259–60), relating a visit by her mother to Paris in 1914, has no critical intervention and no use of the historic present, while the one preceding that, recalling their first reunion, includes indirect discourse in this past tense narration: 'Elle m'a annoncé qu'elle allait partir, rentrer en Russie le soir même, elle avait déjà retenu sa place dans le train' (p. 257).

Ne sachant pas elle-même l'anglais, elle faisait soigneusement contrôler la façon de parler des jeunes Anglaises qui se présentaient par une amie qui s'y connaissait, et ne choisissait que parmi celles qui avaient la prononciation la plus pure.

Véra leur faisait bien comprendre qu'elles n'étaient engagées que pour donner leurs soins à 'la petite', 'la grande' n'en avait pas besoin. (p. 261)

This passage is a clear illustration of how the re-emergence of narrative authority out of dialogue establishes that hierarchical distance between quoting and quoted speech which gives the narrating voice the power not only to replace reported utterances with indirect propositions, but also to represent these with an interpretative (here ironic) gloss.

As the first voice's narrative authority finally becomes overtly asserted, the fiction of the critical interlocutor's independence loses its importance, and so its discourse too, like those of recalled characters, can be integrated into the authorial narration of which it was only ever a projection. Thus the narrator can assimilate into its own discourse the critic's role of analysing in the present the past events of childhood: 'Il me semble maintenant que c'était peut-être là un effort de sa part pour équilibrer entre Lili et moi les avantages, les chances . . . Je parlais très bien le russe, quelque peu l'allemand, je n'avais pas besoin en plus de l'anglais . . .' (pp. 261–2).[31] Even where it remains within the recalled period, the first voice now no longer recreates but analyses: where words like 'rancune' or 'mépris' were earlier deemed inadequate (p. 127), now we are told of 'les passions obscures, les réactions sauvages de Véra', the 'puissant système de défense disposé autour [de Lili] par sa mère' (p. 262). The appearance of metaphors of military aggression, familiar from Sarraute's earlier works and which describe tropistic undercurrents not fully perceived by the child, seals the identification of the narrating voice here as firmly adult and with an authorial status which makes its interlocutor superfluous:

Celles qui commettaient tant soit peu l'imprudence d'amener Lili à mettre en branle par ses plaintes, ses pleurnicheries, ce dispositif toujours en état d'alerte,

---

[31] Again, when Natacha meets her mother for the first time since her 'dumping', retrospective analysis and subsequent information, until now the domain of the second voice (and regularly rejected as irrelevant), appear in the narration: 'Je ne peux qu'imaginer, l'ayant mieux connue depuis, sa froideur calme, cette impression qu'elle donnait d'invincibilité, comme si elle avait elle-même reçu une impulsion à laquelle il lui était impossible de résister . . . c'est ce que mon père, au moment où elle le quittait, a dû ressentir . . . je l'ai compris beaucoup plus tard' (p. 257; cp. pp. 138, 219).

devaient se dépêcher de battre en retraite . . . Si elles osaient se défendre, elles rece-
vaient la volée de mitraille de ces mots lancés par Véra sur son ton sans réplique:
'Lili-ne-ment-jamais'. (p. 262)

Enfance thus continuously consolidates the authority of its narrative
voice while appearing to dissolve it. This consolidation of one voice
and concomitant subduing of the other is important above all in the
way it serves as a strategy to control how the text is read, through the
alignment of the second voice with the projected reader. However,
if, as Chapter 1 argued, writing distances the reader from the
authorial intentions behind the text, no matter how much those
intentions are focused on the very issue of reading, then it should be
possible to read Sarraute's text differently from the way she
prescribes. The freedom of actual readers will be the subject of
Chapter 5; to conclude this discussion of *Enfance*, I would like to give
a brief example of how one might read even the text's intentional
definition of its own meaning (or at least what one infers as
such[32]) against that intention. I shall consider two images *Enfance*
provides of its own textual dialogue, one positive and one negative,
and look at how each can be read as relating to the text which
contains it in ways other than those which initially propose
themselves.

The view of dialogue which *Enfance* promotes, through scenes
like the 'Femme et mari' one discussed earlier, is one where narrative truth is the result of the joint activity of teller and addressee.
This view, seen by many critics as the very principle of *Enfance*, is
embodied in a *mise en abyme* towards the end of the work, when
Véra's mother tells Natacha about her own childhood. The grandmother is not only a narrator here, but is also a good listener when
she plays narratee to Natacha's narratives: 'Je lui raconte tout ce qui
s'est passé à l'école et elle le rend intéressant, amusant, par sa façon
de l'écouter . . .' (p. 227). Teller and listener by turns, the old woman
and the child enact a model dialogue.

The grandmother is also a reader, and by reading aloud to
Natacha becomes for her a source of literature, so linking the act of
reading to that of producing a text of one's own, in this case, her

---

[32] This is obviously an extremely important qualification and requires more than paren-
thetical acknowledgement; I shall return to it at the end of Ch. 4, in the context of the way
dialogue operates across each participant's image of the other.

narration of her childhood.[33] Reading is not just linked to composition, however; by casting the grandmother as reader as well as listener, and as source of literature as well as oral storyteller in dialogue, Sarraute also conflates again oral communication with writing, and so the listener in *Enfance* with the remote and ungovernable reader of the text. This attempt to cross the barrier of writing to attain an (ostensibly) unmediated form of communication is emphasized in Véra's mother's choice of texts: the genre she mediates is drama (e.g. *Le Malade imaginaire*), which is both internally fully dialogic and as an artform bridges the divide between speech and writing, event and text, through the actor's direct address to the audience in the dramatic performance.

The emblematic relationship to *Enfance* itself in which the dialogues between Natacha and Véra's mother are cast, is emphasized by the fact that both talk about their lives. Natacha tells the old woman about her immediate experiences at school, an immediacy recreated throughout the text by the first voice when its narration slips into the historic present in order to circumscribe even more carefully its present discourse within the confines of the child's experience. The grandmother, on the other hand, tells of the past, of her youth in Russia, in a narration which both in its retrospective focus and in its referent is doubly representative of the narrative focus of *Enfance*, and which thus places Natacha in a situation similar to that of the narrator's listening double: 'Installée par terre, adossée aux genoux de grand-mère, l'écoutant parler de son enfance, je voyais revenir les vastes places enneigées aux reflets bleutés, les façades à colonnes des palais peints de délicates couleurs' (p. 230). The grandmother's narration recalls to Natacha her own forgotten past, as she hears her own earlier childhood in the other's recollections in the same way as the second voice of *Enfance* does. The dialogue becomes a way of recalling to the listening child a past life which she had left behind, much as we saw the opening words of *Enfance* act as a stimulus to the narrator's memory, though there on the level of the signifier rather than of the referent. There is another difference here of course—the fact that the interlocutor is a different person

---

[33] The relationship between writing and reading has been explored by Antoine Compagnon (1979: *passim*), for whom all writing is a rewriting of what one has already read. This imbrication of reading and writing in each other is of course given a particular twist by Sarraute when, as in *Entre la vie et la mort*, she defines the model reader as the *alter ego* of the writer (see Ch. 4, s. 2).

makes for a more authentic dialogue than one where both voices are aspects of the same consciousness.

Yet the particular way in which the old woman's discourse is presented here also illustrates the issues of power and control which pervade the text as a whole, and it is this which allows us, through closer analysis, to read the passage as a negative rather than positive *mise en abyme* of *Enfance*. The presentation of this dialogue replays in microcosm the way the text as a whole, while seeming to enact a meeting of different perspectives, in fact simulates such difference, and by simulating it seeks to pre-empt it at the moment of reading. The dialogue between Véra's mother and Natacha, like the textual dialogue generally, is represented in a fundamentally monological way. Only towards the end, when the old woman talks about her children, a subject distant from Natacha, are her words given as direct speech. Her memories of childhood in Russia, on the other hand, while they appear to be uttered directly, are in fact narrated by Natacha; the avoidance of personal pronouns only dissimulates the status of the grandmother's words as indirectly quoted. Thus, that part of the dialogue which recalls to the listening Natacha her own past, far from being presented to her in its 'irreducible other-ness', is represented by her, assimilated into her own narrative which then feigns the appearance of the grandmother's direct discourse: 'Un jour de la semaine sur deux on ne parle entre soi que le français . . . un autre jour l'allemand [. . .] Des Françaises, des Allemandes, des Anglaises surveillent sans cesse, ne laissent rien passer . . .' (p. 230). In this way, an ostensible dialogue which is in several respects a microcosm of the whole text, on a closer look reveals itself to be a dissimulated monologue ('Et les fêtes, la visite de la tzarine [. . .] On ne peut être plus loin des petites rues d'ici [. . .] de mon école'), and as such even more representative, but unwittingly, of the text which contains it.

This dissimulation is heightened by the fact that the illusion of direct speech is double, in line with the double narratorial frame in which the utterance is held. The impression that Natacha's representing discourse is autonomous is as illusory as was that regarding the grandmother's words: her childish idiom comes from the narrator, whose presence is concealed by the conflation of its 'je' with that of the child. Thus the suggested independence of the grandmother's voice is undermined by Natacha's self-effacing control, and Natacha's narration is in turn revealed to be dictated by the narrating adult's dissimulated presence. This situation enacts in miniature the way in which in *Enfance* as a whole, the impression of two autonomous voices working out the truth of the writer's childhood between them is also an illusion, with here again the same consciousness responsible for both, while giving the first voice power over the second within the dialogue.

Given this underlying domination concealed behind a series of representations of juxtaposed voices at the different levels of narration, the image of the reciprocal relationship of Natacha and her grandmother as alternately narrator and narratee ceases to be an accurate emblem of the text. Instead, another sequence suggests itself as a more suitable *mise en abyme* of the way the dialogue of *Enfance* conceals the control of every level of exchange in the text by one of its participants. This control, most clearly manifested in the way the second voice's interventions almost invariably serve to confirm the narrator's authority, culminates in the author's inscription of the reader's role within the text, in the same relation of subordination to the narrator. A solitary game played by Natacha before Véra's mother arrived, and which she claims no longer to have need of once the old woman is there, illustrates in microcosm the dynamics behind the text's various levels of interaction.

Before the grandmother came on the scene, Natacha used 'cocottes en papier' to teach herself difficult lessons. These were paper figures of her classmates which she directed in a kind of primitive puppet-show: 'Je les dispose sur ma table, côte à côte, en plusieurs rangs et moi, leur maîtresse . . . pas la vraie qui nous enseigne cette année . . . une maîtresse que j'invente . . . je m'installe sur ma chaise en face d'elles' (p. 220). It is possible to see this scene as a figure of Sarraute's writing in two ways. One which initially suggests itself and which is in keeping with her own diagnosis of contemporary literature and of her position within it, associates the child Natacha with a kind of writing previously criticized in works like *Entre la vie et la mort* (e.g. pp. 50–5), where literary invention focuses on the creation of characters and is associated with mimicry ('J'aime beaucoup imiter les gens et souvent mes imitations font rire . . .', Natacha tells us: *E* 220[34]). In the homemade puppet-show too,

---

[34] Natacha's childish writing has already been associated with literary cliché—in her 'first novel' with its consumptive hero and kidnapped princess (pp. 83–8), and in the school exercise on 'Mon premier chagrin' where she avoids lived experience in favour of a fictional account of the death of her dog, 'un modèle de vrai premier chagrin de vrai enfant' (p. 209).

characters are caricatures: 'Des inspecteurs de toutes sortes . . . des gros poussifs qui ne prononcent que quelques mots en soufflant . . . des méchants livides et maigres qui sifflent des remarques aigres-douces ou acerbes . . . et moi aussi je me transforme, je change comme je veux mon aspect, mon âge, ma voix, mes façons . . .' (p. 221). Certainly the fact that this scene just precedes the other major *mise en abyme* (one short section describing a serious childhood illness, a likely threshold experience, separates them) would suggest that it is intended to figure a stage, of writing as of childhood, to be outgrown. It thus seems to be a negative *mise en abyme* (what Ross Chambers (1984: 29) calls an 'antimodel') of the narrative situation of the whole work.

However, in light of the way the structure of discourses in *Enfance* both derives from and conceals undeniable strategies of control, it is possible to read this scene as a model rather than an antimodel of the text. The image of a chorus of voices, some knowing and others ignorant, all monitored by an authoritative figure—a child using the words of an adult—who lends them words and sets them against one another, bears a certain similarity to the way the voices of *Enfance*, reported by an adult in the voice of a child, are subjected to a series of authorities. These culminate in the consciousness which underlies both voices heard at the topmost level of narration and which controls any errors they might make, just as in the game, wrong answers given to the inspector can be rectified by an author who is both on stage and running the show, in control both within the fiction as a character and behind it as creator.[35]

The structure of control which operates in *Enfance*, and which the 'cocottes en papier' sequence figures, seems designed to exclude the possibility of any unknown voices coming into the act. Even the inspectors who come from outside the classroom, the scene of the fiction, have their roles written out for them and are at the mercy of the other voices within the class:

Cet inspecteur est un peu dur d'oreille . . . 'Qu'a donc répondu cette élève? . . . Je transforme aussitôt la mauvaise réponse . . . Elle a dit cela? Il m'a semblé pourtant . . . — Non Monsieur l'Inspecteur, toute la classe l'a entendue . . . N'est-ce pas?

---

[35] This 'puppet-master' approach to fictional characters was openly used as an authorial principle in one of the prose texts of *L'Usage de la parole*, 'Ne me parlez pas de ça', of which this scene is highly reminiscent. There the authorial voice admired in the characters 'cette docil-ité qui fait un des charmes de ce jeu' (*UP* 123), an attitude far removed from the Bakhtinian ideal of a full dialogue between the author and his autonomous characters.

(d'un air doucereux) mes enfants? . . . et toute la classe en chœur, comme un bêle-ment . . . Ooooui Maadaame . . .' (pp. 221–2)

In so far as this projected dialogue is a pact which keeps outsiders in their place, it figures the way the reader of *Enfance* enters the text only to find his interpretative role already incorporated into it in the shape of the critical voice, his possible criticisms both absorbed structurally and disposed of thematically by the work whose narrating voice rarely takes any criticism on board.

Yet the fact that we can read passages like the two just examined 'against the grain', reading a model of the text's apparent enactment of dialogue as its antimodel and vice versa, indicates that the passages themselves may solicit, or at least tolerate, readings other than those they seem officially to promote. Thus if the originally identified dialogic motivation of *Enfance* is countered by an authorial desire to establish narrative authority both within the text and in relation to the way it is read, this reaffirmation of control over the text is itself outdone by what I called in Chapter 1 the text's 'unconscious irony' (p. 27). This is an effect of the way its language, which transcends both the expressive intention of its writer and the interpretative scope of any given reader (while simultaneously defining those subjects), refuses to be confined to the expressive function assigned to it and retains its ability to be read otherwise.

The impression *Enfance* initially creates of wanting to relativize its authorial discourse, to undo the claim to authority and truth which autobiographical discourse makes in a particularly emphatic way and which, given the combined distortions operated by memory and narration, even it can never entirely justify, is thus first of all dissipated by the text's increasingly overt assertion of narrative authority. This seems to illustrate one of the conclusions of Chapter 1, that a certain kind of monologism is inherent to all language use, even to the claim that truth (in this case biographical truth) is dialogic, as well as to the invitation to dialogue which accompanies this claim. The desire to ensure correct interpretation leads to an attempt to control the reader's response, an attempt epitomized in the way, in *Enfance*, the reader's (passive) role is figured within the text itself. Yet despite this tendency, relativization of the authorial discourse does unavoidably take place, as its monologic intention, objectified in the (written) language of the text, rejoins the totality of possible significations of that text and is reconstructed by the reader out of them.

Before moving on, in the two final chapters, to the question of reading as such, I wish first to explore further how (what we can infer as) Sarraute's authorial intentions are exceeded, even to the point of being contradicted, by the language of the texts. I shall focus specifically on the relationship between the authorial subject and its language in *Tu ne t'aimes pas*. The less overtly autobiographical nature of this text seems to allow a more thorough engagement with the question of identity than ended up taking place in *Enfance*—the authorial subject's loss of unity is much more emphatic in *Tu ne t'aimes pas* than in the dualism of the earlier text where Sarraute finally succumbed to 'les pièges que pose l'écriture autobiographique' (Vercier 1985: 164) and which she at first appeared to have found a way around. Yet if, as Lacan teaches, language use is inseparable from the construction of the ego, if the reconstruction of a unitary identity is a function of speaking as such, and not just of speaking about one's life (though it will obviously be accentuated here), we can anticipate that the language of the fragmented authorial subject in *Tu ne t'aimes pas* will remain to some extent marked by that unifying force which the autobiographical discourse of *Enfance* illustrated so vividly.

3

THE SELF AND LANGUAGE:
AUTHENTICITY AND CONVENTION

Tu ne t'aimes pas, written immediately after *Enfance* and published in 1989, shares with it the structure of a fragmented authorial voice engaged in internal dialogue. The authorial status of the dialoguing self is less explicit than in *Enfance* where the autobiographical project emphasized the identity of narrated, narrating, and writing selves; none the less, Sarraute's conversations with Simone Benmussa while *Tu ne t'aimes pas* was being written show her affinity to its 'nous' in terms of both the general lack of a unitary sense of self, and the particular experiences that plurality of voices describes, such as the death of its partner (see *TTP* 122; Sarraute 1987*a*: 151–6). With the absence of the unifying impetus inherent in more openly autobiographical writing (and which defeated, in *Enfance*, the attempt to undo it through a dialogic structure), comes a much more radical disintegration of the authorial voice. Instead of a binary opposition between two perspectives which could be characterized in a relatively stable manner as respectively close to childhood sensations and alienated from them, and consequently reliable and unreliable, we get in *Tu ne t'aimes pas* a view of the mind as composed of innumerable voices, no one of which predominates in the text. The more rigorous dispersal of speaker-authority here than in *Enfance* leads to a more sustained use of direct discourse to represent the utterances of 'outsiders' too, a more enduring authorial refusal to subsume the words of others into its own determinedly multiple discourses.

The absence of a defined reader-figure in *Tu ne t'aimes pas* also distinguishes it from *Enfance* (and indeed from *L'Usage de la parole* which immediately preceded *Enfance*). Not assigning the reader a clear and limiting role within the text would appear to grant him more freedom, to permit a more unconditioned response to what he reads and a more active role in the establishment of meaning than *Enfance* finally allowed. On the other hand, the absence of the reader from the text could simply mean that he has ceased to matter, that his reception of the message is no longer seen by Sarraute as in any way vital to its meaning, for the meaning of authentic writing, as we have seen, is *expressed* rather than inferred, and readers, for Sarraute, are notoriously unreliable as partners in dialogue. After all, to an outlook which sees the artist as privileged with access to an authentic mode of expression, the contribution of an absolutely other reader can only be inferior.

This second, more sceptical interpretation of the reader's absence from *Tu ne t'aimes pas* is supported by the fact that its internal dialogue has an undeniably self-sufficient quality, greater than that of *Enfance* or *Entre la vie et la mort* where the status of the *alter ego* hovered between that of writing self and reading other. For the voices of *Tu ne t'aimes pas*, self–other relations with all their attendant traumas are something now past: 'Il y a longtemps que nous ne sommes pas allés de ce côté' (*TTP* 156). It seems that the engagement with a reader may have become equally superfluous. Paradoxically, of course, this indifference to the reader, by declining to promote a specific way of reading, facilitates an authentically dialogic response to the text (the final chapter will consider in general terms what such a response might be).

This lack of acknowledgement of the reader as other, and withdrawal from intersubjective communication into the (highly vocal) arena of the self's many voices, inevitably casts into question the degree to which *Tu ne t'aimes pas* can really be said to pursue authentic dialogue, assuming otherness as the fundamental value in dialogue.[1] In arguing that even Sarraute's most overtly dialogic texts ultimately hold on to a monologic aesthetic of expression, I do not aim to present her as failing to reach a certain standard of truth established by theory. Rather, as I shall suggest at the end of this chapter, what happens to dialogue in *Tu ne t'aimes pas* as in *Enfance*

---

[1] Arnaud Rykner is one critic who sees both *Tu ne t'aimes pas* and *Enfance* as enacting a real self–Other dialogue: 'Même lorsque le narrateur se laisse aller à être son propre interlocuteur, comme dans *Enfance*, il devient autre, il devient l'Autre: sa voix se dédouble, voire se démultiplie comme dans *Tu ne t'aimes pas*. Le Je n'est Je que dans le rapport qu'il entretient avec un Tu, que lorsqu'il se détache d'un Tu qui est encore lui et ne l'est déjà plus' (1991: 20). Yet Rykner never resolves (or indeed acknowledges) the conflict between the always already socialized self implied in this dialogic view of identity, and the simultaneous affinity he notes of the Sarrautean self to Husserl's 'intentional consciousness' and its process of 'phenomenological reduction', the solitary return to a primordial *Lebenswelt* or 'protofondation qui seule permet une saisie du monde qui soit à la fois authentique et consciente de sa propre préhistoire' (p. 64).

may well tell us something about the nature of language and of dialogue in general. Both texts demonstrate how using language at all, whether in speech or in writing, necessarily unifies the self in spite of itself. Looked at in the light of the theories of subjectivity and language discussed in Chapter 1, this repeated collapse of the non-authoritative, differentiated authorial psyche into a unitary discourse in fact appears as a necessary aspect of linguistic self-representation. In this way, Sarraute's critique of lifeless conventional language yet faith in and pursuit of authentic expression in her own writing merely magnifies contradictions also inherent in more self-conscious articulations of the limitations of the linguistic subject and the dialogic nature of truth. Even these are bound to betray their stated beliefs to the extent that they believe in what they say and try to convince their addressee of it (as Chapter 1 argued, this is true even of Lacan, despite the lengths to which his prose goes to exceed its own conscious agenda).[2]

But this unavoidable monologism is not the whole story: given the alienation which is constitutive of linguistic communication, the addressor can never quite evacuate the transindividual aspect of his discourse and limit it to its intended meaning—and nor can the reader, however much he may wish to submit to the writer's intention, read only this. This is what permits readings of texts like those of the two images *en abyme* of the dialogic structure of *Enfance* discussed at the end of Chapter 2; in the present chapter, the inability of Sarraute's discourse to escape convention entirely and become thoroughly individual, purely expressive, will be illustrated on the basis of *'disent les imbéciles'* as well as of *Tu ne t'aimes pas*. With the transcendence of the text's inevitable monologism, the possibility of some kind of dialogue returns; for the alienation which appears to prohibit it (by leading each speaker to posit the response of understanding he desires to his monologic expressive intention) simultaneously makes it possible by preserving the reader's otherness from the text's attempt to define him.

---

[2] On the way deconstructionist theories of the conventionality of language and the nature of meaning as an effect of that language enact the 'Cretan liar' paradox (where the statement by a man from Crete that all Cretans are liars must disprove itself in order to be true), see Prendergast (1986: 18).

1. The subject as social being: Sarraute and Lacan

In order to gauge both the extent to which the Sarrautean self is conceived as existing dialogically, and the ways in which it is independent of or even hostile to dialogue, it will be useful to consider it in the context of Lacan's theory of the role of dialogue in the constitution of the subject.[3] In using Lacan's work in this way I do not wish to imply that it represents the truth about dialogue or the subject, or by extension that the value of Sarraute's vision should be measured by its closeness to or deviation from his. Instead, I see reading one in terms of the other as instituting a relation not of mastery but of dialogue between them—with all the complications and issues of power which I have suggested are inherent to that relation. (I shall return to the question of what is involved in establishing such a dialogue at the end of Chapter 4, as part of a discussion of the way reading, and specifically a critical reading such as mine, replays as a linguistic act the irreducible monologism involved in writing.)

Tu ne t'aimes pas, in representing the mind as an ongoing conversation between innumerable participants, illustrates Sarraute's stated conception of the self in her own conversations with Simone Benmussa, not as a singular entity reducible to social roles based on outdated literary models (writer, mother, etc.), but as 'quelque chose d'incommensurable' (Sarraute 1987*a*: 76). The self is empty in the sense that it contains no solid unchanging kernel, yet it is full of contrasting selves whose constant commentary qualifies any attempt to present to others a stable, unitary personality:

---

[3] The divergences which will become apparent in the following discussion, between Sarraute's and Lacan's views on the individual's relationship to language and the world, make it expedient to avoid as far as possible using the term 'subject', associated with Lacan, to refer to the Sarrautean protagonist (whether the plural authorial voice of *Enfance* or *Tu ne t'aimes pas*, or its earlier 'chevaliers': see Ch. 2, p. 58). While this figure is a subject in the Lacanian sense to the extent that it has access to language and is conscious, it is not perceived by Sarraute as embodying the 'fallen' aspect of Lacanian subjectivity, the idea of the mind being structured, and so limited, by language (entry into the Symbolic denying access to the incommensurable self through the creation and repression of the unconscious). I shall therefore generally use the word 'self' rather than 'subject' to refer to the image of authentic existence presented by Sarraute, and follow Arnaud Rykner in seeing that self become a subject once it interacts with an other (in language): 'L'être sarrautien est un être social qui doit affronter des subjectivités étrangères, lesquelles donnent consistance à son existence et lui permettent de se constituer à son tour en sujet' (1991: 19). However, I shall argue that Sarraute presents this transformation of the incommensurable self into a subject in interaction as a negative move, a loss of personal authenticity.

Suppose qu'un journaliste vienne interviewer l'écrivain. Il veut l'écrivain? Il va recevoir ça aujourd'hui, c'est ça qu'il est venu chercher [. . .] Mais c'est une petite part infime de tout le reste [. . .] Il y a toujours une multitude en nous, puisque nous sommes si nombreux . . . et qui souffle [. . .] 'Mais qu'est-ce que tu racontes! Qu'est-ce que tu vas leur dire?' (pp. 82–3)

The social persona is merely the appearance beneath which, in the familiar Romantic opposition, lies the formless reality of tropisms: '[Les personnages] ne sont qu'apparences, par derrière se déroule la vie anonyme des tropismes' (p. 119). A primary feature of this sense of self as 'rien, rien, rien' (p. 163) is its passivity: it is when it is ingesting impressions from outside that the self is ineffable, not when it is active: 'Le monde entier est là et s'engouffre à chaque instant, se transforme à chaque seconde, passe à travers moi. Ma propre personnalité n'existe pas à ce moment-là. Je ne sais même pas ce qu'elle est. Je ne suis que ce qui passe à travers moi: ce que je regarde, ce que j'entends . . . le monde entier' (p. 163). It is significant that Sarraute here equates personality with self-consciousness ('Je ne sais même pas ce qu'elle est'); this tendency will be central to the assessment of how far her thinking on the self is compatible with Lacan's subject-in-dialogue.

The way relations to another unify the incommensurable self and give it an identity is a major theme in Sarraute, as Arnaud Rykner has emphasized (see n.3). Before looking at the way this phenomenon is represented in *Tu ne t'aimes pas*, a brief reminder of Lacan's account of how identity is mediated through the other will be helpful. The infant's experience of the mirror stage lays the foundation for the later assumption of a linguistic identity imposed from outside. Here the infant projects its perception of the integrity of another figure back onto itself, and so intuits its own identity on the model of that other. The calling into being of the social subject is completed by the way its parents (in the paradigmatic family structure) refer to it and name it, replacing the mirror's unifying power with that of language. That aspect of the self which cannot be named (desire of the mother) is repressed in the Oedipus complex, a move which creates the unconscious. Hence the subject of language is only part of the self whose originary division (the *Spaltung*) brought it into being. Every engagement with others and their language deepens the gulf between the subject and its truth, in a repetition Lacan calls the *refente* (1966: 842).

When relations become mediated by language, they consolidate a distinction between self and other not acknowledged prior to this. Language, by letting us name other things, circumscribes our sense of ourselves as different from those things, just as the first encounter with the Symbolic order gave the child a fixed place in the family (via the *nom du père*). Anika Lemaire sums up the fate of the Lacanian subject for whom access to the Symbolic order means 'l'impossible coïncidence du (Je), sujet de l'énonciation, et du "Je", sujet de l'énoncé' and so 'amorce la dialectique des aliénations du sujet. Le sujet se fige en ses énoncés, en ses rôles sociaux et la totalité de ceux-ci s'édifie peu à peu en un "moi" qui n'est plus qu'une objectification du sujet' (1977: 127). The *moi* is an imaginary construct, 'par un autre et pour un autre' (Lacan 1966: 374). Thus for Lacan the reductive influence of the other on the self is inseparable from the fact of using language, and as such is generally invisible to us. The dependence on the other for one's identity explains the aggression inherent in human relations and which, I have suggested, is manifested in dialogue in the attempt both to project onto the other the response of recognition one desires from him and to prevent undesirable responses:

L'homme *obligé de se façonner en référence* à l'autre ou contre l'autre, en rivalité, obligé d'attendre de l'autre la reconnaissance ou le jugement, est naturellement enclin à toute la gamme des conduites agressives, depuis l'envie, en passant par la jalousie morbide et l'agressivité réelle, jusqu'à la négation mortelle de l'autre ou de soi-même. (Lemaire 1977: 277)

So far one can see a clear kinship between Lacan and Sarraute. Lacan's focus on the way social roles and the language which supports them reduce an indefinable self to a false *moi* encourages comparison with Sarraute's critique of the way individuals draw on received novelistic models to constitute fictional social personas for themselves. Well before the ineffable Sarrautean self was given such extreme structural acknowledgement as it gets in the multiple voices of *Tu ne t'aimes pas*, her work already addressed its uncharacterizability and the illusory nature of the *moi* which conceals it when, as Rykner has it, the self becomes a subject in interaction. In *'disent les imbéciles'*, the sense of being 'rien . . . un vide . . . un trou d'air . . . Infini' (*DI* 126) is complemented by the experience of acquiring an illusory identity, imposed by others, which turns one into an object. One character, confronted with a photograph of himself, feels alienated in this image which fails to match his sense of self, just

as for Lacan the mirror-image alienates the small child by imposing
an illusion of integrity on the formlessness of existence: 'Qu'est-ce
que c'est que ça? mais ce n'est pas moi . . . — Allons donc, vous ne
vous reconnaissez pas? — Si, si, bien sûr . . . Je retrouve mes traits,
je les ai vus reflétés dans des glaces, fixés sur des pellicules, mais
jamais je n'ai vu . . . je n'ai jamais imaginé . . . Avouez que ce n'est
pas ressemblant . . .' (p. 30). Aside from the several instances where
the self is objectified through reflection of its image in mirrors,
photographs, and even in people's eyes, it also undergoes the
Lacanian experience of being reductively—and arbitrarily—
defined through others' language: 'Lui on le connaît . . . il n'y a pas
plus délicat, plus modeste, je dirais même plus humble . . . oui,
humble . . . Non? Pas humble? Humble ne vous convient pas? Je
crois que j'ai trouvé: orgueilleux plutôt? Vous voyez, orgueilleux lui
va. Un monstre d'orgueil [. . .] C'est évident, qui ne le voit? Vous
êtes cela. Vous êtes un monstre d'orgueil' (p. 77).

It is always social pressure which leads Sarraute's characters to
accept false social identities, just as the Lacanian subject is exposed
to 'tous les mensonges ou aliénations voulus ou non [. . .] toutes les
distorsions inscrites au principe même de la dimension symbolique
conventionnelle de la vie en groupe' (Lemaire 1977: 108). But the
phenomenon of having one's identity conferred from without is not
distasteful to all: for some, being the object of a gaze can arouse a
'délicieuse sensation d'être enfermée en sécurité dans cette forme
que dessinent nos regards déférents' (*DI* 96). As the object of admiration of a group, a 'maître' can say anything, however irrelevant
(like crying 'Debout les morts!' in a conversation about the Moors[4]),
secure in the knowledge that his ideas will be admired on the basis
of his social status rather than for their intrinsic merit. Here the
other's gaze is empowering rather than restrictive:

C'est leurs regards réunis sur lui qui lui donnent cette aisance, cette liberté de
mouvements, tout en le contenant à l'abri d'une forme . . . la sienne . . . qu'ils
modèlent, qu'ils caressent [. . .] Il regarde son gros poing couvert de poils roux qui
s'abat sur la table . . . c'est à lui, tout cela, c'est lui. Il a envie de se tâter pour
s'assurer que c'est vrai, il lève le bras plus haut, il abat son poing plus fort, sa voix
claque: 'Debout les morts! Debout les morts!' (p. 71)

This image of the alienated subject who relates to himself, via
others' perceptions of him, as to an object, to the point of looking at

[4] This misunderstanding was already treated in *EVM* 143–4; it will reappear in *Ici*, 108–9.

his hand as something distinct from himself yet in which his identity is somehow contained, reappears in *Tu ne t'aimes pas*, this time to be analysed by the authorial voices: the man who gazes at his hand on the table has 'dans son regard tant d'amour . . . C'est ainsi chez ceux qui s'aiment . . . leur amour va d'abord à tout ce qu'ils peuvent apercevoir d'eux-mêmes . . . leurs mains, leurs pieds, leurs avant-bras . . . et puis dans la glace leur reflet' (*TTP* 20).

Embracing one's alienated image, including seeing one's body from without, is thus a symptom of self-love; it is the inability to cooperate in one's objectification that leads to the diagnosis 'Tu ne t'aimes pas'. The several voices of the self in this novel[5] are incapable of such self-observation: contemplation of their reflection has never exceeded 'de brefs moments, plutôt d'étonnement . . . Est-ce moi, vraiment? . . . Mais venait très vite un autre et encore un autre reflet . . . Et puis nos regards occupés ailleurs ne s'arrêtaient guère pour contempler' (p. 21). Nor is the body ever an object of awareness for the voices of *Tu ne t'aimes pas*; it exists in the realm of the real and so functions without being conceptualized, independently of consciousness:

— [. . .] Nos mains sont des objets utilitaires, des ustensiles limités à leur fonction, elles n'ont rien à faire ici . . .
— Et tout notre corps à nous, en ce moment nous ne sentons pas sa présence, c'est comme s'il n'existait pas [. . .] (p. 21)

The reflections of the self which others provide no more enable it to establish a stable identity than does contemplation of its own body: 'Ces images de nous-mêmes que les autres nous renvoient, nous n'arrivons pas à nous voir en elles' (p. 15). The Sarrautean plural self is the exception in society, an aberration among those unitary individuals who see themselves 'reflétés dans les yeux des autres' (p. 15): 'Chacun d'eux est sain, normal, chacun d'eux s'aime, et nous . . . on ne s'aime pas' (p. 12). It is impossible to pin down as an

---

[5] Although *Tu ne t'aimes pas* is more a series of first-person (plural) reflections on the nature of the self than a work of fiction, the label 'roman' appears on the cover of the first Gallimard ('Blanche') edition. Valerie Minogue, in the *Notice* to *Tu ne t'aimes pas*, discusses the genre of this text which 'n'a pourtant rien d'un roman conventionnel. Au contraire, il réalise un pas de plus vers ce roman "abstrait" que Sarraute envisageait déjà en 1950, dans l'essai "L'Ère du soupçon", où elle note dans le roman "une évolution analogue à celle de la peinture—bien qu'infiniment plus timide et plus lente", évolution au cours de laquelle "l'élément psychologique, comme l'élément pictural, se libère insensiblement de l'objet avec lequel il faisait corps"' (*OC* 1959; *ES* 73).

object of love this being which is made up of 'tant [de personnes] . . . comme des étoiles dans le ciel . . . toujours d'autres apparaissent dont on ne soupçonnait pas l'existence [. . .] Je suis l'univers entier, toutes les virtualités, tous les possibles' (p. 17).

In Sarraute's view, then, self-definition from the point of view of the other is clearly not an *integral* part of being conscious. It is on this point that her notion of subjectivity (as existence in/with language), whether illustrated in the multiple entity of *Tu ne t'aimes pas* or in the distressed reaction of the young man in '*disent les imbéciles*' who fails to recognize himself in a photograph, diverges most sharply from that of Lacan. By *Tu ne t'aimes pas*, fifty years into Sarraute's writing career, such unwelcome definitions are, moreover, no longer even perceived as the threat they were earlier: the infinite self is so confirmed in its difference from the fictional characters who populate the real world and believe in their reflected images that it can recall even hostile engagements with indulgence. However much its interactions with others may compromise it, it knows now that it will always recover its internal multiplicity: 'Quelle souillure peut-elle trouver une place dans notre mouvante immensité? Quelle trace peut-elle laisser?' (p. 70). What then is for Sarraute the nature of the 'authentic' self, and what kind of consequences does her portrait of a self happy with its own (admittedly considerable) company have for the question of intersubjective relations, both within the fictional universe and in terms of the text's interaction with a reader?

For Sarraute, as we have seen, there are two modes of existence in the world, distinguished by the way in which one reacts to images of oneself; these images can be perceived directly by the self (in mirrors or by viewing one's own body, a necessarily incomplete mode of self-objectification), or they can be provided by others who communicate to us verbally or visually the way we appear to them. Unquestioning acceptance of these images as equal to the self distinguishes the vast majority of individuals in Sarraute's universe from those whose experience of such imposed definitions on what is felt subjectively to be infinite causes distress and alienation. None the less, the status of each mode of being is not stable: just as the solid individual, evocative of a character from a traditional novel, can undergo a vertiginous loss of identity if the certainty of his reflected image is taken away, the formless self which gets its most extreme articulation in *Tu ne t'aimes pas* can find itself lured by others into asserting a reductive self-definition. Thus the 'maître' in '*disent les imbéciles'*, immediately after his 'Debout les morts!' apotheosis and his admiration of his 'gros fort poing des forts tempéraments' (*DI* 75), experiences a total loss of identity on the basis of a loss of confidence in his admirers' judgement:

Cette place que vous m'avez attribuée avec tant de générosité . . . je me demande s'il n'y a pas eu une méprise . . . Vous vous en souvenez, quand je levais le poing, quand je frappais la table, quand je roulais de gros yeux globuleux injectés de sang . . . c'était vous, vous qui me poussiez . . . un effet de suggestion, d'hypnose [. . .] Je n'ai pas pu y tenir, je me suis échappé, je suis dehors de nouveau . . . un souffle, une ombre, un vide où tout s'engouffre . . . (p. 76)

By contrast, the 'nous' of *Tu ne t'aimes pas* can ruefully recall a time (significantly past) when outside pressure led them to construct 'un beau "je" présentable, bien solide' (*TTP* 37). This construction (of the self as a character who never seeks revenge) quickly went out of control:

— On ajoutait ceci . . . et encore cela . . .
— Comme la pipe qu'on plante au milieu du visage . . . le chapeau de feutre qu'on pose sur la tête . . .
— Oui, d'un bonhomme de neige . . . (p. 39)

However, this effigy dissolved again once the self escaped the objectifying power of the other and returned from the intersubjective encounter to the authenticity of its own internal dialogue: 'Avec quelle rapidité, quand il est resté seul parmi nous, il a fondu . . .' (p. 39).

The temptation to turn one's authentic self into an object is thus the result of associating with others who believe in their own characterizations, a fact which augurs ill for the whole idea of intersubjective relations. Self-objectification is contagious, and any engagement with it, even the very attempt to tear away the mask which others present to us, ironically leads to the self constructing an identity of its own (that of the aggressor). Both *'disent les imbéciles'* and *Tu ne t'aimes pas* provide strikingly close examples of this. In the earlier novel, the riposte 'C'est vous que ça juge' to one individual's criticism of a prominent figure's idea, sparks off an extended reaction in the mind of the addressee who is immediately objectified by its pronoun ('Vous. Vous. Vous. Plus d'infinis, d'espaces sans bornes': *DI* 133). Reduced to a *moi*, the self responds in kind: 'Sous le "C'est vous" il y a . . . ça saute aux yeux . . . il y a "Ce n'est pas lui" [. . .] Nous avons été mis en balance. Placés à chaque bout de la bascule. Nous nous faisons face, lui et moi' (*DI* 135). By destroying the absent 'lui' whose idea he has attacked, the 'moi' hopes to free himself from his accusers' imprisoning definition, for he only exists as 'vous' in opposition to this other figure.[6]

The imprisoned 'moi' accuses his designated opponent of wilfully turning himself into a character by matching his demeanour to a familiar model of genius. Yet though he perceives that figure's falsity, he cannot destroy it without engaging with it on its own level, thus becoming embroiled in a demeaning battle of egos. In the attempt to dismantle the persona of the 'genius', the limitless self becomes highly individualized, evident in the way the pronoun 'je' proliferates during what turns out to be a struggle to the death: 'Je tourne autour de lui, je bondis, je mords, j'arrache des lambeaux [. . .] Je ne peux plus m'en détacher, je me colle à lui, je pèse sur lui, je l'étreins, je reçois sur moi son souffle, sa sueur, son sang' (p. 138). Utterly counterproductive, the attempt to unmask an opponent, by forcing the self into a position of aggression which unifies him ('Tout ce que je sais, c'est qu'au point où j'en suis, il faut que lui ou moi l'emporte': p. 138), makes him an easy target for his interlocutors' reductive characterizations of him in turn. Their stereotypical images of him—'roquet aboyant aux chausses, les chiens aboient la caravane passe, le pou dans la crinière du lion, la grenouille et le bœuf'—and his reduced state as single aggressive impulse overlap: 'et je saute et je jappe et je pique et je me gonfle' (p. 139).

In the comparable nightmare recalled in *Tu ne t'aimes pas*, the object attacked by the ineffable self is not a character but a concept, 'bonheur' (denounced already by Sarraute in the essay 'Le Bonheur de l'homme', 1984*a*). What is striking about this passage is that the concept of happiness it explodes by showing its inadequacy to lived experience has much in common with the ideal of dialogue, to the point of merging with it: 'Où est ici cette totale liberté? Cette absence de toute contrainte? Ce détachement parfait? Ces nobles sentiments que personne n'a encore éprouvés? Ces conversations à travers lesquelles on voit circuler les belles, puissantes, vivifiantes idées?' (*TTP* 69). Similarly, the reality it replaces it with, 'cet

---

[6] 'Lui' is the pronoun of character in fiction, comparable to the 'moi' of psychoanalytic discourse. For Ann Jefferson, 'to see a character as a *he* is to see him as a "character", and so to be denied any communication with him' (1980: 103).

insupportable esclavage, ces jalousies, envies, mesquineries, agres-
sivités . . . et ces conversations d'où tant de conformisme, d'ennui se
dégage', expresses a marked lack of faith in the power of communication. In an attempt to discredit those who claim to live in happiness and who thereby dominate others (like the self) who lack such
unifying concepts to apply to their lives, the plural self of *Tu ne t'aimes
pas*, like the imprisoned 'moi' of *'disent les imbéciles'*, is transformed
into an agent of destruction (and so bears out its own scepticism
regarding communication):

> Alors plus rien ne nous retient, aucun scrupule, aucun respect de la vérité. Tout
> nous est bon pour essayer de venir à bout de ces destructeurs, de ces tueurs . . . nous
> lançons sur eux n'importe quoi . . . n'importe quelles pitoyables et basses histoires,
> quels humiliants déboires colportés par leurs plus vils ennemis, probablement
> inventés . . .
>
> Et nous sommes repoussés de toutes parts, chassés avec dégoût . . . nous rentrons
> salis, les mots qu'on a crachés sur nous nous couvrent, dégoulinent . . . (pp. 69–70)

Even recollection of the event from the safety of hindsight awakens
the clichéd language of convention—'nous jeter à corps perdu [. . .]
nous perdre corps et âme [. . .] ne pas nous rappeler que "Charité
bien ordonnée commence par soi-même"'—which the self rejects
as 'pris au-dehors, ce ne sont pas des mots de chez nous' (p. 70).[7]
The internal multitude has its own language, and reference to the
body is not part of it, for, as I mentioned earlier, the body is not conceptualized, it is simply there, unobtrusively doing its job in the
realm of the real. The relationship between language and the body
is not that simple, though, and I shall return to it in connection with
Sarraute's validation of her own language's authenticity.

The 'true' state of the Sarrautean self is thus solitary and passive,
for any kind of social engagement is doomed to end with it drawn
into a struggle which falsifies its infinite nature (another example
from *Tu ne t'aimes pas* follows a perceived insult which caused an
immediate though short-lived unification: 'Je m'aime. — Nous
avons de nouveau osé aller jusque-là', p. 102). Withdrawal from
intersubjective relations is the necessary condition for personal
authenticity; only in *intra*subjective dialogue can the cliché-ridden

---

[7] Similarly, in *'disent les imbéciles'*, the self's obligation to argue on others' convention-
bound terms forces him into cliché: 'Quand on s'est mis dans un si mauvais cas, quand on a
fait un si dangereux faux pas, quand on a été, ainsi, fait comme un rat, on ne sait plus à quel
saint se vouer' (*DI* 140).

language of social intercourse be replaced by the genuine, expressive discourse 'de chez nous'. But this disdain for dialogue with others raises the question of the nature of the relationship between Sarraute's text and its reader. How can Sarraute reconcile her view of what communication does to the self with her activity of writing which manifests a desire to communicate that view none the less to a reader?

The fact that Sarraute persists in writing for a reader despite the gloomy view of communication her writing depicts, is related to her belief that the writer can forge an exceptional language; this allows her to set her own work outside the complex of domination and sub-mission she describes so frequently as unavoidable when humans address one another. (The fact that it is not outside that complex, as the treatment of the reader in *Enfance* shows, only bears out the accuracy of her observation of the issues of power which are involved in communication.) Seeing her own highly poetic lan-guage as expressive rather than conventional, originating in a self which is not a symbolic construct, she perceives the ideal recipient of this authentic address not as a symbolized other encountered only in language and thus unknowable, but as another unsymbol-ized self, known prior to the intervention of a mediating language. (This reading double, to be discussed more fully in the next chapter, is of course a prominent feature of *Entre la vie et la mort* and *Enfance*.[8])

In so far as the Sarrautean self and its ideal interlocutor/reader are obliged to manifest themselves in language, what distinguishes them, in her view, from the alienated subjects of conventional lan-guage is an absence of self-consciousness. This is what marks the limit of Sarraute's apparent affinity to the Lacanian concept of subjectivity: for her, the alienation of the truth of the subject in language is confined to language use which is not only conscious but *self*-conscious, aware of its status as utterance, and of its speaker. It is not the mere fact of using language which turns the self into a singular *moi* for Sarraute; it is the use of language in a particularly self-reflexive way, epitomized in speech about oneself,

---

[8] In *Les Fruits d'or*, though the good reader is not characterized as the *alter ego* of the writer, his contact with the text is likewise evoked through the sensory metaphors of touch and taste, and is even claimed to take place prior to the language which names those experiences: 'C'est ce parfum qu'ils dégagent, mais ce n'est pas un parfum, pas même encore une odeur, cela ne porte aucun nom, c'est une odeur d'avant les odeurs' (*FO* 153).

which objectifies not only the speaker but also, by extension, his interlocutor.

Thus the self-objectifying, self-loving majority are marked by the reflexivity of their language. It is a language the self of *Tu ne t'aimes pas* claims to lack: even when it assumes it, carrying out the splitting of the self into subject and object explored in depth in *Entre la vie et la mort* and epitomized linguistically in the reflexive verb, this language is always seen as consciously borrowed from others:

> Attendez un instant, ne m'enfermez pas . . . pas entièrement . . . *je me suis scindé* en deux . . . une opération que vous recommandez, je sais la faire aussi, je sais *me regarder* du dehors, je peux *me voir, me connaître* [. . .] J'ai su assimiler vos enseigne-ments, j'ai retenu vos classements, j'applique vos règlements, je suis d'ici, de chez vous, un des vôtres. (*TTP* 208–9; my emphasis)

The language of others is a pernicious one: it kills what it names by conceptualizing the ineffable (oneself, the other, two decades of emotional life in 'vingt ans de bonheur': p. 47). The speaker of this language thus commits a sort of linguistic suicide by suppressing his presence as expressing source (Lacan's 'sujet de l'énonciation') in favour of a linguistic sign which objectifies him. His language is full of reflexive verbs like 's'aimer', which triggered *Tu ne t'aimes pas*, or 's'amuser' (p. 131); he is liable to use phrases like 'Que je me sois fait ça à moi', where 'le voilà plus net que jamais, ce dédoublement' (p. 138), or even simply 'Si c'était moi' (p. 140). This way in which reflexive language, where the self objectifies itself in a pronoun, cuts itself off from the living sensation in which it is born and which it should express, reaches an extreme in the use of the future perfect. In Sarraute's example, 'Je m'amuse', which already kills its speaker by naming her as an object, migrates even further from the life and the event in which it originated by becoming 'Ce que je me serai amusée' (p. 131). As a result, 'd'un seul coup ce qui était en train de s'accomplir s'est accompli . . . Cela s'étale derrière nous, immobil-isé, offert, comme un souvenir . . . pour le voir il faut qu'on se retourne . . .' (p. 132).

The fault of inauthentic others, then, is their alienation from the truth their own consciousnesses can provide. The seat of truth for Sarraute is the tropism, and the tropism is conscious, if only just. (Its ambiguous location 'aux portes de la conscience' (*ES* 97) is exploited by Sarraute in ways to be looked at more closely later in this chapter: it belongs to a physical realm prior to conceptualization,

yet is both a source of language and can—though with difficulty—
be articulated in language.) Self-ignorance is ignorance of the
tropism which emerges from within us, and fidelity instead to a view
of life and, worse, of ourselves which comes from without, frozen in
a second-hand language.

Thus Sarraute draws truth more closely into the orbit of the
individual mind than do the psychoanalytic theories of Freud and
Lacan. Psychoanalysis 'detranscendentalizes' the Romantic opposition between illusion and reality by circumscribing it within the
self (but a self structured by the social phenomenon of language),
locating absolute truth in the unconscious rather than the cosmos,
with consciousness the locus of illusion. Sarraute takes the demysti-
fication of truth a step further by situating it within consciousness,
but only when it is in touch with its own tropistic activity. For
Sarraute, it is when consciousness becomes self-consciousness that
it enters the alienated realm of illusion. In the context of irony, the
fact that Sarraute locates the truth of the self in consciousness rather
than in the unconscious explains why, as we saw with *Enfance* and as
reading *Tu ne t'aimes pas* will confirm, her work ultimately seems governed by the principle of verbal rather than epistemological irony.
For unlike the way in which epistemological irony acknowledges the
speaker's own Socratic ignorance, in verbal irony the truth of which
the inadequate utterance so obviously falls short is itself in fact consciously known, and as such has the potential to be expressed.

Sarraute's criticism of how individuals rely on external definitions of themselves for a sense of identity illustrates the way her version of the self's externality to itself is located a notch higher in
consciousness than is Lacan's. For her, this dependence on the other
operates on the level of *values* (just as the dialogic encounter does,
see Ch. 2, pp. 58–9), rather than being an a priori implication of
living in language; for this reason it can be rejected. The other's
definition of one's identity matters because of who he is, not as such:
'On m'a dit de vous que vous êtes quelqu'un. — Quelqu'un? Moi?
— [. . .] Ah vous voulez savoir qui . . . vous avez bien raison, si un
imbécile me l'avait dit . . . mais je ne vous l'aurais pas répété . . .'
(*DI* 144). Moreover, the loss of this other-constituted identity does
not entail a loss of consciousness or necessarily of language: 'Si tout
à l'heure, lorsqu'il sera seul, la nuit, étendu dans son lit, il perdait de
nouveau ses contours [. . .] redevenait immense, un océan' (p. 145).
In Sarraute's ontology, the self which is left behind when identity

flees is the conscious self of *Tu ne t'aimes pas* which still possesses its own language, its 'mots de chez nous' (*TTP* 70).

Thus Sarraute can strive to exempt her own literary language, as long as it emerges from the authenticity of the writer's solitude and poetic endeavour, from any participation in turning self or other into a *moi*, or sensation into a coded structure. In her view of communication, the Lacanian *moi–moi autre* axis of language (see Ch. 1 n. 20) is replaced by a 'self–*moi autre*' opposition, where it is the conventional language of the other which objectifies speaker, addressee, and referent. Yet her representation of the ways in which the other's language alienates himself, his interlocutor, and his referent from their truth, has some relevance, as I shall show, for her own authorial language too. For even her own poetic discourse, by its very nature as language, cannot avoid reproducing to some degree the alienation it condemns: it confers a unitary identity on its author who, in seeking to ensure her addressee's reception of her discursive intention across the written symbols in which it is embodied, projects an ideal sameness onto his real otherness, so imposing an image on him. (While *Tu ne t'aimes pas* no longer represents the model reader-as-double, the very fact that a text which is offered to the reading public is made up of the self's addresses to its listening subselves, aligns its real readers with those subselves as co-addressees and so perpetuates, if less explicitly, the characteristic Sarrautean conflation of the ideal reader with the writing self.) Thus even as she renounces intersubjective dialogue, Sarraute demonstrates the very limitations of the linguistic subject which give rise to the need for dialogue. The final section of this chapter will examine how language unites the multiple speaking voices of *Tu ne t'aimes pas* into a *moi*, while Chapter 4 will deal with the way in which Sarraute projects the ideal reading she desires (as well as the pernicious reading she wishes to ward off). Now, though, I wish to look at how the social conditioning she censures as inauthentic goes more deeply than conventional social behaviour, to manifest itself even in the language she uses to combat it. How does Sarraute establish the authenticity of her (certainly distinctive) language, its source within the self rather than in the convention-governed social world, and how does that very authentication reveal its own irreducible conventionality?

2. *Metaphor and metonymy*

We have seen how much Sarraute's criticism of conventional discourse and its effects on its speakers and hearers has in common with Lacan's account of the conventionality of language in general and its consequences for the subject. The vital difference between them is that she equates convention with self-consciousness and so with a manner of *wilful* self-representation which the conscious individual can reject. Lacan (after Jakobson) sees language as structured along the axes of metaphor and metonymy which organize it as a self-contained entity (Lacan 1966: 505–9, 799–800; Jakobson 1956: *passim*). Similarly for Sarraute (always taking into account the different level on which her attention is focused), the distance from truth at which conventional social intercourse operates can be measured as the space of social metaphors and metonymies which alienate those who engage in such relations from the reality in which they live, and which by blindly repeating they turn into a self-sufficient substitute for truth. The metonymic drive in the social (and aesthetic) construction of characters is ridiculed in *Entre la vie et la mort*, where the writer finds that his possessions, accidentally acquired and relating to himself only in terms of their proximity, are seized on by his admirers, distorted, and used to define his personality:

C'est surprenant, c'est agréable . . . comment ne pas se sentir un peu ému, flatté par cet intérêt . . . une curiosité presque avide avec laquelle ils observent tout autour d'eux, le plus discrètement possible [. . .]
   Qu'est-ce que c'est? D'où ont-ils ramené ça? De chez lui? C'est sur lui que ç'a été prélevé? [. . .] C'était exquis, ce thé préparé par vous, paraît-il un mélange savant de qualités rares . . . infusé dans une théière d'une forme étrange posée sur une sorte de récipient . . . — Mais c'est une simple bouilloire . . . j'avais renversé le couvercle pour que la vapeur . . . — Non, ils ont dit que c'était un samovar . . . — Un samovar? Chez moi? Ils l'ont vu? — Oui. (*EVM* 128–30)

The writer becomes assimilated into society's discourses by being turned into a character, a process in which an eye for metonymy is extremely useful and where the failure to anticipate such metonymic extrapolations leaves one at the mercy of other people's eagerness to caricature: 'A-t-il oublié, mais connaît-il seulement le rôle si important des gants, des cannes de Balzac, des pantalons de Baudelaire, de tant de pipes, de gilets brodés, de plastrons, de lampes, de monocles' (p. 132). In this process, metonymy is finally arrested by metaphor, as a selection is made from the potentially endless list of the individual's real and imagined attributes, and from the chosen elements a figure is constituted whose outlandish distance from the truth is humorous precisely because of the foundation of similarity on which it is constructed:

Ce thé préparé dans sa chambre, cette théière, cette bouilloire . . . ces gestes, c'est une question d'arrangement, de présentation [. . .] il suffit de les transformer légèrement . . . de ralentir les mouvements . . . de lents gestes solennels comme ceux d'un prêtre quand il lève le ciboire [. . .] ça se faisait dans un silence religieux . . . c'était un rite sacré . . . (p. 134)

It is not just the social mania for characterization that is governed by the derealizing force of metonymy and metaphor; at the most basic level of social constructs, conventional clichéd language betrays the same distance from reality. Proverbs serve as primitive and reductive metaphors for human behaviour in all its unpredictability and illogicality, by constantly translating it into the terms of the familiar. Thus 'Nul ne dit autant de sottises qu'un homme d'esprit' (*DI* 56) covers all sorts of excesses which would otherwise defy reason, subjecting them to a seemingly infallible law (again the metaphorical equation depends on an initial metonymic relation between the 'sottise' and the person it is claimed to be representative of, who can then paradoxically be confirmed as an 'homme d'esprit'). The law of cliché claims authority over the body too: a physical attribute or gesture is interpreted as a sign, so that the hand which hesitates over how much change it should give as a tip becomes a metonym of its owner, instantly defined on that basis as 'un pingre' (p. 112).[9] Once labelled in terms of familiar concepts, the victim becomes vulnerable to all kinds of other metaphorical transformations: in common opinion, avarice is a social evil similar to all other vices, and so this gesture of hesitation is not only defined as a sign of meanness, but as a result is assimilated to the vice of alcoholic excess and subjected to the law 'Qui a bu boira' (p. 114), thus defining its agent forever. From the hand to the person to the diagnosis and the equation with vice of all sorts, the same trajectory is followed as in the case of the 'homme d'esprit': from perceptible reality through metonymy to a metaphorical generalization which can then be offered as proof of that metonymy's truth. ('Pas de fumée sans feu' (p. 152) repeats this derealization of reality through the

---

[9] The scene echoes a passage from Maupassant's *Une vie* (see *OC* 896 n. 1).

same metonymic and metaphoric process: an event becomes a sign of something greater to which it is connected, just as smoke signals fire; the fact that smoke signals fire then 'proves' by analogy that it is valid to extrapolate from a detail to a whole in any context, just as the fact that drinkers will always drink 'proves' that the young husband is a consistent miser.)

A prime example of how the code of proverbs and clichés which pervades conventional discourse relies on metaphor and metonymy to reduce reality to the terms of the familiar, occurs in the same section of *'disent les imbéciles'*. The inauthenticity of such expression is illustrated by the very way the faceless 'ils' who have diagnosed the young man's gesture as that of a 'lamentable grippe-sou' (p. 116) cite the authority on which their diagnosis is founded:

Que pouvons-nous contre les règles qui nous régissent, des préceptes fondés sur la sagesse, sur une expérience qui remonte à l'Antiquité? Celui-ci: tu le connais bien, à quoi bon essayer de l'oublier? Elle se bouche les oreilles . . . Doucement, fermement ils écartent ses mains . . . Il faut que tu aies le courage de l'écouter: Ab ungue leonem. (p. 117)

The proverb here does more than just express a metonymy (the lion's clawmark reveals the whole beast) and imply a metaphoric equation between lion and miser which again validates the young man's metonymic definition as a miser. The fact that only a short phrase is needed to suggest a universal truth actually *enacts* the metonymic principle which the proverb as a whole expresses. Not only is the stock of human character-types so circumscribed that a single gesture is immediately translated into a whole personality; the language in which that outlook receives expression is similarly so limited and familiar that a few words serve to indicate a whole utterance. Public language is so predictable that it has almost become superfluous, and its predictability is the result of its constant reference to a received and familiar reality rather than to anything original, expressed for the first time. Thus the validity of this highly limited language and frame of reference cannot be guaranteed by its speaker, for he is not its expressive origin; instead he must refer back to a past original speaker from whom it has been inherited. Expression is replaced by quotation in this register of language where an utterance is deemed to be true on the strength of its origin in a nameless and probably unknown representative of classical antiquity, but who merely by being ancient authorizes the truth of contemporary opinions. The fact that the opinion is articulated in a foreign language only emphasizes its externality to its speaker who not only quotes another's ideas but does so in the other's language.[10]

This invocation of an absent ancestral authority to ground a highly conventional language is strongly evocative of Lacan's identification of the *nom du père*, and a scene from *Tu ne t'aimes pas* underscores the resemblance.[11] The plural self's interlocutor here is another of the many mystified subjects of conventional language who populate Sarraute's works; a bad 'reader', he is unable to imagine any of the fictions suggested by the 'nous', in which an absent other might experience typically Sarrautean embarrass-ment or distress (*TTP* 140–1). Not surprisingly, he is also unable to perceive the inadequacy of his words to their referent—'pity', for example, is to him a sufficient label for an indefinable sensation which the Sarrautean self, at pains to find words true to experience, can only define negatively as not jealousy, almost but not quite melancholy or nostalgia (p. 147; the use of negative definition in *Enfance* was discussed in Ch. 2, pp. 80–1). The fact that this sub-versive and unnameable feeling is directed towards one's father (and that the interlocutor can't conceive of such a lack of respect: 'Ça me dépasse', p. 145), again relates the opposition between con-ventional and authentic language to the issue of ancestral authority, now invested more immediately in the literal father rather than in Roman antiquity. The conception of reality which the 'nous' pos-sess, specifically here their sympathy with the son's nameless feel-ings for his father, locates them among 'ces gens sans pudeur qui osent lever les yeux sur leur père dénudé [. . .] des gens qui manquent de ce respect qu'on doit à un père, de ce respect qu'on se doit' (p. 148). The affinity to the *nom du père* is obvious, always bear-ing in mind the specificity of Sarraute's view of what conventional language is, and her belief that authentic expression can transcend it. It is because for Sarraute too the father is the representative of the Law (however it is conceived) that the 'nous' who reject the

---

[10] Nor is quotation always acknowledged as such, for even when ostensibly based on personal experience, the discourse of the alienated social subject is derivative: 'Un jour . . . nous étions à Rome ensemble . . . — A Rome? — Oui, rappelez-vous . . . nous étions jeunes . . . et le guide . . . Oui, ça, il l'a déjà entendu, il a lu quelque part, il ne sait plus où, cette histoire, elle s'appliquait à quelqu'un d'autre . . .' (*DI* 73).

[11] For Lacan, 'c'est dans le *nom du père* qu'il nous faut reconnaître le support de la fonction symbolique qui, depuis l'orée des temps historiques, identifie sa personne à la figure de la loi' (1966: 278).

conventional reductive language deemed appropriate to him—and to oneself: 'ce respect qu'on se doit'—are 'des hors-la-loi, des parias' (p. 148).

Inauthentic language thus fails to make contact with its referent, distanced from it and distorting it through reductive metonymies and simplistic metaphors. Yet clearly, given that these mechanisms are those which Jakobson, and after him Lacan, identify as the fundamental axes of language, not even Sarraute's quest for authentic expression will be able to escape them entirely. How do they feature in her own idiom and how does she distinguish that use of them from one which stifles the reality to be expressed?

In the scenes from *'disent les imbéciles'* and *Tu ne t'aimes pas* just examined, metaphors abound which are not the product of the mystified language of self-loving others, but stem from the authorial voice(s). When the young wife in *'disent les imbéciles'* approaches the anonymous others who will only offer her received truths about 'the mark of the lion', we are told that 'elle embrasse leurs genoux'; on hearing what they have to say, she—implausibly in any real sense—'se bouche les oreilles . . . Doucement, fermement ils écartent ses mains . . .' (*DI* 117). Similarly in *Tu ne t'aimes pas*, the 'nous' imagine that the conventional thinker must regard preconceptual reality in terms of familiar metaphors[12] for a threatening absence of differentiation:

— C'est tout mou, flageolant, bourbeux, qu'on y mette le pied et on s'enlise . . . des marécages . . .

— De la soude caustique où l'on va se dissoudre . . .

— Un grouillement de choses fuyantes qui se cachent dans des trous sombres, des fentes humides . . . (*TTP* 145)

Yet their own perception of reality is itself also couched in metaphor. If Sarraute rejects one set of metaphorical equivalents of 'ces choses', it is to replace them with another (or at least a simile which operates on the same axis of substitution as metaphor does), one which is held to preserve the life and movement of its referent:

---

[12] These metaphors are also of course highly typical of Sarraute's early imagistic prose— she has explained her recourse to 'banal' imagery as necessitated by the shortcomings of her readers: 'Il faut au lecteur une image tout à fait facile [. . .] Si je ne donne pas une image [. . .] banale, volontairement banale, le lecteur perd pied' (Sarraute 1987*a*: 148–9, cp. p. 197; see also Ch. 2 n. 3). This paradox, the result of the fact that language is not only expressive (the aspect Sarraute emphasizes) but also communicative, illustrates well the impossibility of evacuating the conventional entirely from the personal and authentic in terms of language.

— Des mots comme sournois, inquiétant, répugnant ne les atteignent pas.

— Elles pourraient faire penser aux maillons serrés d'une trame toujours mouvante qui se tisserait sans fin . . . s'étendrait toujours plus loin . . . (p. 146)

This simile, by drawing attention to the ever-changing nature of
tropistic reality, explains, moreover, why the language which
attempts to express it is forced to trace a metonymic path. This is
illustrated at the phonetic level in *'disent les imbéciles'* when an 'objet
de piété' becomes an 'objet piégé' (*DI* 52): the response to the inadequacy of one metaphor is to follow it with an alternative in a way
which demonstrates clearly both the metonymic move from term to
term and the way that Sarraute, like her characters, attempts to
make that movement meaningful and approach some kind of sta-
bility through maintaining similarity between the terms. In this
example, it is as though the desire to make a series of different words
say the same thing, and so refer beyond themselves to a truth not
itself constituted by the language used, acknowledges its own
impossibility and compensates for it through phonetic rather than
semantic similarity.

In fact, the same dynamic governs the meandering dialogic representation of *sous-conversation* in *Tu ne t'aimes pas*, where the juxtaposition of utterances takes the metonymic impetus in all expression to
an extreme (and is thus as much a metaphor of language's
metonymic motor as of the internal infinity of the mind). As the
writer's guests in *Entre la vie et la mort* go from object to object in an
attempt to pin down the social persona which will sum up their host,
Sarraute's attempt in *Tu ne t'aimes pas* to express the truth of a volatile
self leads her on a similar path though in a different sphere (utterances rather than personal attributes). Given the linear nature of
expression, the movement from voice to voice can only ever reproduce as a sequence something held to be ineffable. Yet the utterances themselves restore the sense of homogeneity they set out to
undermine, their general consensus (which I shall discuss in the
next section of this chapter) freezing an original metonymic
tracking of the ever-changing nature of tropistic life into an image of
unity in diversity. This recalls the way the figure of the priest froze a
series of observed actions and objects, none of which on its own provided a key to the individual. Just as the cane, the trousers, or the
gesture can never really sum up a whole person, no single utterance
can sum up a whole self. Yet the sequence of utterances in *Tu ne*

t'aimes pas as so many 'attributes' of the 'nous', demonstrates both the potentially endless accumulation of details which is a response to the impossibility of expressing the inner void, and the way that accumulation is controlled through the unifying concept of a plural self but which can speak in a united chorus as 'nous'.

If Sarraute's own authorial discourse is forced to mediate the reality to be described through the dual prism of metaphor and metonymy, how can it be preserved from the lifelessness which marks the reductive language of social interaction? Within the mind, 'rien ne porte de nom' (*TTP* 148). Instead of language there is sensation, and it is through positing an area of overlap where physical sensation ends and language begins that Sarraute can assert the existence of a living linguistic register adequate to the tropism. Thus it is in sensation, in the tropism, that the proliferation of Sarraute's linguistic tropes must originate, reaching outward from within the body to communicate to the reader those tropisms which themselves reach out from the self to bind it to others. Authentic language rushes outward from within the self, escaping the control of the social speaker (the self as subject—see n. 3) and brushing aside his conventional language: '[Les mots] nous traversent, nous sommes un espace vide, ouvert, rien ne se soulève sur leur passage, ils repoussent, bousculent notre délégué et de la bouche du porte-parole par lequel ils l'ont remplacé ils sortent . . .' (p. 107).

Involuntary (thus true) sensations, occurring at the outer limit of consciousness where the physical and the psychic merge, manifest themselves uncontrollably in the body which can thus be trusted to reveal what the mind might choose to conceal.[13] In this way we can read off a person's emotions from the signs his body offers us: 'L'énorme machinerie aussi compliquée que celle qui fait respirer nos poumons, battre notre pouls, d'un seul coup, sans qu'il sache comment, sans qu'il puisse expliquer pourquoi, lui fait monter le sang à la tête, son visage rougit . . . "Jaloux? Moi!"' (*DI* 16; cp. *TTP* 88–9). This immediate readability of the body means that Sarraute

[13] In Jean Pierrot's view, one of Sarraute's main achievements is to have 'mis en lumière le rôle essentiel que dans tout dialogue humain effectivement réalisé, jou[e] chacun des corps mis en présence, en tant que récepteurs et qu'émetteurs d'informations incessantes, à partir desquelles s'opèrent ces corrections et ces adaptations continuelles en quoi se résolvent tous les dialogues réels' (1990: 461). For a detailed discussion of how Sarraute uses the body to anchor truth, see Jefferson (1992: 40): 'The body [. . .] forms the basis of the writing which is simultaneously making it the focus of the intersubjective relations that it depicts and appealing to it as guarantor of the truth of that representation.'

can give us the physical reaction of someone who overhears himself defined as gifted but not intelligent, rather than describing his response less accurately in emotional terms: he feels 'une sensation inconnue, étrange, c'est elle que doivent éprouver ceux qui gisent, la moelle épinière blessée, quand ils veulent se relever et s'aperçoivent que leurs réflexes habituels ne jouent plus, que leurs jambes sont paralysées . . . un point vital en eux a dû être atteint' (*DI* 36).

Yet even the body, the source of truth for Sarraute, is already metaphoric at the point at which she invokes it. The example given illustrates this well: the shock which the individual feels when he hears his intelligence denied is comparable to what a victim of para-lysis feels when he realizes that a part of his body he took for granted no longer functions. Though the word is not used, the idea is that of numbness—numbness as a reaction to such a damning diagnosis and numbness too at the loss of a part of one's person, here one's intelligence. Sarraute's description is an imaginative elaboration on a familiar correlation between psychic trauma and physical numb-ness; she is returning from language not so much to the body as truth but to the body as already a metaphor. To make this point is not to detract from her merit as a writer—it is in what she does with the metaphor that her literary achievement lies—but simply to draw attention to the necessarily conventional basis of the image if it is to be effective (a condition of which Sarraute is well aware: see n. 12). As readers, we accept that the physical sensation described is a true correlate of the sensation experienced precisely because our famil-iarity with this bodily metaphor is such that we no longer even regard it as one. We relate to the body here as an already familiar image rather than as a set of brute physical reactions.[14]

Even where there is a natural connection between the physical sensation described and the psychic sensation for which it stands

[14] There is a similar instance of the bodily vehicle of a dead metaphor being reactivated in *Tu ne t'aimes pas*, this time in relation to the experience of being 'wounded' by another's words. Here too the return to the body as the ultimate index of truth or falsity (i.e. whether the self had actually been insulted or not) is in fact a return to and imaginative development of famil-iar metaphors of public discourse:

— Peut-être s'en trouve-t-il encore ici qui ne sont pas certains, qui voudraient demander à encore quelqu'un d'autre, parmi ceux qui savent, si ce que tu as reçu en plein visage était de vrais crachats?

— Si quand il a poussé ce rugissement, posé sur toi sa lourde patte, enfoncé en toi ses griffes, c'était vraiment blessant? (p. 99)

(blushing and embarrassment, for example), to see the physical phenomenon in terms of this connection is itself an indication of the
way consciousness is inevitably governed by symbolization. By seeing a sudden blush (or any other physical reaction) as a sign of an
emotion, Sarraute is giving it the status of something to be read, and
is thus engaging with it from within an order where things stand for
other things, rather than simply being there. She has already given
it the role of symptom before she refers to it: it is not because it happens to be in the text that we can make the identification of jealousy;
rather it is because a symptom of jealousy must be provided that it
is introduced. From the start it is a symbol rather than a brute phenomenon. And of course symptoms, as well as being metaphoric
(they represent something different, be it an emotion or a virus), are
in the first instance metonymic (they are linked in space—on the
body—to what they represent, whether that is physical or psychic).

Behind every alienating form imposed by society there may well
be a truth, but this truth can only be represented as another
metaphor, even within a language like Sarraute's which strives to
undo the distance between words and experience. Using the body
to ground authentic language fails to halt this endless linguistic
regression; instead it brings about the construction of yet another
set of metaphors—albeit metaphors which, in their intimate reference to the body, are 'faites pour pénétrer jusque dans les recoins
intimes des sensations du lecteur', in the words of Valerie Minogue
(*OC* 1751).[15] To represent the body as source of truth by describing
the way it physically betrays actual emotion is not quite to go back
from language to the body, but rather to make the body linguistic,
by defining it as something to be read, as signifying. Moreover, of
course, the symptoms manifested by fictional bodies in a literary
text are not simply there to be deciphered but are linguistic constructs mapped on to, rather than produced by, the characters who
bear them. Thus Sarraute must first write on to the body what
she then presents that body as reading off from the self. Her

---

[15] Minogue's sketch of such metaphors as they occur in *Portrait d'un inconnu* is worth quoting at more length: 'D'autres impressions morales sont traduites en impressions sensorielles;
en goûts et en saveurs, âcres, douceâtres ou écœurants; en odeurs, vapeurs, relents, qu'on
hume, qu'on renifle, qu'on flaire; en surfaces moites, molles, visqueuses, gluantes, auxquelles
on touche avec dégoût, ou en matières douces, veloutées ou soyeuses, qu'on caresse avec
plaisir [. . .] Ailleurs, le lecteur se voit plongé dans des évocations de lésions, de maladies ou
de soins médicaux [. . .] Il serait bien difficile de rester impassible devant des images d'une
telle vigueur et dont la portée est ressentie d'une manière si intime, si physique' (*OC* 1751).

demonstration that the body is the source of language necessarily takes place entirely in language and not in the Real (whatever the claims of the voices of *Tu ne t'aimes pas* that the body for them is outside conceptualization: *TTP* 21). Because invoking the body as a prelinguistic guarantor of truth (see Jefferson 1992: *passim*) necessarily symbolizes it, it automatically loses its authority to underwrite the truth of expression, for in so far as it is represented, it is the effect of the metaphoric and metonymic order it claims to guarantee. Sarraute is thus ultimately caught in a similar 'engrenage', though at a more fundamental level of conceptualization, to the young wife in *'disent les imbéciles'* who sees the conceptual cornerstones of her reality come loose from their referent: 'Ça va la reprendre. Tout va se remettre à bouger. Le pingre ne va pas tenir en place. Il va s'éloigner, remplacé par le Prince charmant. Et puis revenir, et puis repartir. Elle a mis le doigt dans un engrenage, le pied sur des sables mouvants, elle est prise dans un affreux dilemme' (*DI* 120).

While metaphor and simile are alike in that both are principles of linguistic substitution, one major difference between them is the way simile advertises its distance from the reality it represents—it does not claim, as metaphor does, to *be* that reality. In this light we might see the way Sarraute's writing repeatedly moves from simile into metaphor as one poetic strategy by which she attempts within language to minimize the gap between language and reality. Thus the sensation provoked by engaging with a particularly distasteful idea is first represented in terms of the simile of unpleasant smells and tastes: 'Réprimer en soi cette répulsion, s'efforcer d'examiner cela comme font ceux qui analysent des crachats, des excréments, dissèquent des cadavres. Mais cela fait plutôt penser à un de ces fruits de mauvaise qualité . . . quand on y a goûté, on a la sensation que les muqueuses de la bouche se contractent . . .' (*DI* 50). The simile slides imperceptibly into metaphor, and the problem of representing sensation, acknowledged in the 'as if' quality of the simile where the body's ability to anchor expression is only a wish, disappears from view. Suddenly the experience of an unpleasant taste seems adequate to describe the much more elusive unease caused by ideas which are only metaphorically unpalatable: 'Que c'est donc mauvais . . . Mais il n'est pas question de le cracher . . . Il s'efforce de le mâcher . . . et il sent comme tout en lui se resserre, se ratatine . . . c'est du poison' (p. 50; cp. *TTP* 131). As simile becomes metaphor, the power of the image is heightened, the reader's sensory identification more immediately appealed to. Yet the fact that such bodily metaphors are part of a lexicon of symbols and have no organic relation to the reality they describe is illustrated here by the way a familiar metaphor recurs in this new context: 'Un engourdissement le gagne . . . une paralysie . . . il voudrait se dresser, appeler' (p. 50). The means with which to represent the real are limited and not tailor-made for the task—a fact of which Sarraute, who gently mocks the solitary, introverted writer's 'goût plus ou moins conscient pour une certaine forme d'échec' (*ES* 150), is herself of course entirely conscious as she strives for ever more immediate metaphors and metonymies.[16]

3. *Sarraute and the Imaginary*

If submission to linguistic convention is inevitable even for the Sarrautean self, a function not only of self-consciousness but of consciousness, what does this imply for its own status and for its relations with others? I wish to look now more closely at the nature of self–other relations in Sarraute, in the context of the way these are conceived by Lacan. Once again, this is not to suggest that the value of Sarraute's representation of subjectivity and intersubjective relations should be measured by the degree to which it reflects Lacan's. Reading one in the context of the other initiates a dialogue between them, a dialogue in which the relations of power could easily be reversed (but from which they can never be evacuated, as I shall argue at more length in the next chapter).

Social interaction, for Lacan, is inaugurated by the Oedipus. At this mythical moment, the child's total involvement with the mother, for whom he desires to be everything in a relationship of mutual absorption, is interrupted by his awareness that she is already in a relationship with the father. As a result, mother and child are each seen to have a fixed place in the elementary social

---

[16] In the *Notice* to Sarraute's critical writings (*OC* 2034–50), Ann Jefferson describes the necessary failure of Sarraute's literary language as the mark of its authenticity, its problematic but real connection to the world it attempts to describe: 'Dès le départ, le langage littéraire se définit chez Nathalie Sarraute comme la recherche d'une expression adéquate, qui pourtant lui échappe. L'authentique sur le plan de l'expression linguistique équivaut à l'insuffisant; mais c'est cette insuffisance même qui assure le lien, quelque ténu qu'il soit, entre les mots et ce qu'ils cherchent à exprimer' (p. 2043).

structure of the family. The father is the representative of language, and so relationships from now on will be between discrete, named individuals rather than unconceptualized bodies.

Given that Sarraute sees the body as a prelinguistic source of truth, it is not surprising that her conception of true relations with others should have more in common with pre- than post-Oedipal relations in Lacan's schema. This applies to relations with inanimate objects too: in *Tu ne t'aimes pas*, when a privileged name associated by the self with 'un petit pont en dos d'âne au-dessus d'une eau verdâtre' (*TTP* 175) is scorned by a prestigious figure, this privileged entity and the self are both turned into objects, into observer and observed watched in turn (and with derision) by another. This experience of suddenly seeing something which had been part of the self from the point of view of another[17] arouses a feeling of lack and nausea—'une déception . . . un manque [. . .] un léger écœurement' (p. 177); there is an obvious parallel with the Oedipal relativization of self and Imaginary other. There, seeing the desired object now mediated by representation (the father's language) also results in a sense of lack. Yet Sarrautean and Lacanian outlooks continue to operate on different levels: this text gives no indication of a fundamental mediation at work in the world, and the conceptualization of the loved object and of the one who loves it is presented as a wilful falsification of entities whose reality is accessible. The culprit here, unsurprisingly, is a 'genius' of self-love; once again, it is other people with their conventional language who objectify the world and ourselves (as well as themselves). What this scene also tells us is that by doing this they further sabotage our true, immediate relationships with those rare others (and objects) with whom we establish an authentic bond at a prelinguistic level—the level of response which in turn gives rise to authentic expression.[18]

---

[17] — [. . .] Recouvert d'une mince couche, d'une pellicule . . .
       — Faite de tous ces contacts, descriptions et reproductions. (*TTP* 177)
[18] Setting aside her belief that language *can* be authentic, Sarraute's descriptions of how others' inauthentic language affects the self's relations frequently recall the Lacanian Oedipus. Words like 'ton père' or 'ta sœur' re-enact something close to the subject's fall from the infantile Imaginary: 'Sous nos yeux un enfant est arraché à cette crèche jonchée de paille soyeuse, emplie de souffles chauds' (*UP* 51). They make him aware of his unchangeable place in the family, 'la même place qui lui a été assignée une fois pour toutes' (p. 52). Interestingly, it is the *mother* here who causes this Oedipal relativization by naming relations within the family in the anonymous voice of the public: 'Elle est à une si grande distance [. . .] On dirait une étrangère . . . quand elle prononce ces mots: "Ton père" "Ta soeur", sa voix résonne comme

What happens when the authentic relationship is broken up? In this passage, the plural self escapes the other's condemnation by strategically joining his camp: 'Nous ne faisons pas partie de ces foules moutonnières qui défilent sur les vieux petits ponts, se penchent sur les eaux glauques [. . .] Heureusement il ne s'attarde pas, il est déjà loin, et nous avec lui, nous nous arrêtons comme lui, nous regardons . . .' (pp. 176–7). This identification with a powerful other entails the blind assumption of his values which are entirely opposed to one's own: 'La force qu'il y a en lui nous soulève, nous sommes projetés hors de chez nous [. . .] Nous en avons été tirés, pas fiers d'y avoir vécu, assez honteux d'avoir pu être aussi amollis, asservis, apeurés' (pp. 178–9). This clearly degrades the original relationship, betraying its authenticity in a shift of loyalties highly evocative of Lacan's concept of secondary (Oedipal) identification, where the subject ceases to desire to be everything for the (m)other and one with it, and identifies instead with the paternal figure as possessor of the (now discrete) object of desire. In what for Lacan is the step which constitutes the subject socially, by giving it a language which symbolizes it as well as everything around it, that object is related to no longer on the mode of being but on that of having (and so can be evaluated as a possession). In *Tu ne t'aimes pas*, as for Lacan, the powerful figure is the one who breaks up and forbids the taboo dual relation, so 'castrating' the self by showing its intimacy with the other (the mother for Lacan) to be based on an illusion (here the self's unique relation to a town which is in fact loved by many). His authority comes from the way he is recognized by others: in the Oedipus complex, the mother herself; here, the great man's coterie (thus in Sarraute's case, the loved object itself does not betray the self by cooperating in the relationship's relativization, but retains its absolute quality). As in *Enfance*, this alienated perspective is associated with adulthood: the self-lover is 'un adulte' opposed to the 'enfant curieux qui veut voir comment c'est fait, qui s'amuse à arracher l'enduit, qui donne des coups partout, démonte, démolit . . .' (p. 62).[19]

---

ces voix anonymes, venant on ne sait d'où, qui dans les lieux publics diffusent des informations' (p. 53). John Phillips has discussed the role of the mother in Sarraute at length (Phillips 1991, 1994: *passim*).

[19] This association of childhood with closeness to truth recurs in the later evocation of true contact with an object (pp. 198–9). As in *Les Fruits d'or* ('Cela ne porte aucun nom [. . .] Quelque chose d'intact, d'innocent . . . comme les doigts fluets d'un enfant qui

The intrusion of the powerful figure, as I have mentioned, creates a lack in the Sarrautean self's relation to the loved object;[20] this too has a Lacanian counterpart in the 'manque à être' which is central to the existence of the subject of language, and which results from the paternal (and symbolic) taboo on fusion with the mother. When the reality of desire is repressed in favour of a symbol (the domain of the father's law), the nature of the word as the absence of the thing gives rise to a subject structured by lack. Again the parallels between Sarraute's perception of social intercourse and Lacan's theory of language and identity are both striking and none the less limited. Sarraute's location of alienation solely in the self-conscious discourse of the self-lover and his admirers, her retention of a belief in an authentic conscious discourse independent of that, strongly oppose Lacan's argument that authenticity and truth are confined to unconscious desire from which any use of language necessarily distances the subject. In his view, *all* language creates a *moi*, and not just the particularly objectifying, self-reflexive language of particularly alienated victims of social convention.

What kind of *intersubjective* relationship (rather than one with an object) can escape the consequences of social mediation? The ideal, least socially determined relationship is evidently that of love, and love, for the self of *Tu ne t'aimes pas*, is correspondingly defined not as overcoming mediation but as somehow never being subjected to it. The loved one is another 'part inséparable de nous-mêmes' which it simply augments: 'On dirait que notre immense masse mouvante s'était encore accrue . . . était plus dense, plus vibrante' (p. 122). Love as a relation comes before self-consciousness in the same way that the body does: it is similarly simply there, unconceptualized: 'Perçoit-on quand on est en bonne santé sa respiration, le mouvement de son sang, le jeu de ses muscles?' (p. 122). Its habitat is prior to individuation and expression, so that to make an excursion 'là-bas où les mots circulent, se posent, désignent' (p. 123), to say

---

s'accrocheraient à moi, la main d'un enfant qui se blottirait au creux de ma main': *FO* 153), truth is found by a single individual communing with an object (there a text, here the rim of a well), and the renunciation of language in favour of sensation which it involves is linked with a return to a lost innocence, erasing the 'enduit' of adult perception.

[20] This recurs in a second attack on another of the self's attachments:

— [. . .] Ce qui avait toujours été là a disparu, ça a peut-être été déplacé, non, ç'a été enlevé, ç'a été anéanti et maintenant il y a là, à cette place un vide . . . et ici, mais c'est ébréché, c'est fissuré, déchiré . . .

— Et nous sommes ébréchés, fissurés, déchirés . . . (p. 178) 'je t'aime', meant that 'une part de nous se détachait, allait dehors, revêtait pour l'occasion la tenue de sortie, celle de deux êtres distincts l'un de l'autre' (p. 124).[21] Yet it is no surprise to note that the nature of love, even before it is dressed up in other people's language, can be grasped by the plural Sarrautean self only in metaphor ('Ça ouvrait, creusait en nous un chemin à travers une même substance, remontait à une même source': p. 123), or in the simile of the body's 'thereness' just cited. In addition, despite the feeling of total unity and the attitude that the distinct public personas of the lovers are a game, the other in his public role manifests an unpredictability, and thus betrays an unknowability, at odds with this. 'Tu' can become 'un étranger confortablement installé chez lui' (p. 125), of whom one can't be sure that he won't 'pousser le jeu trop loin' (p. 126). Although this fear is not realized, the very fact that there is room for it points to the awareness of an irreducible difference between self and loved one, an awareness which challenges the perception of this other as 'une part inséparable de nous-mêmes' (p. 122), expelled only by the intrusion of a conventionally minded third figure.

This mode in which the Sarrautean self relates to the loved other or to a privileged object (incorporating it into itself rather than treating it as a distinct entity), in its opposition to the kind of conceptualization Lacan sees as inaugurated by the Oedipal moment, invites comparison with the mode of being he terms the Imaginary. The pre-Oedipal, Imaginary self desires to be what the other (in the first instance the mother) desires, for it has not yet renounced the desire to *be* in favour of the desire to *have*, or acquired symbolic representation in a signifier. It consequently appears in Symbolic terms as a lack,[22] just as the self of *'disent les imbéciles'* or *Tu ne t'aimes pas* feels itself to be empty and nameless ('Nos flots agités toujours changeants ne peuvent porter aucun nom': *TTP* 129). Yet (to state the obvious) the Sarrautean self exists and speaks in a text, and so is necessarily in the Symbolic. Its self-characterization as undifferentiated and unconceptualizable thus presents itself as a nostalgic reconstruction from

---

[21] The way this conventional phrase can actually kill the shared emotion it names is the subject of the short prose text 'Le Mot amour', in *L'Usage de la parole*, pp. 63–79.

[22] 'En s'identifiant à l'objet du désir de l'autre, soumis passivement, assujetti, dépendant, l'enfant n'est pas un "sujet" mais un manque, un rien parce qu'il n'est pas situé ou repéré individuellement dans le circuit symbolique de l'échange' (Lemaire 1977: 141).

within a differentiating and conceptualizing language. We have seen the way Sarraute's struggle to forge an authentic, expressive idiom must operate within the constraints of language's metaphoric and metonymic structure, thus without ever eliminating entirely the alienation characteristic of conventional discourse. Similarly, we can expect that the self she presents as formless and passive, preferring to merge with objects on the level of sensation than to seek to communicate with other individuals as a subject (love itself is now past) will, by virtue of having language (even if it speaks only to itself), necessarily bear the marks of the active, symbolized consciousness in which its multiple voices originate. The language of this ineffable authorial self cannot but impose on it a conventional symbolic singularity not unrelated to that embraced by the subjects of self-conscious language, by constantly recreating a monologic unity among the multiple, metaphoric voices.

In fact the very way the body is used by Sarraute as a touchstone for truth draws attention to the metaphoric status of the 'masse agitée' of the self. The body, as Jean Pierrot and Ann Jefferson have separately pointed out (see n. 13), is integral to the Sarrautean dynamic of dialogue; thus the disembodied voices of the self become personified: 'Cela ferait rire ceux qui du dehors nous observent, s'ils voyaient en nous ce que nous y voyons par moments . . . tant de jeunes gens fringants, d'adolescents se rassemblant chez des "vieillards croulants" et tant de vieillards chez des jeunes . . . et partout tant d'enfants . . .' (p. 32).[23] They fall asleep and wake up ('ils se secouent, ils se grattent': p. 92); they 'can't believe their ears' (p. 76). The metaphoric status of their bodies is concealed by the fact that they generally map directly onto the single body which contains them: when 'we' go for a walk or when 'we' can't believe our ears, for example. The fiction of a plural self thus relies tacitly on an awareness of the body as a unit, an awareness which in the Lacanian scheme of things launches with the mirror stage the whole process of self-objectification completed by the assumption of language and the acquisition of the status of subject (Lacan 1966: 93–100).

[23] This perception of the voices of the self as so many independent subselves distances somewhat Sarraute's idea of internal multiplicity from that of Roy Schafer with whom she otherwise seems to have much in common (see Ch. 1, s. 3). Schafer warns explicitly that the narrative structures the self adopts should not be taken to be autonomous subselves, and he criticizes the concept of multiple selves as 'itself only a narrative structure that begs the question' (presumably by positing an unproblematic notion of the self to start with; Schafer 1981: 40).

At one point, the fictional status of these bodies is acknowledged, as one voice laments that the lack of bodies keeps them from behaving in a certain way: 'Si nous avions des corps, des visages, on pourrait nous voir en foule nous bousculant, nous serrant les uns contre les autres, tendant le cou pour regarder ce qui se passe maintenant là-bas, chez eux, ce qu'ils sont en train de faire de nous' (p. 108). The image would be true if only it really referred to a body (or bodies) instead of having to posit one in which to ground itself. In the absence of the truth which the body guarantees ('Et on verrait dans nos yeux, sur nos lèvres une expression . . .'), there is only a verbal construct which sometimes acknowledges but more often conceals its metaphoric status. Thus, while it criticizes others for 'executing' not the real self but an effigy which 'les mots fournis par nous leur ont permis de fabriquer' (p. 109), the bodies which the text associates with the real self are similarly the creation of the text's language. As a reader, one can find oneself, uncomfortably, in the same position as the misled others here, for the metaphorical bodies of the self's many voices which one is led to imagine are not so different from 'cette poupée [. . .] ce mannequin qu'ils ont construit à l'image de ce que nous avons fait apparaître devant eux'.

It is not only the voices' bodies which are metaphorical, relying for grounding on the idea of the single physical body of the self which really does walk and talk and have observable digestive processes ('Pourtant en nous aussi deux cigarettes . . .': p. 23). This recourse to physical singularity in order to establish their truth underlines the metaphoric status of the whole notion of plurality which is itself a product of the attempt to express a self originally held to be empty. A proliferation of utterances results from the attempt to articulate the self yet remain free from the limiting effects of language on that self. Such are those limiting effects, it is not surprising that the exchanges, despite the surface variety of voices, can regularly be reduced to one train of thought (a unity reflected in my use of the singular pronoun 'it' to refer to this multi-voiced self).

Throughout the text, the dominant tone of the different voices is one of consensus. All work together: 'Tâchons de nous rappeler' (p. 16), and they do. Conclusions on the nature of the self are concurred with once articulated:

— [. . .] Décidément, nous ne sommes pas faits pour le Bonheur . . .
— Pas faits . . . c'est ça . . . pas faits [. . .]
— Cette tare . . . nous n'avions pas vu sa gravité [. . .] (p. 57)

If other people are analysed as being (wilfully) unitary, the self which makes this diagnosis is also a block, the pronoun 'on' blurring the fact that this plural self is acting as a unit: 'Et comme maintenant on la comprend' (p. 137). Every recognition of a self-loving other cannot but unify the self too:

— Mais maintenant que c'est tombé en nous subitement . . . cette illumination . . .
tout s'est éclairé d'un coup . . .
— Et ça ne pourra jamais s'effacer, ce que nous avons vu. (p. 169)

As with *Enfance* (though less dramatically), a structure of dialogue which at first sight subverts narration in fact fails to evacuate it totally, along with the singular perspective it implies:

— [. . .] Dans ce visage à peine visible, pas même des yeux . . . juste le regard . . .
— Il regarde intensément sa main posée sur la table.
— Et dans son regard tant d'amour . . . (p. 20; cp. pp. 37–9).

In fact this singularity is a necessary consequence of the novel's whole concern: to talk about the nature of the self as it does implies a self which can be conceptualized, even if only in terms of its incoherence. Although in the novel an external perspective on the self as a unitary entity is associated with the construction of a *moi*,[24] yet every time one voice talks about what 'we' are like it betrays a similarly external point of view on a similarly homogeneous self:

— 'Je' 'me' . . . Voyez-vous ça . . .
— Mais ce n'est pas tout: Je m'aime.
— Nous avons de nouveau osé aller jusque-là. (pp. 101–2)

Here, the voice that conceptualizes what 'we' have just done speaks for the whole self, participating in the very homogenization it opposes. There is a sense that every speaker is fully aware of the characters of all the other members of this community, and this undoes the impression of the self as infinite and unknowable: along with 'ceux d'entre nous que le Bonheur et sa perfection agacent' there are 'nos possédés de l'esprit de contradiction', 'nos "éternels enfants"', 'ceux qui rampent prudemment', and 'vous qui êtes toujours [. . .] mus par votre bon cœur' (pp. 54–6). Thus one voice can speak for 'nous tous ici' (p. 56), despite the previous

---

[24]　— Tous unis. Quelle discipline. Quel ordre.
　　　— Tous soumis à un pouvoir central puissant [. . .]
　　　— Un 'Moi' . . . C'est ainsi que nous pouvons le nommer . . . (p. 100)

assertion that 'nous sommes ici plus nombreux que nous le savions' (p. 55).

Tu ne t'aimes pas, despite its much more radical fragmentation of the authorial voice than was undertaken in *Enfance*, thus never really abandons singular expression. At first sight it seems that Sarraute has found, through the fictional structure of the interior dialogue, a way around the paradox of ironic self-expression where the articulation of the limitations of the conscious self is either itself informed by those limitations or disproves them (and a way which forgoes explicit appeal to the reader, ever more marginal in Sarraute's universe). Thus she can apparently avoid the contradiction of conceptualizing a 'manque de "conscience de soi" ' (p. 71), by ascribing the observation to only one of the self's many voices. Yet the tacit agreement of the other voices does make this assertion ultimately self-contradictory. The multi-voiced structure in fact permits the Sarrautean self to be self-conscious in its own fashion, to focus on itself in a way which, though less affirmative, is no less reflexive than the 'Je m'aime' of the others. (The discussion of the 'manque de "conscience de soi" ' is also noteworthy for the way the 'nous' there act in such a singular manner that the pronoun could easily be replaced by 'je'—'Nous étions seuls enfermés avec une de ces fortes personnalités': p. 71. In addition, the structure of dialogue here dissimulates a highly monological narrative thread, with the ability of the other voices to identify an event without the speaker naming it demonstrating how far the different perspectives are reducible to one.)

This representation of an incommensurable self whose elements take turns to speak but whose whole dimensions are never given, again links Sarraute to the stance of the verbal ironist. The ironic utterance is manifestly not the whole truth, and so can be seen to act out in microcosm the inadequacy of language to truth; yet the speaker, knowing his own real sense (an attitude to his utterance—see Ch. 1 n. 25) which he could conceivably formulate, merely gestures to this inadequacy without actually being limited to what he articulates. Similarly, the way *Tu ne t'aimes pas* suggests an infinite number of internal voices behind any one utterance in fact gives Sarraute enormous power over her interlocutors, these being in the first instance the self-conscious others represented in the novel, but ultimately the readers who engage with it. Readers are kept from identifying any single utterance as true, for the fact that the self has many other voices implicitly relativizes it (but only in terms of other possible utterances the self could formulate and not with reference to any inherent inadequacy in the self's language or to any outside perspective). This power that the self's multiplicity gives it over others is illustrated by its social interactions in the novel. It is always more than it appears to be, concealing its vastness from the one-dimensional selves it encounters. It is frequently not fully present in conversations: 'Nous sommes là, par-derrière, vacants, détendus, écoutant à peine les propos anodins qui s'échangent' (p. 105; cp. *Ici* 106). When others form a personality for it on the basis of its words (which are only those of one of its 'delegates'), the greater self looks on in amusement at those who have taken what it says at face value, just as the verbal ironist enjoys having his words taken seriously by those not in the know:

— Quant à nous . . . et c'est de là aussi que nous vient ce détachement, ce contentement, nous, nous sommes toujours là, nous les observons . . .
— Contre nous ils ne peuvent rien . . .
— Nous, il n'y a pas moyen d'en venir à bout . . . (p. 110)

Though infinitely more vast than other individuals, the greater self knows its own infinity, just as the verbal ironist knows his own mind.

If others are consistently seen as singular, this is because they are encountered through their language, and language necessarily singularizes the self by forcing it to represent itself in a symbol. Yet if representing the self by 'nous' instead of 'je' cannot avoid this singularization,[25] the distinction between the Sarrautean self and those who submit to convention becomes less absolute. The text does implicitly recognize that speaking makes even its own 'nous' into a single unit: when one voice acknowledges that 'les porte-parole que nous envoyons au-dehors continuent à se servir de ces "je", de ces "moi"', it is told 'Il le faut bien, sinon comment arriveraient-ils à se faire entendre?' (p. 87). Yet the other's public use

---

[25] This impossibility can be understood in terms of Émile Benveniste's definition of the pronoun 'nous' as identifying, along with the speaking subject, an element *external* to it. It thus specifically does not indicate the kind of multiplicity of 'je's presented by *Tu ne t'aimes pas*: 'L'unicité et la subjectivité inhérentes à "je" contredisent la possibilité d'une pluralisation. S'il ne peut y avoir plusieurs "je" conçus par le "je" même qui parle, c'est que "nous" est, non pas une multiplication d'objets identiques, mais une *jonction* entre "je" et le "non-je", quel que soit le contenu de ce "non-je"' (1966: 233). The 'non-je' is precisely what the 'nous' of *Tu ne t'aimes pas* excludes.

of 'moi' and 'je' is censured on the grounds that this must be the register in which his inner self speaks too:

— C'est ainsi que se parle à lui-même celui qui s'aime . . .
— Oui, nous ici, entre nous, ces 'moi', ces 'je', nous ne les employons pas . . . (p. 86)

The other, known only through his language, is characterized on that basis in much the same way as the self was misrepresented in the 'mannequins' which others created and which were a source of amusement to it. Others are no more than what they appear to be; encountered in language, there is no evidence for the self observing them that they possess another scene on which authentic mental activity might be taking place.

Maintaining the distinction between a true self and false others becomes ever more problematic as the text progresses. It is acknowledged that the self's public manifestations of unity, though generally presented as a conscious artifice, can also be the unintentional effect of utterly sincere behaviour. This happens when emotional language, which for Sarraute is true in coming spontaneously from within, unifies the self; yet this unity is considered as qualitatively different from the public images others present. The fact that what might look to others like a *moi* isn't one, is not seen to have repercussions for the self's own diagnoses of others but instead offers yet more evidence of others' inability to grasp the self's enormity. An outburst of anger where 'il n'y avait aucun délégué, qui aurait pu le choisir, l'envoyer? Nous n'étions qu'un seul élément traversé par un seul mouvement . . . Saisis tout à coup, envahis, ça déferlait en nous, jaillissait de nous en paroles précipitées, véhémentes' (p. 211), results only in the fact that 'nous [. . .] leur avons donné pendant quelques instants ce que leur donne constamment celui qui s'aime [. . .] celui entre tous le mieux doué pour s'aimer' (p. 214).

This acknowledgement that the self can appear to others as 'un seul bloc serré, refermé sur soi' (p. 212), however authentic its spontaneity lets it remain, none the less concedes the unifying nature of even intensely unselfconscious language. The representation of such periods of singularity as emanations of its internal truth rather than as the product of a set of conventions is reinforced by the fact that the language which created this single self has been forgotten. The suggestion is that the words' one-off, expressive nature makes them unrepeatable, and so they have the truth of a unique event rather than being elements of a structure which pre-exists and survives its use in any utterance:

— Quelles paroles?
— Impossible de se les rappeler . . . Et même sur le moment nous n'avons pas dû les entendre . . . (p. 211)

The point is explicitly made that this speech, if it is conscious, is (in keeping with where Sarraute locates linguistic inauthenticity) not self-conscious: the self didn't even hear its own words. It is also, significantly, indifferent to its addressee, emphasizing that truth for Sarraute seems in the end to have little to do with intersubjective cooperation: 'Impossible de revoir ceux qui les écoutaient, qui nous regardaient' (p. 211).

The impossibility of divorcing completely the nature of the authentic self from that of the inauthentic others surrounding it appears clearly in the discussion of the 'genius of self-love' who, paradoxically, bears no sign of his nature. Those signs of self-love previously identified in the novel—the self-objectifying gaze, the presence of an internal tribunal 'qui applique les lois du Ciel' (p. 192)—are absent in his case: 'Chez lui, on a beau chercher, on ne trouve aucun signe' (p. 191). He further defines things according to an internal rather than a received law: 'Lui seul a le pouvoir de [. . .] nommer [le Mal, le Bien]' (p. 192). Thus his diagnosis as '[le] plus grand génie dans l'art de s'aimer' (p. 193) rests purely on the sensation he arouses in the 'nous':

— Nous n'arrivons toujours pas à [. . .] désigner ce que nous avons entrevu quand il nous est apparu pour la première fois [. . .]
— Nous pouvons seulement affirmer que c'est en lui, nous en sommes plus sûrs qu'avant, nous ne nous sommes pas trompés, c'est tout à fait certain . . . (p. 190)

How is the self to maintain its difference from this individual in the absence of any concrete indications of his self-love? Eventually, almost as a last resort, the very absence of signs of self-love is seized on as its supreme sign:

— Et si ça se trouvait dans l'absence même de ces signes . . .
— Des signes qui 'brillent par leur absence' . . .
— C'est ça . . . quel espoir, quel soutien dans ces mots qui viennent sans être appelés, qui se présentent d'eux-mêmes, à point nommé . . . (p. 191)

This diagnosis allows the features of the self-lover to be entirely sublimated. He is not self-aware in the manner of those examined earlier; he is simply there, unselfconsciously being himself, for he has so assimilated the objectifying quality of self-love that he has no need to monitor himself from without. But if the other can be unconscious of the principle governing his attitude to the world and himself, the same can presumably be true for the 'nous' which seem to share so many of his characteristics. For the genius of self-love sounds very like the Sarrautean self in his adherence only to his own law, in his lack of self-observation, his irreducibility to another's judgement: 'Peu importe comment il est. Personne n'est capable de le juger' (p. 192). Like the 'nous', he is indefinable: 'Tous les mots qui se présentent ne sont pas de taille' (p. 193). If what distinguishes this individual from the 'nous' is his 'certitude [. . .] absolue', his 'inébranlable assurance' (p. 192) in his particular sphere of activity, this applies to the plural self too in its own sphere: in its contentment with its own company and above all in its faith in its own expression of truth. What's more, the self's diagnosis of the other as a self-lover is itself clearly governed by an internalized law: the way the phrase 'briller par son absence' spontaneously provides the key to the other's nature (in a logic as paradoxical as that which associates 'sottises' with an 'homme d'esprit') is an example of how a familiar cliché can give rise to a perception which is then accepted as true—albeit, in this case, with a sense of desperation which gently mocks this reaction. As the other's social self-assurance is seen to be determined by the laws of an entirely assimilated self-love (his genius lying in this assimilation), the authorial self's certainty regarding its expression of truth is also shown to rest on an internalized linguistic code which unifies the self without its knowledge and dictates the way it understands the world.

Given this inescapable kinship of the plural self with the most refined form of what it defines itself in opposition to, it is not so surprising that it should react to the 'genius' by desiring, like him, to be the arbiter of good and evil for another (according to its own 'internal tribunal' where subjective truth is good and the submission to others' views is evil). It attempts in vain to persuade a victim of the great man's cult that his views are determined by his leader's personality rather than being independently formed: ' "S'il avait promené sa main sur les margelles des puits, sur les parapets des vieux petits ponts, avec quelles délices vous aussi . . ." ' (p. 201). Yet while its attempt to free the other from the influence of the 'grand' is motivated by a desire to lead him to the truth, this truth is undeniably what the self, rather than its interlocutor, identifies as such. Although it describes its addressee's imagined moment of physical contact with the rim of the well as a return 'chez vous' (p. 200), its own strong investment in that image, to the point of making it part of the self, makes this evocation more an invitation 'chez nous'. Its actions may be animated by

— [. . .] notre besoin de répandre la vérité, de libérer malgré eux . . .
— De faire reconnaître ce qui ne peut pas être reconnu . . .
— Et qui est là pourtant. C'est sûr. (p. 202)

Yet this ultimately leads it to participate in the same imposition of values (though of different values) as the great man practises.

The failure of the other to adopt the self's conception of truth means that the self can only repeat its conviction 'seulement pour nous. Pas pour essayer de nous faire entendre' (p. 202). Yet of course the one who still hears when all the fictional interlocutors stop listening is the reader, and the representation of a belief maintained in the face of general hostility and in apparent unawareness of the reader's presence works to convince us all the more of the sincerity of that viewpoint. In the two final chapters, I shall look first at the ways in which Sarraute attempts to persuade the reader into her own perspective and away from an undesired approach to the text, much as the 'nous' of *Tu ne t'aimes pas* attempt to convince the credulous other of his enslavement to the 'genius of self-love'. Finally I shall consider the way the actual practice of reading relates to yet also exceeds what Sarraute proposes. On the basis of how we have seen her writing repeatedly challenge the structural limitations of language by attempting to establish for it a visceral source in the self, one way in which the reader can transcend the role her texts provide for him is by recognizing that, even at its most apparently physical, her language remains subject to the axes of metaphor and metonymy. Such a reading, which takes its lead from her own illustration of the way others' language is alienated from truth by its conventional structure, far from being reductive, rather acknowledges dialogically Sarraute's texts and their ambition to express the truth of the self (body and mind) as complex constructions within a transindividual Symbolic order.

The reader's ability, indeed his obligation as recipient of the text's alienated discourse, to read as symbol what is presented by the author as truth, corresponds to the alternative between the same object seen in Symbolic or Imaginary terms: 'Un terme d'un ordre symbolique peut être imaginaire, s'il est considéré absolument ou symbolique, s'il est une valeur différentielle corrélative d'autres termes qui le délimitent. C'est l'intelligence de ces corrélations latérales qui suspend l'imaginaire, parce qu'elle fonde le concept' (Lemaire 1977: 106). Whereas Sarraute considers the represented body as an absolute, allowing it to stand as an index of the truth of her language, for the reader that truth-founding body, encountered in the text, is always already linguistic. Located from the start in language, the reader–text relationship is always a mediated one, in contrast to Sarraute's ideal of reading which is self-loss in the text: 'Ce qui s'est emparé de nous, cette fois, ce qui a tout occupé en nous, ce qui a fait en nous place nette, c'étaient les mots d'un vieux poème' (*TTP* 79). Reading as a kind of unmediated Imaginary relation where one can merge with the text seems now, for the self-sufficient internal multitude of *Tu ne t'aimes pas*, to be the only viable form of dialogue: the self–other relations of the earlier novels, equally envisaged in Imaginary terms,[26] are doomed by the struggle for domination which they involve. Yet as the quotation illustrates, domination is undeniably also a feature of the privileged relationship of reading—the difference is that here, for Sarraute, there is no struggle, for from the start the text has mastered us, 'a fait en nous place nette'.

Tu ne t'aimes pas then clearly fits into the whole question of the subject–language relationship looked at in Chapter 1, and it does so doubly in both its sensitivity to the way the conventional language of others objectifies them, and in its demonstration of the structural impossibility of escaping the pitfalls of convention (alienation and objectification), even in a language which constantly strives for authenticity and originality. It exemplifies the ironic predicament of being aware of the limited nature of the subject of language but being by definition unable to transcend that limitation as it informs one's own discourse. Sarraute's reaction is to pursue the possibility of a truthful discourse in contrast to the alienation governing the

---

[26] The nephew's experience, in *Martereau*, of dialogue as a 'jeu de miroirs où je me perds—mon image que je projette en lui ou celle qu'il plaque aussitôt, férocement, sur moi' (*M* 241), is a near relative of the Imaginary defined as 'une opposition immédiate entre la conscience et son autre où chaque terme passe l'un dans l'autre et se perd dans ces jeux de reflets' (Lemaire 1977: 112).

way others express themselves, yet, as we have seen, the truth-claim of tropistic writing faces the problem that the body which guarantees it is necessarily already symbolized. This situation is an instance of a conflict Celia Britton has pointed out in Sarraute's work, between opposing deterministic and idealist-humanist world-views, and in which the latter is presented as a solution to the former. However, as Britton argues, the humanist position which is supposed to transcend the view of intersubjective relations as 'alienated, self-referring, and dehumanised' is not only superseded by that view but is actually *produced* by it (just as the body which is seen as conquering linguistic alienation is itself a product of that alienated language): 'Ideas of pure creativity, and so on, arise simply as inverted *reflections* of determinism—its mirror-image, rather than a true critique of it' (1982: 583).

Britton sees an awareness of historical change as a way out of this deadlock (Sarraute's solution—idealism—to the deterministic world of others being as static and unchanging as that which it opposes). I prefer to focus on how a certain conception of dialogue allows us to read Sarraute's work both on her own terms yet beyond them, but still taking our cue from them. Sarraute gives us at once evidence of the need for dialogue, by showing (consciously and unconsciously) language as a symbolic structure which undermines the claim to express truth, and evidence of the obstacles to it, for her writing enacts how the nature of the subject of language leads it to try to control the language which informs it, by halting the deferral of signification in a transcendental signified of its utterance. The resulting assertion of the truth of one's own utterance becomes a request for the interlocutor's assent to one's intentional meaning (a request to be studied in the next chapter in terms of Sarraute's representations of readers), rather than for the uninfluenced response which is valuable specifically for its 'otherness' to the speaker. If linguistic expression requires a dialogic response to make it true, it also resists dialogue by claiming to be true.

What kind of text–reader dialogue can we then envisage, bearing in mind that writing simply intensifies problems central to all communication? The written text is only ever potentially part of a dialogue, for it is always only the opening move in one, unable to acknowledge its interlocutor's response and respond to it in turn. As an address which cannot know who its addressee is, or defend itself in terms of its reception, it has a much higher stake in establishing that response in advance than spoken dialogue does. In the case of Sarraute, I have suggested that the reader's capacity to transcend the role offered to him may manifest itself in his recognition of the impossibility of establishing an absolute opposition between expressive and conventional language. As a linguistic subject, Sarraute is unable to see her own language from without in the way she can see others' utterances, and so remains affected by the illusory integrity and alienation that language use reinforces in the subject (and to which she is so sensitive) even when it is intended to subvert it. This is where dialogue, with its inclusion of another perspective (in this case the reader's), comes in as simultaneously necessary to the establishment of any provisional linguistic truth, and impossible for the text to determine. For even if the authorial subject is aware of his or her own conscious limitations and invites another to help overcome them, that awareness and that invitation, once articulated (alienated in the 'writtenness' of language in general), must themselves be informed by those same limitations (as was vividly shown by *Enfance*).

Only the reader, as other, can read Sarraute's language as she reads other people's, as a structure which reveals its conventional basis even as it tries to position itself outside convention. The distance from its intentional source (the addressor) which language affords the addressee and which writing augments, does not just cause the writer's attempt to write the reader's response into the text; it is also what allows the reader to read even his represented role model as part of the text rather than as the true way to approach it. The other perspective his own linguistic subjectivity provides means that he meets the Sarrautean self in the Symbolic order rather than in Sarraute's Imaginary (which he indeed only construes through it), and so does not achieve entirely that self-loss in the text which she advocates. It need only be added that the reader's own subjective limitations and desire to procure assent in turn replace Sarraute's, with the result that any interpretation of her writing requires to be further engaged with by an other in turn. And so on. The idea of dialogue with which we began, that of a cooperative constitution of truth in the intersubjective encounter, thus seems to give way to a less optimistic but perhaps more realistic one where the prejudices inherent in one subject's language give way to those of another, yet with the consolation that every new set at least has the potential to recognize and engage with those to which it is responding. The fact that language is simultaneously shared and individual (both 'système de signes' and 'assumé comme exercice par l'individu': Benveniste 1966: 254), creates undeniable obstacles to communication; yet while these may be considerable, they are not insuperable.[27]

---

[27] Although for Anika Lemaire they do seem to cast doubt on the overall communicative efficacy of language: 'La psychanalyse nous a appris à [. . .] discerner les traces [de l'Imaginaire] aussi dans le langage où les mots recouvrent des symboles cent fois démultipliés et dont l'organisation finalement tient à un fil si ténu qu'il n'est pas aberrant de se demander si le langage est vraiment l'agent du dialogue inter-humain' (1977: 113).

4

READING AND OTHERNESS

The readings of *Enfance* and *Tu ne t'aimes pas* in Chapters 2 and 3 dealt with the way their textual dialogues, being located within the authorial self, point up the insufficiency of a singular discourse when it comes to articulating the truth of that self (a predicament associated in Chapter 1 with Romantic irony). I have set this dimension of Sarraute's writing in the context of the Lacanian understanding of dialogue as alone permitting the constitution of the subject's truth. This conception of dialogue is also prominent within the field of narrative theory: the Bakhtin/Voloshinov school has demonstrated (with particular attention to Dostoevsky) the tendency within modern fiction to favour ever more unmediated representation of characters' discourses and their productive interaction over an omniscient narrative perspective which would translate these into its own, necessarily limited terms.[1]

None the less, we have seen how a singular authorial discourse reasserts itself in the internal dialogues of *Enfance* and *Tu ne t'aimes pas*, along with the singular identity informed by that discourse. This re-emergence of a claim to speaker-authority out of its ostensible dissolution enacts, I have argued, the way all language use turns its subject into a *moi*, and, being motivated by a particular expressive intention (even if that intention is to articulate an ironic scepticism regarding expression), is unable consciously to overcome its own monologism. (It will still, of course, retain the unintentionally dialogic quality of being formed out of other discourses.) Thus the establishment of a transindividual dialogic truth will only take place in the context of this conscious monologism. Moreover, I have suggested that the alienation of the linguistic utterance from its intentional source (see Derrida 1967*b*, 1972) may lead speakers— and even more so writers—to attempt to ensure that their intention is recognized by implicitly projecting that recognition onto their

---

[1] Sarraute too admires the way Dostoevsky forgoes authorial analysis to let his characters themselves express 'ces mouvements subtils, à peine perceptibles [. . .] des ébauches d'appels timides et de reculs' (*ES* 33) which accompany their ongoing struggle to 'se frayer un chemin jusqu'à autrui' (p. 37).

addressee within the address itself. In the novel, this attempt finds its most extreme form in the representation of model readers within the text.

In the next two chapters I wish to move beyond the consideration of the internal dialogism of Sarraute's texts to focus more closely on their address to their reader and on his response to them. While Bakhtin himself in his writings on literary dialogism provides no specific theory of reading, David Shepherd has argued that aspects of his work seem 'relevant and useful to a reader-oriented project' (1989: 91). Bakhtin, he explains, sees the whole text-as-utterance, as well as the utterances it contains, as 'oriented towards and shaped by an anticipated response', that of the reader and his role of 'active understanding' (p. 92). This view of the text-reader interaction is modelled on *spoken* dialogue—Shepherd notes a 'constant sliding throughout ["Discourse in the Novel"] between speaking and writing, listener and reader' (p. 94). While the mediated nature of written communication may be paradigmatic for spoken dialogue too, the distance between published writer and anonymous reader is certainly much greater than that between speaker and listener. Authors sensitive to the way the process of publication and dissemination distances them from their readers are thus liable to try to shape more emphatically than happens in spoken utterances the desired response to their texts, in order to pre-empt undesirable readings to which they would be unable to give a corrective response.

Chapter 5 will discuss the issues around reading which are central to Sarraute's work from the point of view of the reader approaching the text. In this chapter I want to look at how her texts anticipate their readers, and how they project the kind of reading they desire. In sections 1 and 2 I shall examine her representation of 'good' and 'bad' readers in *Les Fruits d'or* and *Entre la vie et la mort*,[2] the two novels which deal most exclusively with readers, writers, and books. The last section will then consider how Sarraute's evaluation

---

[2] Alan Clayton (1989: 39–40) sees *three* kinds of represented reader in Sarraute: the good double, the bad readers who read Sarraute as though she were a traditional novelist, and a third group who, in their criticism of Sarrautean language, provide a kind of textual self-parody. However, this last group can be assimilated to the company of bad readers; moreover, their criticism is overturned by the text itself. I have discussed (Ch. 2, s. 1) the ironic function of this subgroup who enact what Clayton calls the 'repentir *feint* d'une écriture qui brave alors ironiquement l'image de ce qu'elle n'est pas' (p. 42).

of ways of relating to a text influences the way she addresses her own readers in *L'Usage de la parole*. While she presents a certain kind of text–reader dialogue as a positive alternative to public intercourse which is clearly shown to define its addressee as an object, this privileged dialogue itself necessarily fails to achieve that mutual presence and recognition of the interlocutor as a subject to which it aspires. Instead it participates in the way all address objectifies to some degree the subject it addresses, by projecting an anticipated (desired, or alternatively feared) response onto him and so turning him into a character. The strongly oral tone of Sarraute's writing works greatly to counteract the lack of mutual presence of author and reader; yet the 'writtenness' of all language means that even the spoken quality of her work cannot bridge this distance entirely.[3]

All Sarraute's efforts to shape the reader's response are simultaneously reminders that he really is other, for if the mediation introduced by language makes the addressee into a projected figure for the addressor, it is also what ensures that in reality he remains irreducible to that figure. The one who receives the message is never entirely identical to the one for whom it is intended. The refiguring of the authorial intention which results shifts power to the addressee who construes an intended meaning from the linguistic evidence (including, it is essential to acknowledge, the image of himself he attributes to the text). This is the view of reading proposed by Paul Ricoeur (see Ch. 1, s. 3), a view of opponents competing for control of the text, and in the process projecting identities and intentions onto each other; it is a long way from the ideal of mutual self-presence and cooperation aspired to in *Les Fruits d'or* or *Entre la vie et la mort*. However, it too has its shortcomings which will be considered in Chapter 5, as we address the complex nature of the actual reading encounter.

In taking account of the more coercive dimension of reading, my discussion here of the text–reader relationship in Sarraute marks itself off from those based on a more consensual notion of dialogue. Alan Clayton, for example, also acknowledges the way the

---

[3] Her composition of plays for live performance (first on radio, later in the theatre) can also be seen in this light, as can the growing number of recorded readings of her texts. The fact that her prose narratives and dialogues increasingly adopt the form of events which unfold as they are read creates a similar effect of immediacy which also works to undo the reader's distance from their intentional enunciation; I shall discuss this aspect of her prose in more detail later in this chapter.

approach of Sarraute's texts to their reader mimes the attempt by their fictional protagonists to find a sympathetic, responsive other—he in fact describes Sarraute in *L'Usage de la parole*, the first of her texts to address the reader directly, as 'pastichant presque ses propres procédés de narration' (1989: 15). Yet while for him this migration of the appeal for understanding from the fictional world to its authorial frame turns the reader into a co-writer, I see it as aiming instead to draw him entirely out of his own world, the terms of which might distort his reception of the text's message, and into the point of view of the text.

One critical work, though not on Sarraute, which does pay close attention to the relations of power underlying the text–reader dialogue is Ross Chambers's study of the nineteenth-century 'art story' in *Story and Situation* (1984). While working from a Marxist perspective, he too identifies a desire by the text for the reader's submission: for him it is the commodification of literature which has forced texts to 'designate themselves as contractual phenomena and produce the transactional situation that gives point to their narratives' (1984: 9–10). Since the eighteenth century, he claims, the writing of literature has become ever more removed from the circumstances of direct communication, to be regarded instead as an 'alienated discursive practice' (p. 12). The text has lost its use-value for an exchange-value, 'its interpretability as a complex sign for which other discursive signs can be substituted'; it has consequently had to make itself seductive in order to acquire a readership which will actualize its meaningfulness by interpreting it. Chambers's analysis thus clearly sees the alienation of the literary text as a historical and economic development rather than, as I have argued, intrinsic to the nature of language as representation. For this reason his focus is on texts that clearly announce themselves as art, rather than on writing in general as inherently alienated and language as inherently 'written'.[4]

Yet whatever the causes adduced for the text's alienation from both author and reader, the consequences for that text are the same. This chapter's examination of how Sarraute's texts provide models

---

[4] In his conclusion, he does call for an attempt to situate the specific phenomenon of literary communication within the total range of modes of verbal communication available to social beings (p. 206); and he claims that literary theorists can correct the 'unproblematic view of the nature of the communicational subject and of the addressee, as well as of the relationship that prevails between them' (p. 207).

of the kind of reader they desire bears out Chambers's identification of the creation of fictional addressees as a major textual strategy of seduction. As he asks, 'When we are seduced, are we not always seduced into conforming ourselves with an image: the simulacrum of one whom we believe can be loved?' (p. 15). Such 'situational self-reflexivity' (p. 24), where texts represent *en abyme* their own communicational function, is for Chambers primarily a feature of 'readerly' texts which, by claiming the status of artistic discourse, assert the power to produce new meanings in new interpretative contexts, yet simultaneously lay down the range of possible meanings they will admit.[5]

As I have said, the reader is not doomed to succumb to the text's seductive strategies; in the case of Sarraute, his distance from the text's expressive intention enables, indeed requires, him to read as a linguistic construct what it presents as an expressed truth. Chambers too (within the terms of his Marxist perspective) sees the reader as able to free the text from the (for him ideological and cultural) limitations of its self-conception, while his own discourse will remain subject to comparable restrictions. In this view, the reader in fact becomes the saviour of the text's own claim to artistic status: he rescues its power to create ever more meanings in new contexts of reading from its own tendency to limit its meaningfulness through strategies of control like the *mise en abyme* of the act of communication.[6]

1. Sarraute's represented readers

A striking feature of Nathalie Sarraute's fiction is the way she repeatedly uses the same restricted context—the conversations of middle-class Parisian intellectuals about art—to represent human

---

[5] 'It is as if for them the deferring of meaning from which they benefit as art requires careful control so as not to get out of hand' (p. 26). Chambers's designation of texts as readerly or writerly draws of course on Barthes's opposition, in *S/Z* (1970: 10), of the *lisible* and the *scriptible*, two modes of writing which make of the reader respectively a passive consumer and an active producer of the text. The limited relevance of this opposition to Sarraute's writing has been discussed by Ann Jefferson (1975: 87–95) who concludes that it fails to account for Sarraute's ambition to create a new language which would still be expressive, but of an equally new reality (p. 94).

[6] Chambers 1984: 27. Thus *mise en abyme*, when it concerns the *reader*, appears to be a textual strategy of self-*preservation* opposed to the ironic self-relativization which the text's *mise en abyme* of *itself* invites (see Ch. 1, p. 24).

relations at a level which she none the less clearly holds to be universal.[7] Why does she always choose the same culturally and socially specific surface situation for 'la mise au jour d'une matière psychologique nouvelle [. . .] une matière anonyme qui se trouve chez tous les hommes et dans toutes les sociétés' (*ES* 95)? One consequence of focusing so exclusively on this particular milieu is that it allows her to represent the way people relate to one another in tandem with the way they relate to art. There is a strong sense in Sarraute that human relationships have a great deal in common with the interaction with a work of art, especially perhaps (given its linguistic nature) with a literary work. For an exploration of this homology, which involves not so much the aestheticization of inter-subjective relations as the humanization of the text, the variety of social contexts available is necessarily restricted.

The comparison of relations between text and reader with those which exist between individuals is perhaps made most explicit in *Les Fruits d'or*. The opening scene plunges us into the whole issue of intersubjective relations and their success and failure; and the two encounters it represents (one recalled within the other) significantly focus on the issue of aesthetic response. A couple[8] analyse an evening just spent with a third individual who showed them a post-card of a Courbet painting he admired. When this action failed to unite the three by calling up an identical reaction to the painting in all (the husband refused to manifest any reaction, despising the other's conformity to current fashion), the woman attempted to compensate by appealing to the host for his reaction to a novel called 'Les Fruits d'Or'. The question failed to restore relations, as the non-committal answer could not be decoded in terms of rejection or acceptance of contact with the asker. A recalled or imagined epilogue to the dialogue between husband and wife shows her return to the host to make him admit that his comment on the book was meant as a rebuff to them: 'Quand j'ai essayé de me rapprocher, quand j'ai tendu les bras vers vous, quand je vous ai demandé pour Les Fruits d'Or . . . vous avez voulu nous repousser, marquer que c'était trop tard, que la rupture était consommée . . .'

[7] Hannah Arendt is one critic to single out for praise the element of social parody in Sarraute: '*Le Planétarium* et *Les Fruits d'or* pris ensemble constituent le réquisitoire le plus sévère jamais adressé aux intellectuels' (1986: 25). Yet she also sees the society represented in *Les Fruits d'or* in broader terms as 'un macrocosme du "je", le je en grandes lettres' (p. 26).
[8] Though they are not explicitly identified as husband and wife, I shall describe them as such for ease of reference.

(*FO* 16). But no definitive interpretation is forthcoming, and the anguish of uncertainty as to her relations with the other remains.

The scene offers a positive and a negative model of dialogue, all in the context of reactions to art and literature.[9] In opposition to the breakdown of contact between the host and his guests, contact which only ever existed through the wife's great effort (pp. 13–14), communication within the couple is unproblematic, their dialogue betraying none of that estrangement which the attempts to communicate with the other dramatize so intensely. Unlike their host's words, their utterances are transparent to each other, and in their analysis of the recalled dialogue the motivations behind the words and gestures of each are not only clear to the partner (while they can also be inferred by the host, he never has the comfort of certainty), but are also openly admitted: 'Tu ne regardais rien.—Non, rien' (p. 7); 'Tu m'amusais beaucoup quand tu cherchais à rattraper ma "gaffe", à me faire pardonner [. . .]—Bien sûr, tu as montré que tu refusais ce qu'il t'offrait' (pp. 11–12). Even the *sous-conversation* which in this section acts, unusually, not to evoke the utterance's (concealed) gestation in the speaker, or its effect on the hearer, but as a highly imagistic expansion on its meaning (unambiguous for both), illustrates that mutual understanding is not a problem. (There is an unusually high proportion of spoken dialogue to *sous-conversation* here, presumably because it does not need to be glossed to be comprehensible.) The source of the *sous-conversation*, in addition, is not always clearly located in one rather than the other, suggesting an identity of perspectives in the couple. In fact, the tone of the exchange which, while not without its disagreements, seems preserved from the pitfalls of public intercourse, anticipates the evocation in *Tu ne t'aimes pas* of dialogue with a loved one as the only unproblematic kind of interaction in language (and a thing of the past for the later novel, after the intervention of death).[10]

---

[9] Sarraute repeatedly compares literature to painting, as when she quotes Paul Klee on the way art makes visible rather than representing the visible to define her own literary enterprise (e.g. 1962: 49; see *OC* 1644 n. 1). Thus the portrait in *Portrait d'un inconnu* can act as a model of a kind of writing which refuses traditional characterization. Like her cultivation of a spoken quality in her writing, comparing it to visual art also seems designed to overcome the alienation of writing through a heightened immediacy. Yet the immediacy of pictorial representation is also illusory: as Paul Ricoeur points out, painterly expression too relies on a restricted semiotic code (1976: 40–3).

[10] Towards the end of *Les Fruits d'or* we see how the relationship of a couple, like that of reader and text, can be dragged from the private into the public sphere, where they resemble

The instances of non-communication—the host's overture and also the woman's subsequent attempt to salvage the situation when that overture is ignored by her husband—are both attempts to talk about art. As with 'Les Fruits d'Or' which is 'le dernier cri' (p. 13), talking about the Courbet painting is associated from the start with conventional behaviour and inauthenticity (p. 6): 'C'est exactement la même reproduction qu'ils ont tous chez eux, qu'ils portent tous sur eux en ce moment.'[11] As such it is rejected in favour of an authentic, and thus private, relation to art (the original creation, not one among innumerable reduced reproductions) by the husband who refuses to play along: 'J'ai essayé de les voir, les fameux Courbet, j'y suis allé à l'heure du déjeuner pour ne rencontrer personne' (pp. 7–8). Relating to art seems to be inherently at odds with social interaction. The third figure who intrudes into the dualism of the couple, causing the wife to detach herself from her husband in the epilogue to their conversation, in order to speak to him alone, destroys the intimacy of the relation to the artwork too by making it public. As in *Tu ne t'aimes pas*, the intrusion of an outsider breaks up the unity of the self with its chosen object, whether that object of love is a person or a work of art.

The familiar Sarrautean opposition between conventional and authentic language operates here too. For the couple whose easy exchange is built on a prior understanding, the outsider seems to speak a foreign language: 'Ce sont des pièces que vous avez sans doute rapportées d'un pays étranger où je ne suis jamais allée . . . Elles n'ont pas cours ici, où je vis' (p. 17). This foreign language is a *currency*, and so gives even the artwork a relative (exchange-) value ('Moi je le dis toujours: Shakespeare et Courbet': p. 6), rather than the absolute status it holds when interacted with directly. Because

---

'un de ces couples admirablement entraînés, ces voyantes et leurs comparses, ces Lud et Ludila qui de la salle à l'estrade échangent leurs questions et leurs réponses devant un public ébaubi et méfiant' (p. 123). Both kinds of relationship, that with the text and that with the loved other, are explicitly associated in the woman's report on her husband's reading of 'Les Fruits d'Or': 'Jacques le lui dit souvent, modeste, détaché comme il est. . . il suffit de se laisser aller, il suffit de s'abandonner à sa sensation, de s'y accrocher, de ne rien laisser s'interposer, d'entrer toujours en contact direct, intime, avec l'objet' (p. 121). Not only is the ideal immediate relationship the woman aspires to with the text in fact mediated by Jacques's authoritative recommendation; his direct words to her also become mediated by the vestigial third-person narrative voice when they are made public.

[11] The choice of Courbet is not entirely arbitrary: the fictional popularity reflects a real fashion for his work at the time of writing (see *OC* 525 n. 1). As a realist painter, of course, he also stands for an outdated mode of artistic representation.

public discourse turns the ineffable selves it talks about into unitary objects which can be compared and contrasted, it is bound to objectify the artwork too, whereas this is something to be related to as another subject,[12] rather than talked about as an object. Ann Jefferson has pointed out how, in *Les Fruits d'or*, the privileged mode of relation to the text is address; talking about it introduces another addressee and so reduces its status to that of referent: 'When the "I" realises that his discourse may be addressed to "Les Fruits d'Or" itself [. . .] the referent of [his] discourse becomes its addressee' (1977: 216). The relation to a text cannot be spoken about (hence Sarraute's refusal, discussed in Chapter 2, to sanction a metalanguage for her work); it can only be experienced as a currently happening event.

Yet we can anticipate that the dialogue with the artwork will not be as unproblematic as Sarraute desires. As the last chapter showed, the structure of social discourse remains fundamental even to the Sarrautean self as a subject of language. Thus the attempt to establish an authentic relationship will necessarily encounter and struggle against the same unifying impetus made so vivid in the host's 'foreign currency' which conceptualizes not only its referent but also its addressor and addressee (its reflexivity is embraced by those who wish to give themselves the illusion of coherence: '*moi* je le dis toujours'). Even the Sarrautean subject who pursues authenticity of expression with such determination cannot undo its own symbolic integrity, and so by extension cannot avoid turning its addressee into a unitary construct. Indeed *Les Fruits d'or* recognizes that the objectifying impetus is not unique to the convention-bound host but can be attributed even to the most sincere individuals— although only when they engage in alienated social interaction. Seen from the host's perspective, the couple become the agents of aggression and he the victim of their reductive characterization: these attitudes are strategic rather than personality traits, and features of this kind of communication. The couple turn their host into an object through their gaze in which he is imprisoned, and which is a function of their distance from him if not from each other: 'L'immense distance où ils se tiennent et d'où ils me voient, pris,

---

[12] Or rather, for Sarraute, as another self which is not considered to have undergone the 'fall' into linguistic subjectivity and convention—that is, whose access to language is not seen as determining its experience of the world (see Ch. 3 n. 3).

enfermé tout entier dans le champ de leur regard' (p. 24). The only defence against this distant gaze which marks alienated social relations, the only way to control the image others form of one, is to offer them one ready-made: 'Cette image de moi que je leur présente en gros plan, ce bon regard ouvert, confiant, que je pose, voilà, tout droit sur leurs yeux . . .' (p. 24). Over twenty-five years before *Tu ne t'aimes pas*, presentation of a unitary self is already seen as a self-conscious act (here a reaction to the threat of being defined by the other), rather than as an involuntary consequence of being conscious; behind this singular image and its wilful deception which is necessary for survival, there lies already the formless Sarrautean self.

Just as this 'true', formless self hides in public behind a self-conscious posture, and so becomes incapable of relating sincerely to another, an authentic relationship of the reader to the literary text also becomes impossible under the public gaze, and is replaced by a sham. The host is still under the imagined gaze of the couple when he approaches 'Les Fruits d'Or' (his resulting self-consciousness strongly evokes the opening scene of *Entre la vie et la mort*, where a writer performs in public the act of critically rereading his writing): 'Je détourne la tête, je marche—regardez-moi—vers la table où le livre est posé sur des feuillets couverts d'une large écriture. Je l'ouvre . . . Comme on pose la main sur un verre pour arrêter son tintement, je fais en moi le silence. Que tout s'immobilise, se fige' (*FO* 26). The public relationship to the text is one of non-response: the host announces to the imaginarily present couple, 'Je suis content de pouvoir vous le dire: rien ne passe, pas la plus légère vibration' (pp. 26–7).[13] Evidently, then, when an authentic reading does impose itself, a reception of the text's address which cannot be ignored ('Il faudrait pour ne rien entendre me boucher les oreilles': p. 27), it will be incompatible with the public sphere. When this happens, the host is led to reject even the imagined presence of the others as reducing his ability to 'hear' the text as it 'speaks' to him:

Mais écartez-vous donc, vous me gênez . . . votre présence, là, autour, nuit . . . quand vous êtes là, j'entends mal, les sons me parviennent brouillés, je me sens,

---

[13]   The archetypal public reader is in this way the critic who, rather than dialogue with the text, regards it as 'une danse solitaire' (p. 32) and makes it the object of a discourse in which it is an entity comparable to others rather than a unique being: as Courbet was related to Shakespeare, 'Les Fruits d'Or' is 'ce qu'on a écrit de plus beau depuis Stendhal . . . depuis Benjamin Constant' (p. 32).

quand vous êtes là, comme dans une salle qui a une mauvaise acoustique . . . sortez, on vous l'a déjà dit, vous êtes inertes, mous, grossiers . . . Votre présence, votre contact est salissant . . . Votre place n'est pas ici, entre nous . . . (p. 27; cp. pp. 111–12)

Relations with the other and relations with the text remain closely matched through to the end of *Les Fruits d'or*. The pernicious public form of each is associated with an oppressive law which again bears a superficial but limited resemblance to Lacan's Law of the Father. Thus the opinion 'Très bon, l'article de Brulé sur Les Fruits d'Or. De tout premier ordre. Parfait' (p. 33), which is both a reaction to a text and a communication with others, is articulated as a truth which may not be contradicted, and carries totalitarian overtones: 'Inutile de fouiller à droite ni à gauche: toute velléité de résistance est écrasée' (p. 33).[14] The alternative mode of relations suppressed by this law is correspondingly described as a kind of primordial formlessness evocative of the Lacanian Imaginary (but within language): 'tous les dérèglements, foisonnements, grouillements, magmas informes, sombres fouillis, nuits traversées de sinistres lueurs' (p. 34).

Given the impossibility, discussed in Chapter 3, of establishing an absolute distinction between conventional and authentic discourse, the attempt to locate the privileged linguistic relation between self and other or reader and text outside conventional public interaction must be a struggle to achieve the unrealizable, reminding us of Sarraute's description of the writer's taste for 'une certaine forme d'échec' (*ES* 150). As was the case with the notion of an authentic self in *Tu ne t'aimes pas*, Sarraute's view of authentic dialogue is projected from within the conventional order rather than being established independently of it.[15] If we look more closely at the way the aggression which characterizes conventional relations is manifested, we can see how the symptoms of a power-based relationship unavoidably recur in some measure in the 'authentic' alternative.

[14] cp. 'Il a été tiré de sa retraite et obligé à jouer son rôle, à tenir son rang. A revêtir la robe rouge et l'hermine, à se couvrir de sa toque et à rendre, devant l'assistance qui se lève et attend en silence, son jugement [. . .] La sentence est définitive: "Les Fruits d'Or, c'est un très beau livre" ' (p. 39). Yet it is possible to break this Law, at the price of exclusion from the community it unites: 'Violant tous les accords tacites, les pactes secrets, enfreignant les règles que le respect d'autrui impose, que dicte la pudeur, bravant tous les interdits, il s'élance' (p. 115).
[15] Making what seems at first to be a similar point, Françoise Dupuy-Sullivan argues that Sarraute in *Les Fruits d'or* is trying to move outside the power relations between reader and text, and concludes with the recognition that such an attempt is bound to fail (1990: 45). Yet

It is impossible not to be struck by the number of references to the *regard* in the accounts of public encounters in *Les Fruits d'or*. The gaze provides a constant accompaniment to the things people say to one another, and confirms the generally hostile function of those addresses. The other's gaze, as we saw in the host's experience with the couple, always turns one into an object—even, in one Kafkaesque case, into an insect: 'Il se débat comme un insecte qu'un souffle a renversé et qui bat l'air de ses petites pattes affolées [. . .] On le prend, on le pose sur un doigt et on l'inspecte de près' (*FO* 117).[16] All the variations of the gaze, down to its withdrawal in an unmistakable gesture of annihilation ('Il l'effleure un instant de son regard vide et détourne les yeux . . .': p. 85; cp. p. 90), build on this objectifying power. The distress it causes to its object increases with the number of observers; witnesses are made into accomplices of the one leading the attack, purely through the fact that they see. Those who refuse to be accomplices must become blind: 'Nous le menu peuple, nous les braves gens qui nous trouvons là par hasard, trop tard pour fuir, nous ne devons ni regarder ni détourner les yeux. Nous devons être aveugles, sourds, totalement inertes' (p. 57). Yet this refusal turns one into a lifeless object oneself: 'Nous devons être [. . .] durs, figés, des objets disposés là, des poupées bourrées de son avec des visages de porcelaine et des boules de verre à la place des yeux.' If one wants to be a living subject in the terms of the public realm, one must be the subject of a *regard* (social subjectivity confers the power—indeed the obligation—to turn others into objects, along with the constant experience of being objectified one-self). For Jacques Lacan, seeing and being seen are part of the whole complex of individuation (the infant encounters this aspect of sub-jectivity in the mirror stage); for Sarraute, they govern the public mode of relating to the other as a character. If social interaction is

in a shift of perspective which suggests her own submission to the power of Sarraute's dis-course, the 'rapport de force' which she identifies as inescapable for the reader of this novel is that with the community of other readers, not with the text itself. The momentary escape from social into solitary reading which she sees *Les Fruits d'or* as offering the reader is not con-sidered by her (as it will be below) to entail also the reader's submission to the text.

[16] The echoes of Kafka's *Metamorphosis* and of Gregor Samsa's gradual blindness and immobility become even stronger later with the experience of the social pariah: 'Ils me regar-dent apitoyés, personne ne peut plus rien pour moi [. . .] Mais c'est de moi qu'à mon insu sort le courant [. . .] Je suis rejeté dans un coin, je tourne sur moi-même enfermé dans l'étroit espace que borne ma courte vue' (p. 134). Hannah Arendt (1986: 22) points to more echoes of *The Metamorphosis* in *Portrait d'un inconnu* (*PI* 46, 116).

based on the illusion of coherent and unitary identities, the gaze fosters this illusion, both for others who see the self as an object, and for the self when it takes for the truth others' definitions of its own identity (or when, as we saw in *'disent les imbéciles'*, it gazes on itself and so defines itself).

What mode of dialogue does the objectifying gaze allow? If the looked-at individual looks back, a kind of deadlock can be achieved. This is presumably why the voyeur, who is in the powerful position of seeing without being seen, savours his perspective so much: 'C'est presque une joie pour elle, une sorte de jouissance douceâtre de le connaître si bien, de voir comme protégé par sa carapace [. . .] il les épie [. . .] Cela l'amuse, elle le sait, de voir sans être vu—il se croit si bien à l'abri des regards' (pp. 58–9). The deadlock of the reciprocated gaze brings only a highly precarious equality characterized by conflict, both with those excluded from the exchange and also, more importantly, between the participants. The two *savants* whose academic discourse alienates their hearers certainly exclude all others, especially the woman to whose request for book-in-hand proof of the excellence of 'Les Fruits d'Or' they disdain to respond: 'Il ne jette pas un regard à la pauvre écervelée. On dirait qu'il n'a pas entendu son appel. C'est sur l'autre, qui lui fait face, que par-dessus leurs têtes à tous il fixe les yeux' (pp. 63–4). Yet their exchange of glances—'Ses paupières mi-closes [. . .] s'ouvrent maintenant toutes grandes sous le regard brûlant. Leurs yeux s'interrogent' (p. 64)—is, like their dialogue, only superficially consensual. Their opaque language conceals a hostility betrayed by the inherently truthful body when an apparently complimentary address elicits contrasting physical and verbal responses: 'L'autre, en face de lui, a une brève contorsion, comme traversé par une soudaine et courte bourrasque, et aussitôt s'apaise et incline la tête lentement: "Oui. Évidemment" ' (p. 65).

In this register of self–other relations, a valuable relation to the text as other is clearly impossible. All these conversations which objectify their addressees also of course make 'Les Fruits d'Or', their ostensible referent, into an object. But subordinating the relation with the text to the public relation with another not only turns that text into an object referred to instead of a subject engaged with; it also embroils it in the conflicts which characterize social relations. Thus it is used either as a weapon to harm the other (as with the announcement in front of a recently published author that 'Les

Fruits d'Or' is the best book to have appeared for fifteen years: p. 55), or as a target which stands for the other (as when the defender of recently published authors attacks 'Les Fruits d'Or' in order to deflate its protector: p. 59). Reading as a relationship with a text, once it enters the public sphere becomes reading for social power. Even those who ask in all humility to be taught how to read in social terms ('Ils consentent à redevenir des petits enfants. Ils sont si démunis, si humbles [. . .] Qu'on ait pour eux un peu de bonté . . . juste un seul geste généreux . . . Qu'on leur montre, qu'on leur explique, le livre en main . . .': pp. 60–2) fantasize about using this social skill to acquire power. If what was explained was something they had seen but rejected as trivial, they could overthrow their teachers and establish their own superiority (the evocation of which exploits once more Sarraute's association of social corruption with adulthood as opposed to the innocence of the child):

> Ils auraient si honte pour ces misérables, ils se sentiraient si gênés qu'ils feraient comme les grandes personnes quand des enfants leur tendent dans leur menotte un caillou, une brindille, un morceau de papier, en disant: Tiens, voilà une orange, voilà du pain, mange, c'est un bonbon . . . ils feraient claquer leurs lèvres, ils rouleraient les yeux, ils dodelineraient la tête pour montrer leur délectation: 'Oh que c'est donc bon. Oh que c'est beau, Les Fruits d'Or. Oui, vous avez raison. Comme c'est admirable. Comme c'est profond.' (pp. 62–3)

Les Fruits d'or, then, claims very strongly that once enacted according to the rules of social interaction, all exchanges, be they with other individuals or with texts, will involve the objectification of the other in relation to oneself, in an aggressive gesture of domination. Yet if, as I have argued, the social order Sarraute attacks is inseparable from the Symbolic order which governs all communication (including, manifestly, her own writing), then the private dialogue of self and other or of self and text which is opposed to social exchanges will not be able to escape this dynamic entirely. How does Sarraute's ideal private relationship, whether inter-subjective or of reader to text, betray its subjection to a Symbolic order, one which, by turning selves into unitary individuals and making all communication mediate, keeps dialogue from being an ideal moment of consensual, mutual presence and introduces coercion and resistance? The novel's closing representation of a single good reader and his address to 'Les Fruits d'Or' (no longer part of public discourse for it has fallen out of favour), aside from being a model for how its own readers should relate to it, also sustains the homology between the ideal reader–text relationship and the human relationship of love, with its prelinguistic shared understanding celebrated in *Tu ne t'aimes pas* (see Ch. 3, pp. 122–3). Before seeing how even this relationship cannot help betraying its 'social origins', let us examine briefly the way it is presented as the ideal of both aesthetic and intersubjective dialogue.

The fact that the fictional novel is addressed at the end humanizes it, giving it equal status with any of the individuals whose dialogues *Les Fruits d'or* represents; moreover, the tone of the reader's address is that of a lover to a loved one, underlining the identity between a true relation to the text and a true relation to another human.[17] Indeed the description of the ideal reader–text relationship here is almost identical to the evocation of love much later in *Tu ne t'aimes pas*. What passes from 'Les Fruits d'Or' to its reader is 'comme une vibration, une modulation, un rythme . . . c'est comme une ligne fragile et ferme qui se déploie [. . .] un tintement léger . . . qui d'eux à moi et de moi à eux comme à travers une même substance se propage' (p. 136). In *Tu ne t'aimes pas*, love, now past, is remembered thus: 'Était-ce une couleur, une ligne, une à peine perceptible nuance, une intonation, un silence [. . .] Ça ouvrait, creusait en nous un chemin à travers une même substance, remontait à une même source' (*TTP* 123). Both descriptions also emphasize physical fusion and anteriority to public language, though given the immaterial and linguistic nature of the text, the metaphoric status of this bodily description is much more explicit in *Les Fruits d'or*:

Ce silence où vous baignez, dépouillé de tous les vêtements et ornements dont vous aviez été affublé, nu, tout lavé, flottant à la dérive, avec moi cramponné à vous, rend très étroit notre contact. Nous sommes si proches maintenant, vous êtes tellement une partie de moi, qu'il me semble que si vous cessiez d'exister, ce serait comme une part de moi-même qui deviendrait du tissu mort. (*FO* 157)

---

[17] Jean Pierrot points out in Sarraute's first novel the privileging of the relation to the artwork over the generally unsatisfactory relation to others: 'Dans l'univers de Nathalie Sarraute, l'intersubjectivité ne prend qu'exceptionnellement la forme heureuse et apparemment réussie qui caractérise, dans *Portrait d'un inconnu*, les retrouvailles du narrateur avec ce portrait auquel il demande, et dont il obtient sans doute, compréhension, appui et reconfort spirituel' (1990: 105). Pierrot too sees this exchange as a one-sided imposition ('une intersubjectivité feinte'), though he reverses the roles and gives power to the one responding to the work (a point I shall return to at the end of this chapter).

The amorous nature of the relationship of reading is in fact explicitly acknowledged: 'Personne n'a le pouvoir d'interrompre entre nous cette osmose. Aucune parole venue du dehors ne peut détruire une si naturelle et parfaite fusion. Comme l'amour, elle nous donne la force de tout braver. Comme un amoureux, j'ai envie de la cacher' (*FO* 136).[18]

The intensity of this relationship both permits and obliges one to abandon the social community, with its destructive language and gaze:

Qu'ils ne voient pas ce qui est là, entre nous, qu'ils ne s'approchent pas de cela, c'est tout ce que je leur demande [. . .] N'importe quel mot venu d'eux, qui se poserait sur nous ou seulement nous frôlerait, me ferait me rétracter, me replier sur moi-même et hérisser tous mes piquants [. . .] Mes yeux vides fixés devant moi ne verront pas leurs regards se rencontrer et échanger l'assurance de leur confiance, de leur entente, de leur supériorité. (pp. 136–7)

Thus the reader renounces public discourse to speak to the text alone. He may continue to hope for an answering human voice—'quelqu'un qui réponde, juste une autre voix . . .' (p. 151)—which would demonstrate an identical attitude to his: 'Il doit y en avoir bien d'autres comme moi à travers le monde. Timorés comme moi. Un peu repliés sur eux-mêmes. Pas habitués à s'exprimer' (p. 156). But such a specular dialogue with an identical other, outside the destructive dynamic of social interaction, is now recognized in advance to be unfeasible—the conventional attitudes of even apparently similar interlocutors would sabotage the exchange by relativizing 'Les Fruits d'Or' in the way already defined as typical of the social response to art: 'Il est certain que cette même impression, que vous leur donnez comme à moi, ils l'éprouvent devant Dieu sait quoi, que j'aime mieux ne pas imaginer' (p. 156).

The decision to remain alone with the text inaugurates a relationship in which it repeatedly seduces the reader: 'N'importe quel petit bout, pris au hasard, s'insinue en moi ou non. Et quand il le fait, il tire après soi tout le reste [. . .] Comme un être vivant' (p. 155).

---

[18] The relationship of love, for Sarraute, is one of identity between self and other (in *Tu ne t'aimes pas* the loved other is a 'part inséparable de nous-mêmes': *TTP* 122). Bernard Pingaud shows how the reader–novel relationship in *Les Fruits d'or* fits this criterion, in a comment which anticipates Sarraute's creation of the writer's double as ideal reader in *Entre la vie et la mort*: 'Celui qui dit "je" à la fin du roman est à la fois auteur (de ce roman) et lecteur (des "Fruits d'Or"), c'est en quelque sorte à lui-même qu'il s'adresse, dans la proximité du vrai contact' (1963: 34).

This counteracts the lack of fidelity of the reader who is often 'prêt à reconnaître que je suis trompé' (p. 155) until the text exerts its seductive power once again. This seductive power, and the reader's ongoing susceptibility to public opinion, are the first indication that this relationship, for all that it shuns the public sphere, does not entirely succeed in escaping its dynamics. The kind of interaction with the text which the reader describes in his final address to it carries unavoidable echoes of the social relations he is trying to escape. The features we have seen to be characteristic of these are the role of the gaze as mediator between individuals, and the hostile footing on which this puts any exchange by turning its addressee into an object. An exchange of glances involves the uncontrollable objectification of each by the other, and if the other's definition is not embraced for the illusion of a coherent self it offers, the only way to resist it is by projecting an alternative image. A struggle results both to counter the other's imposed image of oneself with one's own, and to impose one on the (often equally resisting) other.

If the ideal text–reader relationship presented at the end of the novel appears to have escaped this complex of aggression and counter-aggression, it is only because one party, the reader, is willing to be the submissive partner of a text which literally captivates it. Opposite the text as a linguistic entity (a state dissimulated by its anthropomorphosis into a lover), the reader is openly represented as somewhat inarticulate.[19] He is unfamiliar with 'le vocabulaire perfectionné de ces savants docteurs' (p. 152) and speaks hesitantly; the soulmates for whom he hopes will be the same, 'pas habitués à s'exprimer' (p. 156). His difficulty in expressing what he feels ('Je le sens très bien, mais je ne sais pas l'exprimer . . . je n'ai à ma disposition que de pauvres mots complètement usés à force d'avoir servi à tous et à tout': p. 152) means that he offers no competition to the writer, no danger of an independent response which would evaluate the work critically (i.e. interpreting it in terms of his own discourse rather than passively 'imbibing' it entirely on its own terms): 'Car enfin, qui suis-je? Qu'ai-je fait? Je n'ai même jamais songé à essayer d'écrire un roman [. . .] Je ne me rends même pas compte, par exemple, en vous lisant, s'il y a eu des difficultés à surmonter, et de quel ordre [. . .] Tout me paraît couler de source. Se développer

---

[19] Sarraute demonstrates the same conviction as her characters that 'la maîtrise d'autrui passe par son asservissement à leur parole' (Rykner 1991: 47).

naturellement' (p. 154). Unable to take a critical stance towards the text, he humbly desires only to 'm'en montrer digne' (p. 153), and so gives himself up to this 'quelque chose qui me prend doucement et me tient sans me lâcher' (p. 153). If the fact of addressing the text appears to give the initiative in the exchange to the reader by making him active, what he actually says to it shows him renounce the power of the addressor and thus reinforces his passivity.

It seems that a primordial fusion of self and other, an Imaginary relation where both cease to be distinguishable, can even in the intimacy of reading only be approximated in a relationship of domination and submission. The creation of sameness always involves the (voluntary or imposed) suppression of one party's otherness. Text and reader here only appear to lose their discreteness through the reader's willingness to give in to the text. This perception of the submissive role of the reader will remain constant right up to *Tu ne t'aimes pas* where a text 's'est emparé de nous [. . .] a tout occupé en nous [. . .] a fait en nous place nette' (*TTP* 79). The dialogue around the text remains subject to the same structure of power that governs the social exchanges represented in Sarraute's novels, with that power, for Sarraute, ideally located at the writer's pole of the exchange.

This gesture of inscribing within the text the response of the good reader as one of submission is, I have suggested, a consequence of the way the author's controlling presence as enunciator is even more attenuated in the written (and published) text than in speech. Sarraute's creation of a model reader simply magnifies the way all address projects the interpretation it desires, an interpretation which is never assured due to the alienated nature of linguistic communication. The total anonymity of the real reader, which is the reason the desired interpretation is projected so emphatically by Sarraute, is itself just the limit-case of the way even the familiar other encountered in the face-to-face exchange, indeed even the lover, can never be known fully. As Sarraute creates an identity for this unknown other to conform to, all speakers (though not so emphatically) counter the unknowability of their interlocutors by conceptualizing them in a personality (which in cases where the other is known is of course established to a greater or lesser degree on the basis of the data he provides).[20]

---

[20] Émile Benveniste comments on how the second-person pronoun is used to represent to oneself a person other than oneself (primarily, though not necessarily, one's addressee). This

The identity Sarraute creates for the reader is that of the double, a feature the next section will consider in more detail. To circumscribe his response further, she also provides a number of *negative* models of readers and their readings. Yet the presence of these is in fact a reminder that the reader really *is* other: if he needs to be seduced into a specular identification with the humanized text, it is because these other, undesirable responses to the text are available. Thus in *Les Fruits d'or*, the idea that readings are uncontrollable because readers are unknowable forms a constant, menacing backdrop to the presentation of the reader-as-double led by the text-as-subject. Yet the novel's presentation of a progression from inferior (powerful) to superior (submissive) readers suggests some optimism at this stage that the desired metamorphosis of actual readers from other into same might be achievable through a reading process which draws them out of their own and into the text's point of view.

2. The reader as self and other

The identification of the ideal reader as the writer's double is of course central to *Entre la vie et la mort*, the novel which follows *Les Fruits d'or*. Yet in this novel the prospect of such a reader emerging from the ranks of the convention-bound reading public, though still desired, seems to be recognized as a fantasy, and the move towards authorial self-sufficiency begins. It is a move which will eventually give rise to the internal community of voices in *Tu ne t'aimes pas* and, more recently, of individual words in *Ouvrez*, words held back by a screen which prevents the self from— literally—'speaking its mind' in public exchanges (exchanges whose insignificance for the self is

enlarged definition of the sense of 'tu' allows one to recognize a certain fictional quality in the 'you' I represent, although Benveniste acknowledges this as merely a possible feature rather than a constitutive element of address: 'Quand je sors de "moi" pour établir une relation vivante avec un être, je rencontre *ou je pose* nécessairement un "tu", qui est, hors de moi, la seule "personne" *imaginable*' (1966: 232; my emphases). The way we 'invent' our interlocutors is vividly dramatized throughout Sarraute's fiction; Valerie Minogue, in the *Notice* to *Le Planétarium* (*OC* 1799–1811), describes how, in the bookshop scene in that novel, 'le lecteur se trouve sur un terrain foncièrement indéterminé, où chaque "personnage" invente l'autre [. . .] Nous trouvons-nous à l'intérieur d'un Alain qui interprète —voire invente—son père, qui, lui, est en train d'"inventer" Alain? ou est-ce le père qui est le "romancier", se plaçant à l'intérieur du fils pour se voir lui-même de la façon dont il imagine que son fils peut le voir?' (p. 1803).

thus emphasized). By *Entre la vie et la mort*, then, faith in the reading public has virtually disappeared, yet the fiction can still be entertained that behind the appearance of conventionality there might hide that ideal reader who could then be 'reclaimed' by the writer. In the central section of the novel, the fictional writer and his text are confronted with what seems to be an undesirable supporter, a man who enthuses about the work in the metalanguage of criticism where words are lifeless objects (because not animated by sensation): 'Des mots sans lien visible entre eux . . . ils tombent durs et drus, ils tambourinent contre lui sans pénétrer. De temps à autre il parvient à en attraper quelques-uns au passage: Symbolisme. Surréalisme. Impressionnisme' (*EVM* 99). Worst of all, this reader's analysis focuses on what he sees as the novel's empty centre: 'C'est un silence. C'est une rupture dans le temps . . . Cette scène dans la salle d'attente déserte d'une gare . . . C'est un temps mort. Un centre détruit. Tout le livre gravite autour de lui' (pp. 99–100). Not only is there no empty waiting room in this novel (thus the bad reader does not even read accurately); the very concept of a decentred structure contradicts the writer's view of his novel articulated previously:[21] 'Il est impossible qu'ils ne le voient pas. C'est là, surgi du néant [. . .] Au centre de cela il y a quelque chose d'indestructible. Un noyau qu'il n'est pas possible de désintégrer, vers lequel toutes les particules convergent, autour duquel elles gravitent à une vitesse si énorme qu'elle donne à l'ensemble l'apparence de l'immobilité' (p. 91).[22] By failing to see that the centre is full rather than empty, the admiring reader seems to be just another of those whose gaze here too turns the text into an object, destroying all hope of contact: 'Leurs regards passent et repassent sur cela distraitement sans le voir [. . .] Ils étalent sur cela une même couche sale d'enduit' (p. 92).

This reader is suddenly redeemed, however, for his response

[21] Again, Sarraute clearly gives the writer and not the reader authority over the determination of textual meaning; the reader's role is purely to confirm the truth of what the writer has felt: 'Tout ce qu'il lui fallait, c'est qu'ils lui montrent qu'ils sentent comme lui cette présence, que c'est bien là pour eux aussi [. . .] juste qu'ils confirment cela' (p. 93).

[22] This view is implicitly Sarraute's too. Aside from the fact that this discussion takes place in the centre of her novel (the twelfth of its twenty-two sections), the fictional writer's view of his work echoes her own perception of the purpose of writing: 'Quand je me suis enfin décidée à écrire un roman, ce ne fut que pour que ces mouvements puissent se développer sur un plus vaste espace et *rayonner d'un même centre*' ('Forme et contenu du roman', *OC* 1668, my emphasis; this previously unpublished lecture dates from the mid-1960s).

turns out to be based on sensation after all: the image of emptiness struck him because of the feeling it produced, not because it suggested that the whole work was a non-referential fabrication.[23] Far from advertising the postmodern emptiness of the linguistic structure which contains it, the image has an inherent expressive power: 'Voyez-vous, ce qui est important, c'est l'impression qui m'est restée. Peu importe le souvenir précis. Seule la sensation compte' (p. 102). The conventional reader reveals himself to be a good reader, as the writer finally looks him in the eye: 'Des yeux limpides d'enfant où il n'est pas possible de trouver le moindre soupçon de rage contenue, de désarroi . . . des yeux paisibles se posent sur les siens' (p. 102). Here the subject's gaze is reciprocated by one which lacks any differentiating quality, placing this exchange of glances outside the social dynamic of aggression and domination, and emphasizing the idea that being a good reader involves bearing no trace of otherness (an outlook of course not without its own aggressive implications, as *Les Fruits d'or* has just shown). The admirer here seems to fulfil that requirement, for in addition to having a clear, unindividuated gaze, he has approached the writer's most recent work through his earlier writings, thus following the writer's own trajectory.[24]

Yet if in this case the menace of an 'aberrant' reading (specifically a poststructuralist analysis of empty centres) is overcome, the scene also recognizes that the identification of the good reader is fraught with danger, for his status as such is never entirely certain. If what starts out as an alienated critical reading can redeem itself in this way, the border between the conventional reader and the ideal reader becomes dangerously permeable, especially given that the latter is capable of speaking in the vocabulary of the former. Even the good reader, previously celebrated in *Les Fruits d'or*, remains, as a separate individual, susceptible to conventional discourse. Aware of this unreliability, *Entre la vie et la mort* takes to its extreme the

---

[23] The empty room does in fact exist in the novel, though not in a railway station; that image came from a little-known earlier work by the writer, thus giving added cause for the reader's rehabilitation and extending the union between writer and reader back into the past.

[24] In *L'Usage de la parole*, the authorial voice is similarly gratified to find that the addressed readers remember the phrase 'Si tu continues, Armand, ton père va préférer ta sœur' from *Entre la vie et la mort* (*UP* 49; *EVM* 56). Yet as we shall see, by this point the readers are perceived to be so far from the author that their familiarity with Sarraute's earlier work comes as 'une vraie surprise' (*UP* 49), and is not enough to reunite her with them.

assimilation of the ideal reader-as-double to the writing self by creating a model reader who, unlike the good but public reader, is *literally* part of that self: 'Une moitié de moi-même se détache de l'autre' (p. 69). The *alter ego* in *Entre la vie et la mort* seems to be the ideal interlocutor because it is connected with the self prior to language: if language aims to convey a prelinguistic sensation to another, the bond of identity between self and *alter ego* should guarantee the realization of that aim. It seems to represent the culmination of a progression towards perfect communication, where language, and thus the text, would become redundant once it led the interlocutors back to a common ground prior to it.

This is not what happens, however, for if the figure of the *alter ego* embodies the desire for an ideal reader identical to the author, it actually ends up illustrating the fact that the reader will *always* be irreducibly other. In order to be a model for the reader, this self-identical double must read, but in the very act of reading it becomes different from the self. The text, at the end, remains necessary in order to call it back again: 'Vous mon double, mon témoin . . . là, penchez-vous avec moi . . . ensemble regardons' (p. 174). The text's language becomes paradoxically a sort of line thrown out to hook a reader who has been (and will be again) made other by the very act of reading it, and draw him in to where the author is. Thus the text simultaneously establishes the distance of addressor from addressee, and attempts to undo that distance by dissimulating the linguistic nature of what connects them in favour of a metaphorically sensory bond.[25]

Before looking at how the double becomes invaded by otherness, we can note that the writer's conception of its initial sameness involves the same kind of domination as that to which the reader of 'Les Fruits d'Or' was happy to submit; here, however, it prevents the double from doing what it is ostensibly required to do, namely read independently. So while on the one hand the writer complains that 'Vous me donnez ce que j'attends', and pleads 'Écartez-vous, oubliez-moi' (p. 70), yet when the double exercises this desired autonomy, it ceases to be condoned as a double and is rejected. If its

---

[25] The text's language is described as secreted naturally, though the 'organism' which secretes it is an image, and so itself already symbolic: 'Cette image dense, lourdement chargée [. . .] palper encore et encore tout autour, appuyer . . . jusqu'à ce qu'enfin de là des mots commencent à sourdre . . . Voilà . . . Des mots suintent en une fine traînée de gouttelettes tremblantes . . . se déposent sur le papier . . .' (p. 166).

value for the writer seems to lie precisely in its additional perspective—'Soyez sûr. Soyez dur. Surtout pas de ménagements. Que
vais-je devenir si vous aussi comme moi . . .' (pp. 70–1)—it is none
the less denied independence from or equal status with the writer
who strictly monitors its input to the text. The writer's desire for the
double's autonomy is thus far from total (the desire for a double and
the desire for an autonomous other are indeed contradictory), but it
allows the fictional double to stand for the real novel's real readers,
with the implication that the closer these remain to the authorial
subject of the text and the more completely they submit to it, the
truer their reading will be. The double, in fact, is invited to read
critically only at an early stage of composition; when the final version is produced (significantly by the writing self alone: 'Maintenant
laissez-moi. J'ai besoin d'être seul': p. 72), its role as reader is simply
to approve it, merging with the writer in a joint 'nous' or an even
more singular 'on': 'Il semble que cette fois nous ne pouvons pas
nous y tromper. C'est là [. . .] Mais regardons de plus près, exam-
inons mot après mot [. . .] Voyons . . . on le prend?' (p. 74). Change
to the writer's final version is resisted ('Vite, replacez ce mot où il
était': p. 74); where surface changes are made, in order to give the
'cela' which is at the heart of the text 'plus d'abondance, plus de
force' (p. 75), a nagging doubt remains that the change might be for
the worse. This degradation is conceived as a loss of human presence in the text's language, a dehumanizing of its voice, as though it
were artificially reproduced (something clearly not associated with
writing *per se*): 'Ne dirait-on pas par moments que [la voix] est trans-
mise par un haut-parleur ou bien enregistrée sur un disque? N'a-t-
elle pas perdu par endroits ses intonations hésitantes, un peu
craintives . . . son léger tremblement?' (p. 75).

For the good of the text, then, the reading double must submit to
the writer, since the writer is the expressive source of the text. But in
Entre la vie et la mort this does not actually happen, for once the double
begins to read, its perspective becomes detached from the (fictional)
text's authorial intentionality. Not surprisingly, in Sarraute's
terms this alienation from the act of enunciation means a fall into
conventionality and artifice (the double's voice, like that which was
already feared to contaminate the text, acquires 'des notes
métalliques', p. 169). By invoking public norms of language against
the writer's unique expression, it is deemed to have sold out, joining
the social ranks of convention-bound bad readers: 'C'est que nous

ne sommes plus seuls comme autrefois, vous et moi. Ils sont tous là
[. . .] j'entends cette rumeur qui monte d'eux et couvre votre voix
. . . La couvre? Ou avec elle se confond?' (p. 169). It has abandoned
its earlier criteria for artistic merit, no longer hoping to engage with
the text as something alive, but turning it into an object by its gaze
and its abstract critical language. The text's creator, who in the
service of sensation intentionally infringes stylistic conventions,
reproaches the double:

A peine vous détachez-vous de moi—mon double qui va se placer à bonne distance et observe—que sous votre regard étrangement tout se transforme . . .
Comme cela paraît terne . . . un peu mou . . . ou par endroits trop dur et clinquant
. . . lâché . . . raide . . . contourné bizarrement . . . mièvre, coquet, ridiculement pré-
cieux, éloquent [. . .] ces termes que vous employez maintenant, que vous avez toujours dédaignés . . . vous vous en souvenez, deux mots tout bêtes nous suffisaient, à
vous et à moi, juste ces deux mots: c'est mort. C'est vivant. (p. 169)

The way that reading turns the double from a projected second
self into a stranger who is part of the public domain seems to
acknowledge on one level the way language introduces difference
not only between self and other but even within the self, between the
self which utters and that which interprets the utterance. Once the
self relates through the language of the text to itself as creator of
the text, it forgoes any immediate relation to itself. And in so far as
the language of the text is the expression of a linguistically structured subject, *all* attempts to relate to oneself will be instances of self-
difference. As a subject of language, the self is other even to itself, for
knowing itself through the medium of symbols it can no more fuse
with itself than with another. By using the double as a model reader,
Sarraute paradoxically affirms that in relations conducted through
language, the addressee will necessarily be different from the
addressor, even when the self is its own addressee. Although
the double starts out as an invalid model for the reader, given the
reader's otherness to the writer, the way the language of the text
comes between even the self as writer and as its own reader in fact
illustrates how the real reader cannot but be other to the writer.

Sarraute, however, while showing the double's metamorphosis,
resists its implications. She maintains an assertion of the self's
integrity by having the alienated double become an entirely
different character; thus the writer can free himself from that part of
him which, reading, had become different. Yet even the self which

exists prior to the creation of the double[26] is subject to the dead language of convention; once again, this is attributed to pernicious outside influences which can be rejected, preserving the expressive language of true literature. This mode of almost wilful alienation in language, the act of surrendering to the language of others instead of remaining within one's own authentic idiom, is consistently for Sarraute the only sense in which one can be (literally) a subject of language: 'Les mots sont ses souverains. Leur humble sujet se sent trop honoré de leur céder sa maison. Qu'ils soient chez eux, tout est à eux ici, ils sont les seuls maîtres [. . .] Il est pris dans le dédale de leurs miroirs, emprisonné dans les entrelacs de leur reflets . . . Il tourne, renvoyé des uns aux autres . . .' (pp. 68–9).

Unsurprisingly, though, the writer's escape from conventional language into authentic expression fails to leave behind entirely those marks of subjection to language which, structurally identical to the markers of alienated social discourse, are (as we saw in Chapter 3) intrinsic to expression and perceptible to a reader. Extracting an authentic utterance from the 'dead' conventional text demands the kind of objectifying gaze associated elsewhere in the novel (p. 92) with bad reading: 'Les revoir . . . A distance cette fois, il les contemple [. . .] Son regard patine sur leurs surfaces luisantes' (p. 69). Here the words of the dead text, already objects before they are gazed on ('tout lisses, rigides et droits'), are held responsible for the nature of his gaze; yet wherever the responsibility lies, being the subject of such a gaze unifies the self and so makes it into a *moi*. This is doubly illustrated by the text, as the first-person perspective of the writer's 'je' takes over and compounds that display of coherence by creating what turns out to be an only superficially autonomous copy of itself: 'Une moitié de moi-même se détache de l'autre: un témoin. Un juge' (p. 69).

If even the rebellion against 'dead' literary discourse cannot avoid turning the writer's self into a *moi*, it is not surprising that the opposition between inherently expressive language and a conventional writing which does no more than rearrange already-spoken

---

[26] And who also reads his own text—this initial reading and rewriting which is not advertised as such breaks down the distinction between writing and reading which the creation of a double established, and so illustrates Antoine Compagnon's description of their inseparability: 'Le travail de l'écriture est une récriture dès lors qu'il s'agit de convertir des éléments séparés et discontinus en un tout continu et cohérent, de les rassembler, de les comprendre (de les prendre ensemble), c'est-à-dire de les lire' (1979: 32).

words with no regard for the unnameable 'cela', can never be established absolutely, remaining instead an endlessly pursued ideal. The writer's restoration of expressive life to his text is condemned to follow the same metaphoric procedure as did the previous alienation of that life in conventional language (see Ch. 3, s. 2): the translation of the original minimal unit of language which bears the tropism ('des bribes de conversation [. . .] une intonation, un accent qu'un mouvement rapide traverse': p. 73) into other words and images. Indeed, the sense in which the relation of the new terms to the original tropistic utterance is an organic one is itself implicitly acknowledged to be purely metaphorical:

> N'est-il pas possible pour qu'il se reproduise avec plus de netteté et se développe de créer des conditions plus favorables? . . . le faire passer ailleurs, dans d'autres images mieux assemblées, d'autres paroles ou intonations, *comme on transplante une pousse sauvage dans un terrain amélioré*, enrichi de terreau, nourri d'engrais, dans un lieu bien clos, une serre où sera maintenue constamment une température appropriée? (p. 73; my emphasis)

If words should not be thought of as 'tout lisses, rigides et droits' (p. 69), it is not, as Sarraute's imagery suggests, because authentic language has an organic origin in the body and mind which host 'le ressenti', but because it is impossible to divorce the self from the universe of words which comprises its language and makes it into a linguistic subject. (Indeed, the way Sarraute's latest work, *Ouvrez*, presents the self in terms not only of the words it speaks but also of those it carries around in silence, goes very much in this direction.) Language is in one sense external rather than expressed from within, but to the extent that language also informs the mind to which it is external, the distinction between inside and outside, between the writing subject and writing as an object, breaks down. Thus if the writer rejects the 'external' language of the dead text, what he privileges instead of it, language as propelled outward, itself projecting images in turn, and all run through by the same current (*EVM* 73–4), is conventional from the outset and can only aspire to be otherwise through the elementary conventional mechanism of metaphor. It is not the unmediated expression of sensation but its symbolized representation; though spontaneous, it will always be 'outside' that sensation.

The mind's inevitable symbolization of experience is thus visibly at work in Sarraute's authorial discourse which consequently cannot avoid enacting language's objectification of other and self. Yet her pursuit of the ideal of a language which might overcome this alienation of the self from itself and from the other persists through the search for ever more potent, more 'immediate' metaphors and metonymies. This paradoxical but determined ambition to undo distance within the very linguistic structure which establishes it perhaps accounts for the almost obsessive way Sarraute's works repeatedly return to the same themes in similar fictional situations. The text is an attempt to undo the reader's distance in a merging of perspectives: 'Vous mon double, mon témoin . . . là, penchez-vous avec moi' (p. 174).[27] Yet the authorial voice as a subject of language can establish communication only within the terms of what language as representation allows. Because language gives form to the ineffable self, the act of addressing the reader confirms addressor and addressee as separate entities even as it attempts to fuse them into one. And because author and reader are and will remain discrete subjects of language, the attempt by one to create such fusion becomes an attempt to compromise the otherness of the interlocutor. If it ultimately proves impossible to draw the reader of the Sarrautean text entirely out of his social universe it is because the author as a subject of language lives there too; thus her whole attempt to evict the social is conditioned by language, the code which gives form to social relations. And it is because the author–reader dialogue around the text takes place fully in the social sphere that the reader remains able to respond, from his position as other, to the text's attempts to suppress that otherness, and so, as Chambers argues, enables the text to function in ever new contexts of reading.

Entre la vie et la mort thus illustrates a double pull in Sarraute's writing. On one hand, there is an attempt to construct an addressee in the addressor's image, in a determined neutralization of the other's difference. On the other, the mediation prominent in the author–text–reader dialogue, and inherent to dialogue generally, reasserts the distance between addressor and addressee (between

---

[27] Arnaud Rykner describes this ambition and implies that Sarraute realizes it in *L'Usage de la parole*: 'Destinateur et destinataire se retrouvent non plus face à face, mais quasiment côte à côte, pour aborder ensemble les épreuves de la quête [. . .] Par-delà le sens délivré de l'un à l'autre, domine le lien créé *entre* l'un et l'autre. Avant ce qui sera dit, vient la nécessité d'établir le rapport avec celui pour qui cela est dit' (1991: 12–13). The attitude of *L'Usage de la parole* to the reader will be the subject of the next and final section of this chapter.

expression and interpretation). When the reader fails to be completely domesticated, and the impossibility of withdrawing his freedom of interpretation is realized, he is both rejected for his determination by convention yet also solicited anew in the hope that this difference could be eliminated: 'Il faut bien le laisser revenir, il ne m'est pas possible de m'en passer [. . .] Où qu'il se place, près d'eux, loin d'eux, il ne pourra pas ne pas être conquis' (p. 171). Yet unlike *Les Fruits d'or*, this novel does not end optimistically as far as the ambition of fusing with the reader is concerned, even if this reader started out as part of the self. He remains under the influence of the group and their mass hypnosis: 'Il est serré contre eux, l'un des leurs, tout pareil à eux [. . .] je le tire, je me cramponne à lui de toutes mes forces . . . restez près de moi, restons entre nous, je vous en conjure, oubliez-les . . .' (p. 172). This pessimism will increase as Sarraute's work continues: when, with *L'Usage de la parole*, the authorial subject comes to address the reader directly, it is not a single soulmate of the kind envisaged in *Les Fruits d'or* which is anticipated as its audience, but the convention-bound public.[28]

3. The reader as other and as addressee

Aside from implying that no hope remains of finding a double of the authorial self within the public, *L'Usage de la parole* also marks a formal change in Sarraute's approach to the question of reading: rather than representing the text–reader relationship as part of a fictional world, it addresses its readers directly, in an openly dialogical move.[29] From this point on, in fact, Sarraute's prose texts

[28] The homogeneity of the readership anticipated in *L'Usage de la parole*, echoing that of the reading public in *Entre la vie et la mort* ('on est comme galvanisés', *EVM* 172), is underlined by Sheila Bell: 'The audience does not manifest individual, potentially contradictory responses; it functions as a collective entity' (1983: 56). By contrast, Valerie Minogue's claim that 'the plural allows a plurality of response and shifts of stance in the reader' (1983: 44) seems debatable.

[29] In taking the narrator of *L'Usage de la parole* to be authorial, and the narratees to represent Sarraute's perception of her readers, I follow her own indications. Introducing, in 1981, a set of tape-recorded readings from *Tropismes* and *L'Usage de la parole* (see Bibliography), she comments on the later collection: 'Sans le vouloir et tout à fait spontanément, dans ces textes je m'adresse au lecteur parce que j'ai comme l'illusion qu'après tant de temps [. . .] j'ai tout de même fini par acquérir quelques lecteurs qui me suivent, qui me sont proches, je ne les

will all cultivate the character of 'work in progress', of being written as we read them. In *L'Usage de la parole*, the creation of the text is fore-grounded in the way questions which spur on the narration are attributed to its readers (e.g. *UP* 22–3). The same impression of narration and reading being simultaneous is clear in the 'aucun mot écrit' assertion of *Enfance* (*E* 9) as well as in its highly dramatic form, a form repeated in the authorial dialogue of *Tu ne t'aimes pas* or the dialogues among words of *Ouvrez*, and one which borrows from drama the illusion of happening in our presence.[30] Before looking at the kind of relationship *L'Usage de la parole* enacts to a present but distant readership, I wish to discuss briefly the way Sarraute's writing cultivates the impression of being a currently happening event, working against the inevitable fate of the published text to be experienced by the reader as a representation removed in time and space from the moment of composition.

Even before *L'Usage de la parole* introduced this new focus on the writing of the actual text rather than of a fictional one, and at the same time on the reception of that text by an addressee ostensibly present to the authorial narrator, Sarraute's writing had always cultivated a sense of immediacy. The action of the earlier novels may take place within a fictional world rather than appearing to unfold in their readers' presence as the later ones do. Yet the way this world subsumes and so dissimulates the act of representation which creates it (by making the act of writing part of the story, as in the early first-person narratives) achieves through opposite means the same apparent simultaneity of event and representation as the inverse emphasis on the process of composition over the story does

---

connais pas mais j'ai cette illusion—j'en ai besoin pour travailler—que nous cheminons ensemble'. That Sarraute sees these faithful readers as indeed ultimately an illusion is demonstrated by the way their closeness dissipates once they become characterized as real, public readers.

[30] The immediacy drama affects merely conceals its real status as endlessly repeatable representation, as Paul Ricoeur has pointed out: 'La dimension théâtrale consiste en cela: oublier la situation de citation que produit la représentation. Le spectateur croit entendre de vraies personnes. Mais que le rideau retombe, et l'illusion aussitôt s'envole, la pièce entière retourne à son statut de fiction *rapportée*' (1991: 43). While the work which comes between *Tu ne t'aimes pas* and *Ouvrez*, *Ici* (1995), abandons this openly dialogic structure, continuing the withdrawal from engagement with its projected readers already visible in *Tu ne t'aimes pas*, its first-person, present-tense accounts of 'trous de mémoire' (see especially sections I–III and XX), among other subjects, remain highly dramatic. I shall discuss *Ici* at more length in the Conclusion.

later.[31] This effect of simultaneity allows us to forget that in reading we are interpreting an endlessly reproducible representation rather than listening to a 'live' address—thus the first-person narrators of *Portrait d'un inconnu* and *Martereau* give the novels a source *within* the fiction and so invite us to forget that the real source of the text is absent (and that a comparable distance separates our own position as readers from the ideal addressees called up by the fiction). This use of fictional representatives of the writing self is alluded to in *L'Usage de la parole*, though the absence of the authorial subject is here explained as a purely conscious choice—the result of timidity—rather than as illustrating a fundamental inability to be present in one's text. The authorial narrator of 'Eh bien quoi, c'est un dingue' describes a fictional character's invented story of another individual terrified by the sight of a crack in a wall and the liquid seeping through it. This obvious allusion to a seminal scene from *Portrait d'un inconnu* (*PI* 148–52; cp. *P* 25–8) implicitly acknowledges that the earlier novel's narrator-character was a stand-in for the real, absent source of the representation, by admitting how on both levels of the fiction in 'Eh bien quoi, c'est un dingue' narrators write themselves into the event they narrate by means of an invented representative: '[Il s'est servi] craintivement, pudiquement, de ce pauvre homme qui se lève, parfois même la nuit, pour regarder, pour arrêter, retenir, colmater [. . .] il l'a poussé devant soi lâchement pour se protéger [. . .] Et moi, qui ai pris tant de précautions, qui ai cru bon de m'entourer d'une double protection [. . .] (*UP* 117).

Sarraute abandons the first-person narrator after *Martereau*, heightening even more the 'event' quality of her writing over its status as representation through this removal of even a fictional representing perspective involved in the action, in favour of an ever-increasing dissolution of all narrating authority. (When the 'je' reappears in *L'Usage de la parole* it will be to enliven with an illusory

---

[31] In fact, the represented event begins to merge with the text which represents it in *Les Fruits d'or*, where the names of fictional and real novel are identical; similarly, *Entre la vie et la mort* makes the represented event part of the act of writing the text itself, when the novel being written reveals itself to be the one we are reading (*EVM* 168). Having the fictional novel, and the fiction of writing it, turn out to be identical to the real novel being read, seems to be a kind of auto-erasure of the fiction, the last stage before attention shifts definitively from an invented story to the act of invention itself. In *'disent les imbéciles'* Valerie Minogue notes 'des remarques d'écrivain [. . .] Une sorte de "voix off" qui commente la substance textuelle au fur et à mesure que celle-ci se sécrète, qui examine et pèse les mots qu'on est en train de lire' (*OC* 1901).

presence not a represented event but the act of writing itself.) A narrative dominated by free indirect discourse and the present tense succeeds in virtually effacing the distance in space and time of the narratorial point of view from the events it represents. Free indirect discourse lets a character's experience be represented at a less conscious or reflexive level than would be possible if he were to speak for himself (see Ch. 1, p. 29; Cohn 1978: 56), while when used in the present tense it minimizes what narrative distance it must inevitably retain from that represented experience. Thus the perspectives of both narrator and character are first deprived of distance from the event (the narrator's perspective is located in the present and in the mind of the character, while the character lacks the distance self-expression would imply); second, they are harnessed together in such a way that each prevents the other from being identified as the point of view which is representing the event. On the level of the story, this dissimulation of the activity of representation gives the character's experience of the events an immediacy which lets the reader live them vicariously, reducing his interpretative distance in favour of a minimally reflective, imaginative participation which is part of the pleasure of reading fiction generally, and of reading Sarraute's in particular.

The kind of narrative perspective Sarraute's texts favour, one which dissimulates their status as representation in favour of the event they relate, also works of course to minimize what she perceives as the public reader's potentially dangerous autonomy regarding the authentic expressive text which needs to be protected against distortion. Thus the discursive strategies whose effects on the reader are pleasurable in so far as they involve him as a vicarious participant in the event, associate that reading pleasure with an element of powerlessness by working to keep him from interpreting the textual discourse in his own terms. (The fact that part of the pleasure of reading Sarraute may reside in the submission she invites of the reader should not be lost sight of in this discussion of the strategies of power involved in the dialogue of text and reader, or indeed in dialogue generally.)

The direct address to the readers of *L'Usage de la parole* seems to be another such discursive strategy: if the projected ideal reader repeatedly falls back into the reading public, as in *Entre la vie et la mort*, thus suggesting that Sarraute now sees as her actual audience readers who don't empathize fully with the intention animating her writing, then the only way to counter the freedom of this plural, distant readership, at least for the duration of the work, is by addressing it directly.[32] The text just mentioned, 'Eh bien quoi, c'est un dingue', aside from alluding to the public's uncomprehending reaction to *Portrait d'un inconnu* (figured in the reaction of the fictional narrator's interlocutor), clearly demonstrates both a lack of faith in its present readership, and the way a direct address attempts to prevent a similarly dismissive judgement of this text: 'Et moi, qui ai pris tant de précautions, qui ai cru bon de m'entourer d'une double protection, comment m'empêcher, pendant que je vous raconte cette histoire, de vous imaginer par moments m'observant avec cet étrange regard, ce sourire, et vous disant à vous-mêmes: "Eh bien quoi, c'est un dingue"' (p. 117).

This is a particularly vivid example of the way direct address reduces the readers' scope for response, for it confronts them with what it takes to be their likely reaction and deplores it in advance. But even aside from this proscriptive element, the very fact of addressing readers who are in reality absent and unidentified at the moment of writing, attempts to reduce their interpretative distance from the authorial utterance by postulating the presence of both parties to each other in the text. The author's voice, fearing to be lost once its utterance is written and open to all kinds of readings, implants itself firmly in the text in a dialogue with readers it posits. In this way, future readers whose engagement with the text will necessarily take place in the absence of its author, none the less encounter an addressing voice which, as long as they agree to identify with its 'vous', appears to be directly present to them.

I have argued that writing simply magnifies an alienation also characteristic of spoken communication. Given that *L'Usage de la parole* focuses on the dynamics of conversation as these are manifested in invented dialogues, it is not surprising to find it sensitive to the way, in face-to-face encounters, the power that goes with being an addressor can be exploited to control a distant addressee. 'A très

---

[32] Though studies of *L'Usage de la parole* comment widely on the way it addresses the reader, they generally overlook its implicit criticism of that readership. Thus Arnaud Rykner sees in the work 'une intimité réelle [...] entre l'écrivain à l'écoute des mouvements intérieurs du préconscient et le lecteur à l'écoute de l'écrivain' (1991: 12). Maurice Nadeau does comment on the way the text aims to overwhelm its readers (though without pursuing why they need to be overwhelmed): 'Quand la guerrière déploie ses troupes, attaque, nous surprend et pourfend au moment où nous nous y attendions le moins, occupée que nous la croyions à de subtiles manœuvres, il n'y a plus qu'à rendre les armes' (1980: 7).

bientôt' describes a relationship between two friends where one talks compulsively to the other whose responses are minimal, yet where at the end of their encounters, 'celui des deux qui a le plus parlé, à en être épuisé, sent au moment où ils vont se séparer comme une faim inassouvie, comme un manque' (p. 24), and immediately arranges the next meeting. The situation closely resembles the way Sarraute's own texts function, both the way they participate in the necessarily one-sided character of all text–reader exchanges and, in Sarraute's particular case, the way each work picks up again obsessively on the themes of the previous ones, as if to complete what they had left unsaid.[33] In the case of the two friends, this uncontrollable 'flot de paroles' (p. 22) turns out to be the reaction to a distance which is sensed in the other despite the intimacy of a friendship in which he appears to the speaker to be 'un autre moi-même' (p. 27). That this hoped-for identity of the addressee, and its disappointment, is equally a feature of the address to the readers of *L'Usage de la parole* is shown in 'Eh bien quoi, c'est un dingue'. There the address of the fictional narrator (who is admitted to be merely a protective front for the authorial voice) rests on a belief in the other's identity with the self (a belief exploded by the retort of the title): 'Il est indispensable que celui qui se met à raconter ait la certitude que l'autre qui est là, devant lui, tout prêt à l'écouter [. . .] que par-delà quelques apparences, quelques détails de peu d'importance l'autre lui ressemble' (pp. 110–11).

The fictional situation of 'A très bientôt' can thus be seen as a figure of Sarraute's complex attitude to a reader simultaneously desired to be identical and recognized to be other. There, protracted address is used unconsciously to counteract the alterity of an interlocutor who, if he is physically present, is mentally absent. The text thus explicitly represents one-sided address like that of its own writing as involving an attempt to bring the otherness of the interlocutor under the speaker's control by circumscribing it in his discourse. At one point it seems to be aware of this similarity

---

[33] For the fictional speaker, 'quelque chose n'a pas abouti, quelque chose est resté en suspens' (p. 24). Examples of comparable obsessive repetition in *L'Usage de la parole* alone have already been noted: the leaking wall from *Portrait d'un inconnu*, and the mother's admonition to Armand from *Entre la vie et la mort* (see n. 24). In the latter case (which we are asked to excuse, p. 49: 'Il faut [. . .] pardonnez-moi, que j'y revienne [à ces paroles], je dois absolument les reprendre encore une fois'), the lack of means to express the 'si grande abondance' of what these words contain leaves the authorial voice as frustrated as the speaker in 'A très bientôt'; he feels 'un manque qui peut devenir parfois exaspérant, insupportable' (p. 49).

between what it describes and how it itself performs, and to attempt to undo it. Just after evoking 'le volume, la longueur' of this 'flot de paroles' which 's'écoule presque toujours dans le même sens' (p. 23), it reverses its own flow by switching its focus to its projected readers: 'Mais vous perdez déjà patience, vous vous apprêtez déjà à vous débarrasser de tout cela, à jeter cela à la poubelle, enfermé dans un de ces sacs fabriqués tout exprès: un flot de paroles de "bavard intarissable", d'"amoureux éperdu", d'"inférieur faisant sa cour"' (p. 23). Yet of course even this contribution by the readers is dictated by the authorial voice and merely creates the illusion that the communication is not all one-way, while in fact intensifying the circumscription of the addressees' otherness by speaking on their behalf. In addition, depicting the readers as capable of offering only reductive clichés reinforces the author's right to engage in a monologue. Incapable, according to the text, of seeing what is really going on in the fictional encounter, those who read it must be *told* the truth rather than being invited to help create it.

The represented speaker ultimately realizes the reason for his obsessive monologues. What reveals his perception of the other as a double ('[ce] avec quoi on se fond [. . .] ce qui en amour comme en amitié s'appelle si bien "un autre moi-même"': p. 27) to be an illusion, is the intervention of a third figure whose relation to the would-be double (he finds him 'orgueilleux', p. 27) modifies the speaker's view of him. Thus here too, as earlier in *Les Fruits d'or* and later in *Tu ne t'aimes pas* (see Ch. 3, s. 3), a third figure breaks up a binary relation of self-loss in the other in a way not dissimilar to the Lacanian Oedipus. Moreover, as with Lacan and unlike in the other cases where the conventional values embodied in the intruder destroy an authentic self–other relationship, the third figure here represents truth, the experience of fusion having been an illusion. A second outsider seems to confirm this lesson in relativity and discredit the whole idea of a binary relation of full mutual knowledge, by claiming an affection for the absent interlocutor which the original speaker knows is not reciprocated; this casts doubt on whether his own affection is returned. Confirmation that it is not comes with the new figure's revelation that in the presence of their shared addressee he too has the same irrepressible urge to speak and the same sense of unfulfilment on parting. The compulsive address is thus revealed to be the effect of the lack of reciprocity both experience in their dialogues with the absent other.

Yet if this third figure destroys the fusion of the first two, the text as a whole resists the seemingly inescapable conclusion that unknowability is always an element of self–other relations, despite the illusions we foster that the other is transparent to us. At the last minute, the possibility of an immediate relationship is reasserted in opposition to the alienation which causes such ignorance of the other. In a move which is the exact reverse of Lacan's (Hegelian) conception of human development,[34] the relativistic triad itself becomes the source of a new authentic dualism which leads both parties to the truth (for Lacan, of course, the Oedipal triangle always relapses into Imaginary duality too, but this is a refuge from authentic subjectivity rather than its fulfilment): '[Il] voit dans l'autre sa propre image, vers laquelle, tel Narcisse, il se tend . . . il se voit, oui, c'est lui-même courant, parlant, serrant la main, sollicitant [. . .] Il crie: Je suis comme vous, exactement comme vous [. . .] Et aussitôt chez l'autre cet acquiescement, si rapide, sans une hésitation [. . .] ah enfin tu as vu, tu as trouvé enfin . . .' (pp. 30–1). The text refuses to relinquish the ideal of a hierarchy of relations in which the mutual otherness of addressor and addressee in dialogue remains an inferior option. Instead of the vain attempt to 'hook' the elusive other through one's discourse, this text pursues the dream of a preferable mode of communication, distinct from the way language mediates inadequately between the opposite poles of addressor and addressee. The members of the new dualism have both been identified as addressors (the same role Sarraute holds in the text–reader interaction); their fusion thus takes place at the same pole of dialogue and so renders that dialogue superfluous.

This is of course in practical terms an unviable model, for even these two know each other only through what they say to each other, and so their perceived sameness is inferred through their words rather than intuited prior to them. But this dilemma, the fact that users of language can only project a prelinguistic mode of being or of relation across the terms of that language, epitomizes the whole 'impossible realism'[35] which drives Sarraute's writing, its struggle to

---

[34] See especially the essay 'Subversion du sujet et dialectique du désir' (Lacan 1966: 793–827; also 292–3, 837). For a summary of Lacan's debt to Hegel, see Dor (1985: 166–73).
[35] The phrase is of course Gerda Zeltner's (1962) who stresses the poetic nature of Sarraute's literary language, despite the realistic impetus behind her writing: 'Elle arrache ces situations humaines au monde de la psychologie et de la description pour les faire s'épanouir sur le plan de la vision et de la poésie' (p. 599). The impossibility of articulating the

express a visceral sensation within the received constraints of the sign system of language. The desire to escape language and accede to the formless tropistic self corresponds to the desire to establish a relation of identity with an other without the need for the mediation of language (which makes that identity impossible, even with the self). But just as tropistic expression is constructed from within the conventional, public structure of language, dialogue (including reading) can only be the product of the alienation of the expressive intention in the utterance, and the addressee's creation, out of that utterance, of his own understanding of its meaning.

Discovering a soulmate this side of dialogue means that for the subject of 'A très bientôt' the effort to seduce the distant other can be abandoned. Yet if Sarraute continues to write for her distant public, it is because in reality there is no such fairy-tale solution to the problem of communication. The final text of *L'Usage de la parole*, 'Je ne comprends pas', closes (and so ends the collection) with the recognition that the ideal dialogue it has evoked, where mutual alienation and intimidation give way to open, truthful communication, is a fantasy, 'rien d'autre qu'un conte de fées' (p. 150). In the absence and impossibility of any ideal reading double, Sarraute must make do with the real readers of *L'Usage de la parole*. How is the threat posed by these readers and their conventional language to be dealt with by the expressive text?

'Ich sterbe' opens the collection, and it can be read as a paradigm of Sarraute's whole literary endeavour in its claim that the writer's living, expressive language overcomes not only the dead language of the other but even death itself.[36] The other and his language are here literally foreign (developing the image in *Les Fruits d'or* of the outsider's language as 'des pièces [. . .] rapportées d'un pays étranger': *FO* 17): 'Ich sterbe' recreates the subtext to the supposed last words of Chekhov, his announcement to his German doctor, in the words of the title, that he was about to die. Relations with this foreign other are, once again, opposed to relations with the

---

tropism is integral to Sarraute's own perception of her literary project, as Zeltner quotes *Le Planétarium* to point out: 'On n'a pas encore découvert ce langage qui pourrait exprimer d'un seul coup ce qu'on perçoit en un clin d'œil; tout un être et ces miriades de petits mouvements surgis dans quelques mots, un rire, un geste . . .' (*P* 33; Zeltner 1962: 600).

[36] This theme is pursued on a more personal level in *Ici* (1995), a collection of twenty short prose reflections on the self's interactions in language (both with itself and with others).

intimately known loved one who is part of the self: 'Il n'y a pas de "je meurs" entre nous, il n'y a que "nous mourons"' (p. 15). Thus death as that which terminates the true dialogue with the loved one emerges as a concern of Sarraute's well before real events introduce it into *Tu ne t'aimes pas* (see *TTP* 122), although here the writer faces his own death rather than that of the loved interlocutor. If death intervenes to abolish true dialogue with the transparent other, already united with the self in a 'nous' before either one speaks, it is inherent from the outset to the dialogue with the foreign other in his foreign language (as Robert Greene comments (1983: 200), 'the soul departs when authentic speech leaves'):

Pas nos mots à nous, trop légers, trop mous, ils ne pourront jamais franchir ce qui maintenant entre nous s'ouvre, s'élargit . . . une béance immense . . . mais des mots compacts et lourds que n'a jamais parcourus aucune vague de gaieté, de volupté, que n'a jamais fait battre aucun pouls, vaciller aucun souffle [. . .] Pas nos mots, mais des mots de circonstance solennels et glacés, des mots morts de langue morte. (*UP* 15–16)

The reason Chekhov chooses the dead language of the foreign (thus absolutely other) doctor is because its otherness illustrates what it should express, namely his impending separation from his wife in the solitary experience of death. By applying this dead language, which kills what it talks about, to the experience of his own extinction he (and ultimately Sarraute) in fact makes it refer: the very lack of an organic relation to a referent which would give it a living pulse makes the language of the other the ideal discourse of death. 'La langue de l'autre' (p. 12) is thus 'colonized' by the expressive subject in the particular threshold situation of death; he exploits its inability to express in order to speak his own similar inability, as it takes him over: 'Rassemblant ce qui me reste de forces, je tire ce coup de feu, j'envoie ce signal [. . .] Ich sterbe . . . Vous m'entendez? Je suis arrivé tout au bout . . . Je suis tout au bord . . . Ici où je suis est le point extrême' (p. 14). That objectification which is the effect of the other's language is given validity by becoming its referent too, in the announcement of the death of the one whom it names and who by speaking this objectification assumes his death: 'Avec ces mots bien affilés, avec cette lame d'excellente fabrication, elle ne m'a jamais servi, rien ne l'a émoussée, je devance le moment et moi-même je tranche: Ich sterbe' (p. 16).[37]

[37] This suggestion that the language of the other can be exploited to express what it metaphorically enacts (objectification being a metaphor for death), seems to make it for

How does this colonization of the language of the other by the expressive subject, in a dialogue which is not the living exchange of same with same but a signal to one who gazes on the self—'celui qui de là-bas m'observe' (p. 14)—in the way characteristic of alienated social interaction, relate to the text's exchange with a public reader-ship which is equally other, and whose presence as addressee is asserted from the first line of 'Ich sterbe'? The 'vous' addressed by the authorial voice are as distant from it as the doctor is from Chekhov in the address it describes. Despite a continuing attempt to assimilate their point of view to the writer's in the slide from 'vous allez voir' to 'ne nous hâtons pas' to the assertion of identical know-ledge in 'cette humilité que nous lui connaissons' (pp. 11–12), the readers of 'Ich sterbe' retain their distance throughout. Thus they are expected to see the recreation of the tropism as a mere pastime: 'Si certains d'entre vous trouvent ce jeu distrayant, ils peuvent [. . .] s'amuser à en déceler d'autres' (pp. 17–18).

To describe the work of writing the tropism as an amusing game is to speak the language of the public as Chekhov did. Yet this is not a similar abdication of life (in this case the tropism) to his; there is no sense that Sarraute is embracing this remote attitude and its abstract discourse as articulating more accurately than her own expressive idiom a new experience of reality as alienation. In her case, the writer's expressive discourse outlives its use of the other's (projected) idiom rather than succumbing to it and the death it embodies. (In fact even Chekhov did not entirely desert the writer's discourse, for his investment of the language of the other with expressive force was so intense that he immortalized even this dead discourse. After three-quarters of a century these words are still on fire, 'une petite braise qui noircit, brûle la page blanche' (p. 12), and so transcend not only the death inherent to them but also the dis-tance in time and space which separates them as written from the moment they were uttered.)

The difference between Sarraute and Chekhov is that whereas

Sarraute in this exceptional situation an agent of what Charles Sanders Peirce called *index-ical* representation, where a sign signifies something by being a trace of it. When the metaphorical deadliness of conventional discourse (in Peirce's terms it is an *icon* of death) is used to express the subject's actual experience of death, it becomes a product of that death, an *index* of it. It thus takes on the character of expressive language as Sarraute sees it, for such language is the organic product of bodily sensation and so an index of it. (For a concise sum-mary of the theory of signs elaborated in Peirce's *Philosophical Writings*, see Scholes 1981: 200–8, esp. 204.)

he used the language of the distant addressee to express its own life-lessness, she merely quotes it—not only in phrases like 'trouv[er] ce jeu distrayant' but also in the way the projected readers' questions are integrated into the text in 'Ich sterbe' and throughout *L'Usage de la parole*.[38] By quoting them, Sarraute turns the readers of her work into its characters rather than its addressees (see Ch. 5 n. 14). If 'Ich sterbe' illustrates how a staged dialogue with the reader not only fails to transcend the limited monologic world of its author but moreover tries to subordinate the addressee by defining his response, it also shows why Sarraute feels the need to exercise such close control over her readers: for her, the alternative to this mono-logic domination is nothing less than death, the death of the living textual voice at the hands of the reading public and its discourse from which the tropism is absent.

Quotation is of course the mechanism by which verbal irony works. Verbal irony is the irony of utterances which by not meaning what they say (by taking an attitude to their meaning, in Sperber and Wilson's terms—see Ch. 1 n. 25) appear to enact the expressive inadequacy of language and to grant their addressee an active role in the establishment of meaning. Yet I have argued that, to the extent that the attitude these utterances take is determinate and stable, what the addressee is called on to do is simply recognize it rather than cooperate in its creation. As we saw with *Les Fruits d'or* and *Entre la vie et la mort*, the role Sarraute accords her reader is similarly not the active participation in the text's realization she initially appears to solicit, but simple recognition of the text's truth in a passive gesture of affirmation. As verbal irony overcomes the deficiencies of its language, Sarraute's text establishes a monologic truth in spite of a largely (but not insuperably) conventional lan-guage, and presents it to the reader for his assent. But by *L'Usage de la parole*, the reader's role seems to have diminished even further, for he becomes the *object* of quotation rather than the addressee

---

[38] Sarraute also uses what Mikhail Bakhtin calls 'hidden dialogue' (1984*a*: 197)—indica-tions in the speaker's words alone that his interlocutor has responded—to represent the readers' input without interrupting her authorial discourse: 'Mais vous n'aviez voulu m'entendre . . . il n'est pires sourds . . . Non, pas vous?' (*UP* 49). Another even more attenuated (more monologic) form of narrative dialogism Bakhtin describes is hidden polemic, where the other's anticipated responses shape the speaker's utterance in what is in the end just a more blatant version of the ventriloquism any represented dialogue with the reader involves: 'Faut-il être à court . . . cela j'ai quelques bonnes raisons de penser que vous le direz [. . .] Mais vous vous trompez' (p. 49).

solicited through a represented ideal double. Moreover, the tone in which the projected readers are quoted is on occasion openly ironic, as when after prolonged meditation on the implications of the words 'Ton père' and 'Ta sœur', the narrator claims to agree with the unreceptive readers that the words are innocent—a claim which the context of the preceding investigation (not to mention Sarraute's whole literary career) undermines:

Non? vous ne voyez rien . . . vous avez beau répéter: 'Ton père. Ta sœur' . . . je le répète avec vous . . . vraiment, ne dirait-on pas que quelque chose . . . là . . . 'Ton père. Ta sœur' . . . Non? rien ne bouge? la paroi est toute lisse, immobile. 'Ton père. Ta sœur'? . . . vous devez avoir raison . . . il n'y a rien . . . rien qui puisse bouger, s'ouvrir, pas de paroi. (p. 62)

Of course quoting her readers in this way immediately acknowledges a new reader of that quotation, for the reality of reading exceeds all possible textual representations of it—which is precisely what gives the reader his dialogic value as absolute Other, able to establish the meaningfulness of the text.

My examination in this chapter of how Sarraute sees the text–reader relationship confirms the conclusions of Chapter 3 that the features she ascribes to conventional discourse cannot be evacuated entirely from her own writing, for they are basic elements of linguistic communication. Thus a major referent of her writing, the way social address includes a specific perception of its addressee and so turns that addressee into a character (which it dominates), is clearly also a feature of it.[39] The power-based social relationships Sarraute condemns are governed by the *regard*, and she strives for a different kind of dialogue with the reader by aiming to make him a co-subject rather than an object of her *regard*: 'Qu'on se donne la peine de [. . .] *l'observer* avec une certaine attention et on *perçoit* [. . .] si l'on parvient à le *fixer* assez longtemps . . . *regardez*' (*UP* 100–1; my emphasis). Yet elsewhere in *L'Usage de la parole* Sarraute herself unmasks this apparently equal coexistence within a single gaze as the kind of false social unity which can be achieved in the context of mutual objectification and which depends on one partner's submission to the other's reductive characterization:

[39]   That this domination is integral to all address is indicated by Émile Benveniste when he notes that '"je" est toujours *transcendant* par rapport à "tu"', a relation inverted when 'tu' becomes 'je' in turn (1966: 232).

Mais il peut arriver à l'un d'entre eux ou à tous deux de vouloir demeurer encore un peu dans cette forme où l'autre l'a enfermé et que l'autre continue à modeler, les rayons que son regard, son sourire laissent filtrer la lissent, la caressent [. . .] Il arrive que se sentant si bien maintenus, soutenus, que se sentant tout à fait confondus, ne faisant qu'un, ils se plaisent à promener autour d'eux un même regard. (p. 90)

If it is in the nature of address to deal with an image of its addressee whose otherness is necessarily beyond the speaker's grasp, a discourse like that of this study, which points out the way this takes place in Sarraute, will share the same reductiveness. In so far as a reader's interpretation of a text is also a response to its address, involving him in a dialogue with it as respondent, as well as with his own anticipated readers as addressor, that response will enact the same kind of definition or objectification of the text as the text's address to him does (and as his to his anticipated readers will in turn—my own use of the first-person plural to suggest to readers of this book an identity of perspectives with mine is an obvious example of this[40]). *Les Fruits d'or* illustrated how even the address to the text, the only kind of discourse Sarraute allows the reader, is governed by the dynamics of objectification and control. If there the reader turned *himself* rather than the text into an object, defining himself reflexively in a way elsewhere condemned by Sarraute ('C'est que moi, pour que je sois détendu [. . .]':*FO* 152), and surrendering to it, it is because his address was in fact written from the point of view of the (real) text which thus established itself as the dominant party in the exchange with the good reader. If even the emphatically uncritical address to the text cannot escape the process of objectification (in whichever direction), the critic's discourse which speaks not only to the text but about it will be all the more unable to avoid turning it into a mastered object (as Sarraute is intensely aware).

This chapter's exploration of Sarraute's attempt to make her readers submit to the discourse of the text thus deals with only one facet (the authorial one) of the mutual definition which the interaction of author and critical reader (the critic being merely a more

---

[40] Ann Jefferson shows this to be a feature of Sarraute's critical writings too: 'En recréant dans ses essais l'expérience de la lecture, elle cherche à impliquer son propre lecteur dans les phénomènes qu'elle évoque, si bien qu'en parlant, par exemple, de Camus, elle se sert d'un "nous" [. . .] qui montre à quel point elle est consciente du fait que c'est le lecteur qui est le destinataire de ses commentaires' (*OC* 2049).

self-conscious reader[41]) across their respective discourses sets in
motion. It not only fails to examine the other side of the issue but
also clearly participates in it (as does the whole reading of Sarraute
it fits into), in so far as it tries to master the texts it engages with by
defining some of their motivations. However, this perception of dialogue, and specifically of reading, as involving each party's definition of its addressee, should not be seen as a kind of dual solipsism
where each remains condemned to engage only with its image of
the other. First, face-to-face dialogue has a reciprocal dimension
which means that impressions can be modified and misunderstand-
ings rectified (despite the lack of total mutual presence there either).
If its temporal nature makes full mutual presence impossible, that
same extension over time does permit a mediated reciprocity where
the other's response leads inevitably to the modification of the
image held of him, an image which in some form or other is indispensable. While the dialogue around the text lacks this reciprocal
quality, the temporal extension involved in reading a text means
that it is still a more modulated process than considering it in the
monolithic terms of a single address and a single response might
suggest. The writer may be unable to monitor the text's reception in
the act of reading, but the fact that this act is made up of the reader's
perception of not one but countless textual addresses, connected to
one another if not back to their intentional source, and of his similarly interconnected responses to these, gives rise to a certain scope
for modification within the duration of each reading. Thus passages
are reread in the light of others whose relation to them has a direct
bearing on their significance; interpretations are formed and then
revised in the light of new information. So although the reader
always has an image of the text before him as he reads, this image
too is constantly being modified and reevaluated.

Aside from objectifying its addressee, Sarraute's work, I have suggested, also reveals its monologic intentionality through its inability
to enact a fully dialogic relativization of the authorial discourse. As
an image of that aspiration and its necessary failure I identified (in

---

[41] This is emphatically not Sarraute's view—for her, as Ann Jefferson puts it, 'le critique
est celui qui s'interpose entre le texte et son lecteur, qui parle pour ne rien dire, et n'a d'autre
projet que celui d'affirmer sa propre autorité [. . .] Le critique cherche fatalement à s'imposer
en "maître" [. . .] au dépens à la fois du livre dont il est censé parler, et du lecteur, qui, à la différence du critique, accepte de se livrer corps et âme à l'expérience vitale qu'est la lecture
pour Nathalie Sarraute' (*OC* 2036–7).

Chapter 2) the dialogue in *Enfance* between Natacha and her step-grandmother, for it betrays the authorial manipulation behind it (and behind the whole text of which I defined it to be a figure). Yet in much the same way, the dialogue I set up in Chapter 3 between Sarraute's texts and the work of Jacques Lacan betrays evidence of the necessarily monologic point of view (mine) in which it originated. If dialogue in general consists of the alternating attempts by each party to persuade the other of the truth of its address, the monologic representation, from a single critical perspective, of such a dialogue between two pre-existing discourses will necessarily be subject to that principle. Thus it will entail the author's own provisional assent to the truth of each discourse in the dialogue as it speaks. In this way, Lacan's analysis of the development of the psyche in terms of Imaginary and Symbolic phases has provisionally been taken as true in order to enable me to initiate a dialogue by 'speaking' on behalf of Lacanian discourse to Sarraute's writing. The difference between setting up that kind of dialogue and creating a fictional one is that when the discourses exist independently of the text which opposes them, the author is the one who assents provisionally and by turn to the arguments he or she wishes to repeat, rather than creating characters who are all in the service of his or her own attitudes. (This was the case with the 'cocottes en papier' scene of *Enfance* which, I argued, because of the way it shows Natacha's total control over the responses of her addressees, represents more graphically than the dialogue with the grandmother does the monologism underlying that novel's dialogic form.)

The fact that the writings of Sarraute and Lacan exist independently of my singular authorial perspective which set them in dialogue with each other makes it possible to take both sides in that dialogue. The initial passive assent to one side of the exchange means that one's subsequent objectifying address to the other is from a point of view which is not one's own and which can therefore be changed. This study has only presented one side of the dialogue, the address, in Lacanian terms, to Sarraute, where Lacan's discourse was taken as true and 'imposed' on her texts. It would be quite possible (and also necessary, if the main dialogue being considered here were between Sarraute's and Lacan's texts, and not between Sarraute's texts and their readers) to establish a Sarrautean response to Lacan, for example using her texts to question his assumption that determination by language is an unconscious process. An exchange from that Sarrautean perspective would present as true a more self-aware subject than Lacan's, and could use his writing against itself to underline the truth of that assertion (so making him 'assent' to it), perhaps criticizing his possession of a knowledge denied to the helpless subject he presents.[42] But in both cases one point of view is taken against the other and, just as in actual exchanges the self's awareness that the other is a subject does not change the way his address turns him into an object, creating a dialogue between two independent discourses also entails positing each in turn as speaking subject to the other as object. The next and final chapter will look not at how Sarraute could answer Lacan in the unavoidably monologic exchange Chapter 3 set up between them (and which would remain so irrespective of which perspective it spoke through), but at how, in the dialogue which has been my principal focus in this study, the reader as a subject can respond to Sarraute.

[42] This is not automatically to assume that such an argument would be equally persuasive. Indeed the theoretical construct Lacan establishes, rather than suggesting by its existence a greater degree of human self-knowledge than it argues to be the case, could be seen to confirm through its unintentional blind spots the blinkered subjectivity it outlines. A case in point is Lacan's failure, like Freud, to question his use of a masculine model of sexuality; both thinkers let the phallic *moi* prevail in their own texts over the subjectivity they oppose to it as true. Malcolm Bowie has commented on this shared blindness: '[Freud] sees clearly that sexualities are cultural products, and that their ideological supports can be analysed, but the sexuality of the patriarchal male is curiously resistant to investigation. It keeps on returning as the unanalysed grid that allows other sexual dispositions to be sorted and evaluated. Lacan, dissident in so many ways, is steadfastly loyal in this area of enquiry' (1991: 157).

READING IN THEORY AND PRACTICE

Sarraute's attitude to the reader is, as we have seen, a highly complex one: while the amount of attention her work gives him makes clear that his cooperation is considered vital ('il ne m'est pas possible de m'en passer': *EVM* 171), his ideal role in relation to the text seems limited to recognizing and acquiescing in its authority. The fact that her novels progressively abandon the representation of such an ideal reader may acknowledge at some level the impossibility of an addressee who on the one hand would be other enough for his affirmative response to have value, yet whose total approbation would deny that otherness. At the same time, Sarraute continues to write, presenting to her real, unknown readers the incapable addressees of *L'Usage de la parole*, followed by the self-sufficient internal dialogues of *Enfance* and *Tu ne t'aimes pas*, and the reflections of *Ici* on solitude and silence. Most recently, *Ouvrez* depicts communication as dominated by self-censorship, with the essence of the self closed off from public view. The title of this short work encapsulates the ambivalence of the later Sarraute's attitude to her readers: the imperative 'Ouvrez' is not in fact addressed to those who approach the book (or at least not explicitly), but by the population of one zone of the self to those in the other. Thus by responding to what we automatically assume is an invitation we become interlopers in the self's internal conversation; yet our presence 'backstage' in the self, if not openly welcomed or even acknowledged in any way which might reassure us as to the validity of our first reading of the title, is tacitly tolerated (see also Conclusion n. 14).

Sarraute's paradoxical persistence in articulating publicly a lack of faith in intersubjective communication suggests that on some level there endures the dream of that ideal reader who might emerge from the reading public and provide the desired total recognition of and adherence to the author's vision. I argued in Chapter 4 that this dream of a double is doomed to remain unrealized; to conclude this study of the Sarrautean text and the reader I wish now to consider the activity of reading Sarraute, not as her work depicts it but in terms of what happens when real readers with their irreducibly other perspectives come face to face with a text.

The act of reading has been theorized in a variety of ways in recent years, and it is in the context of some of the most important branches of reader-based literary theory that I want to discuss what is actually at stake when we read Sarraute. We might begin exploring the relevance of theories of reading to her work by establishing where the ideal reader her writing projects fits into the spectrum of theoretical readers. Already in her first novel, *Portrait d'un inconnu*, she offers the reader, in the description of the narrator's reaction to a painting he sees in a foreign museum, a model of the privileged response to the work of art. (As previously mentioned in Ch. 4 n. 9, Sarraute makes no distinction between the ideal response to literature and to painting: both involve unmediated intimacy with the aesthetic object.) This early description, paradigmatic for a view of reading which has remained remarkably constant throughout her work, establishes through its imagery common ground with a particular tendency in contemporary theories of reading, one which, while claiming to identify the reader as co-creator of the work, surreptitiously gives the text control over him by regarding his role as already inscribed within it.

Seeing the 'portrait d'un inconnu' profoundly affects the way the novel's narrator subsequently represents the world. To the extent that it exemplifies the mode of representation whose mastery by the narrator is the novel's story, the portrait is a *mise en abyme* of the novel, with all the potential for subversive irony this structure implies.[1] Yet given that the portrait is represented in terms of the narrator's *response* to it, a response sanctioned by the expressive ability it confers on him (emphasizing the ideal unity of reader and writer), the scene can be read as the kind of seductive *mise en abyme* discussed by Ross Chambers (1984: 33–5), one which in fact aims to restrict the reader's freedom by providing a model for how the novel should be read (see Ch. 4, pp. 140–1). Not surprisingly, the mode of reading which the scene promotes appears to be active but is in fact entirely determined by the portrait. The painting's ideal 'reader' already

---

[1] For a discussion of how *Portrait d'un inconnu* is explicitly concerned with questions of characterization and narratorial discourse, see Jefferson (1980: 58–67, 119–33). The portrait which transforms the narrator's approach to the representation of reality in the novel is based on one seen by Sarraute herself, 'à Amsterdam ou à Anvers; probablement à Anvers' (*OC* 1751 n. 3).

shares the artist's world-view before he approaches the work, in that a priori unity of the poles of artist/writer and viewer/reader that Sarraute would continue to desire for the reception of her own writing. Thus the way he reads and responds to the painting's representation of an individual corresponds to the way he perceives and responds to people in general. What the painting does is teach him how to *represent* what he already feels; the revelatory rightness of its depiction of its subject gives him access to a mode of truthful representation which he develops during the rest of the novel, in his invented narrative of the old man and his daughter.[2]

What is this mode of representation whose truthfulness the narrator of *Portrait d'un inconnu* must endorse in order to be its ideal 'reader' (and become a Sarrautean writer)? Its refusal to name its subject is only one, specifically linguistic, aspect of its representational integrity. It confidently refuses to give in to a temptation already entertained by the narrator when he observed that to give his characters 'au moins un nom d'abord pour les identifier [. . .] serait déjà un premier pas de fait pour les isoler, les arrondir un peu, leur donner un peu de consistance' (*PI* 66; on the way the character's name is 'pour le romancier une gêne', see *ES* 74–6). It rejects the kind of typological portraiture in which he had previously and unsuccessfully engaged, in his attempt to articulate the peculiar quality of the father and daughter who obsess him. The reductive, caricatural nature of his description had already been pointed out to him by a friend in terms of just the kind of representation the 'portrait d'un inconnu' rejects (the friend compared the narrator's 'Hypersensible-nourrie-de-clichés' to outdated forms of portraiture of the 'Jeune Fille au Perroquet' type: p. 45).[3]

---

[2] This is exactly the same role that Sarraute identifies Flaubert's *Madame Bovary* as having played in her own formation as a writer: 'J'avais observé, étant encore très jeune, que les gens avaient parfois l'impression d'éprouver des sentiments qui leur paraissaient vrais mais qui n'étaient que la copie de sentiments véritables. Une sorte de trompe-l'œil. Dans *Madame Bovary* j'ai trouvé ce qui *confirmait et éclairait mes propres observations*' ('Roman et réalité', *OC* 1649; my emphasis; this previously unpublished lecture was first given at the University of Lausanne in 1959).

[3] This friend is 'le vieux frère, l'"alter" ' (*PI* 43), and as such is a clear forerunner of the double in *Entre la vie et la mort*. He too functions as a critical reader by suggesting layers of complexity in the father and daughter which the narrator had failed to recognize. But, as with the later double, his intervention, however valuable, does not change the fact that writing is an inherently solitary occupation: 'Je savais que je ferais mieux de rentrer chez moi, me terrer dans mon coin, examiner tout seul, sans la montrer à personne, ma découverte, faire encore un effort, pousser plus loin, tout seul' (p. 48).

The portrait's depiction of its subject is distinguished by a fragmentary, undefined quality which instead of compensating for the inconsistency of character simply articulates it. By privileging the 'piecemeal' nature of touch over the totalizing quality of sight[4] it seems to reject the notion of unitary identity established, for Lacan, through visual perception of others and of one's reflection: 'Les lignes de son visage, de son jabot de dentelles, de son pourpoint, de ses mains, semblaient être les contours fragmentaires et incertains que découvrent à tâtons, que palpent les doigts hésitants d'un aveugle' (p. 80). The raggedness of the old-fashioned costume figures the abandonment of classical realist representation, along with the perception of identity it promoted. Hence the narrator's sense of recognition: for him too, the human subjects who surround him are ragged entities, 'ces lambeaux informes, ces ombres tremblantes, ces spectres, ces goules, ces larves qui me narguent et après lesquels je cours' (p. 66). Despite its physical dissolution, or rather because of it, the portrait expresses an intense humanity: 'Ses yeux [. . .] paraissaient avoir tiré à eux et concentré en eux toute l'intensité, la vie qui manquaient à ses traits encore informes et disloqués [. . .] L'appel qu'ils lançaient, pathétique, insistant, faisait sentir d'une manière étrange et rendait tragique son silence' (p. 80).

The portrait's incomplete, fragmentary state thus concentrates the humanity of its subject in what *is* represented, namely the eyes. These express an intense appeal to rescue the 'inconnu' from the crisis of representation which has led to his remaining trapped in this (albeit disintegrating) conventional form like 'ces êtres enchantés dans le corps desquels un charme retient captifs les princes et les princesses des contes de fées' (p. 80). The viewer's response is to this appeal, and as such is primarily not aesthetic but emotional—it is not specifically to the *representation* of the unknown man but to the way the *represented* figure addresses him.[5] The appeal, moreover, allows for only one kind of answer, and so once the viewer perceives it, he is deprived of all independence in his relation to the work: 'J'avais beau, comme je fais toujours, chercher de toutes mes forces

---

[4] Albeit from within visual art; the painting thus enacts the same struggle against expressive impossibility—the same taste for 'une certaine forme d'échec' (*ES* 150)—as the Sarrautean attempt to capture what precedes language from within language.

[5] The way the viewer here responds to a human appeal in the work, engaging with it on the level not of its representational technique but of the individual whose portrait is the work of art, anticipates the humanization of the literary artwork in *Les Fruits d'or* (see Ch. 4, s. 1).

à me retenir pour rester en lieu sûr, du bon côté, je sentais comme il lançait vers moi, avec un douloureux effort, de la nuit où il se débattait, son appel ardent et obstiné' (p. 81). Response to art thus depends on hearing its appeal and, more importantly, is determined by that appeal:

Il me semblait, tandis que je restais là devant lui, perdu, fondu en lui, que cette note hésitante et grêle, cette réponse timide qu'il avait fait sourdre de moi, pénétrait en lui, résonnait en lui, il la recueillait, il la renvoyait, fortifiée, grossie par lui comme par un amplificateur, elle montait de moi, de lui, s'élevait de plus en plus fort, un chant gonflé d'espoir qui me soulevait, m'emportait. (p. 81)

The song may appear to arise from both of them together, but in fact it is called up by the painting and strengthened by it; the spectator simply offers a timid affirmation of the work's address, and is then overwhelmed by the force with which the work amplifies this response. The gaps in the fragmentary artistic text thus have a double function: they not only intensify the way what *is* represented expresses a living subject's appeal for a response to it; they also allow the reluctantly but still predominantly representational text to absorb and magnify that (predetermined) response.

This idea of the fragmentary text as accommodating the reader's response but thereby controlling it, characterizes the theory of reading developed by Wolfgang Iser (1974, 1978), a theory which, while claiming to show how the reader completes the text, fails to evacuate the notion of textual control. The rest of this chapter will place Sarraute's view of reading in the context of the main issues raised by reader-based literary theory, in order to help ascertain how that view relates to the reality of reading her texts. First, though, we need to address the question of *why* the Sarrautean text, with all its gaps, none the less resists any independent input by the reader, beyond the affirmative response of recognition. (The fact that this distinction between responding and adding something new is unsustainable is of course what makes the desired fusion both unattainable and constantly sought anew in her work. The way difference invariably reappears in the relationship of text and reader is, as we shall see, equally evident in theories of reading which claim to eliminate it.)

If Sarraute can claim that the portrait's viewer provides the impossible minimal 'réponse timide' of simple affirmation, it is because he is held to be from the outset entirely in agreement with what the incomplete portrait expresses; this identity of perspectives means that he will not fill its gaps with heterogeneous material from his own experience. The reason the reader of the fragmentary text must not import extraneous elements into the spaces between the representational fragments is because these gaps are *themselves* representational: they correspond to the artist's reading of the real world as itself lacking solid definition. Moreover, neither in the world nor a fortiori in the text are these gaps places of emptiness: they are filled, but with a matter which resists conventional representation (and so they appear empty to the conventional gaze). This amorphous reality can only be conveyed by the true artist who finds within the lexis of representation (be this linguistic or visual) tools adequate to the task. The narrator of *Portrait d'un inconnu* perceives the hidden reality beneath the painting's fragmentary surface (a depth which heightens the investment of sensation in that residually conventional surface) just as he perceives it in real life, and just as he will learn, through his encounter with the painting, to represent it in turn. If he seeks in those around him 'avec un acharnement maniaque la fente, la petite fissure, ce point fragile comme la fontanelle des petits enfants', it is to find in this gap not an empty space awaiting his free invention but 'quelque chose, comme une pulsation à peine perceptible [. . .] une matière étrange, anonyme comme la lymphe, comme le sang, une matière fade et fluide qui coule entre mes mains, qui se répand' (pp. 66–7). It is because the reader of the painting personifies its own perspective on reality that Sarraute can afford to suggest that his response completes it, whereas in fact all he does is confirm what it already contains, the deeper reality it expresses through the gaps in its fragmented surface.

Thus a superficial impression of incompleteness masking a fully determinate, if elusive, reality characterizes the artist's perception of the world, his representation of that perception, and the reception of his artistic representation by a reader who ideally endorses its identification of a deeper unformulated truth underlying the fragmentary surface of reality. This ideal reader who provides recognition without addition is, as *Entre la vie et la mort* showed (see Ch. 4, s. 2), an impossible dream. In the following discussion of theories of reading I shall look first at those theories which argue for the kind of ideal reading Sarraute desires, and see how they too fail to overcome its impossibility. Section 2 will focus on the opposite pole of reader-response criticism, where reading is considered as precisely the kind of convention-bound, public activity Sarraute abhors and tries to prevent through her ideal reader. This second view has its own limitations, however, and these will be discussed in the final section, in the context of the special importance those aspects of reading which it fails to consider take on when we read Sarraute. On the basis of this analysis of theories of reading, the most valuable approach to reading Sarraute is, I shall suggest, one which recognizes the shared determination of reader *and* text by conventional constraints on the production of meaning, and which as such paradoxically manages to be faithful to her text without being determined by it. Conceiving the text–reader relationship in this way may require us to re-evaluate the nature of the alienation which defines it (in its mediation through writing and publication) and which, as anticipated and countered by Sarraute, has been the focus of this study.

This view of both reader and text as shaped by the wider linguistic community clearly sits well with the Lacanian understanding of identity as linguistic and situated within a transindividual Symbolic order. It is also integral to the approach to reading developed by reception theorist Hans Robert Jauss. Jauss expands the text–reader dialogue to include the whole society to whose questions the text is produced as an answer.[6] He addresses too the way historical change, altering the social context of reception (the 'horizon of expectations' into which the text is received), also alters the aspects of the text engaged with. Thanks to a 'dialogical relationship of the present to the past [. . .] the past work can answer and "say something" to us only when the present observer has posed the

[6] 'The reconstruction of the horizon of expectations, in the face of which a work was created and received in the past, enables one [. . .] to pose questions that the text gave an answer to, and thereby to discover how the contemporary reader could have viewed and understood the work' (Jauss 1982: 28). This is the fourth of seven theses presented in the essay generally regarded as the 'manifesto' for reception theory, 'Literary History as a Challenge to Literary Theory', delivered as an inaugural address at the University of Constance in 1967 (and first published in German as 'Literaturgeschichte als Provokation der Literaturwissenschaft', in H. R. Jauss, *Literaturgeschichte als Provokation*, Frankfurt am Main: Suhrkamp, 1970). Jauss later spells out the 'eminently social, i.e. socially *formative* function of literature' (p. 40), taking the example of how Flaubert's innovative use of free indirect discourse in *Madame Bovary* had the effect of jolting the novel's first readers 'out of the self-evident character of [their] moral judgment, and turned a predecided question of public morals back into an open problem' (p. 44). There are obviously clear affinities between Jauss and Bakhtin; these have been explored by David Shepherd (1989: 102–3) and will be touched on in the Conclusion to this study (see esp. n. 16).

question that draws it back out of its seclusion' (Jauss 1982: 32). Such overtures, repeated through time and across societies, permit 'the successive unfolding of the potential for meaning that is embedded in a work and actualized in the stages of its historical reception as it discloses itself to understanding judgment' (p. 30).

In an introduction to the collection of Jauss's essays which contains his 'manifesto' for reception theory from which I have just been quoting (see n. 6) Paul de Man emphasizes that the 'horizon of expectations' is never consciously available to those whom it defines. (It is the condition of existence of conscious engagement with the text, be it by its author or by its readers.)[7] He goes on to compare the literary historian's attempt to recreate through interpretation the horizon of expectations of the moment of the text's first appearance to the dialogue between psychoanalyst and analysand where neither one knows the experience to be identified (Jauss 1982: p. xii). Located outside the focus of consciousness, this set of undefined expectations is moreover intersubjective: de Man points out that 'the passage from the individual to the collective or the social aspects of the work is implicit in the model of the "horizon"', and salutes Jauss's 'far-reaching synthesis between the private and the public dimensions of the literary work' (p. xiii). By adding a temporal dimension which accounts for our ability to engage with works of previous generations and reconstruct their horizons if not our own, Jauss usefully reminds us that the language in which text and reader find each other also has a history—the horizon of expectations of the text's composition is a constitutive element of our present horizon, and this makes it accessible to us (pp. 19–20).[8] Engaging with a text thus appears as a process which transcends the individual mind (of writer or reader) to become a function of unacknowledged contemporary social attitudes and of history (both literary and social). It is this wider perspective on the

[7] Indeed Robert Holub points out Jauss's own blindness to the 'historical situatedness' of his particular theory of literature, his failure to acknowledge the 'horizon of expectations' informing his own approach to literary texts, and giving rise notably to his association of literary value with novelty (1984: 60–3).

[8] Criticism of Jauss's theory of 'horizons of expectations' tends to emphasize the difficulty of isolating and defining discrete horizons, and so highlights the shared community of language which underlies and unites these. Thus Susan R. Suleiman asserts that 'Jauss's notion of the public and its expectations does not allow for enough diversity in the *publics* of literary works at a given time'; she argues for 'the "multiplication" of horizons of expectation, the realization that even in the distant past and in a single society there was no such thing as a single homogeneous reading (or listening) public' (1980b: 37).

act of reading which will allow us to transcend the understanding of that act in the oppositional terms of text versus reader, an understanding which underlies not only Nathalie Sarraute's writing practice but also the works of prominent theorists of reading.

1. The assenting reader in theory

Sarraute's ideal reader finds, as I have mentioned, a striking and unexpected echo in the work of one of Jauss's fellow 'Constance school' reception theorists, Wolfgang Iser. In his theory of reading, Iser, like Sarraute, seems to assert that the artwork requires the response of an independent outsider to complete its 'indeterminacies' if it is to live. Yet just as the 'portrait of an unknown man' overwhelmed its essentially passive viewer who was unable to 'me retenir sur la pente où je me sentais entraîné' (*PI* 81), Iser too, as has been widely observed,[9] repeatedly collapses the otherness of the reader's perspective into a structural element of the text which ostensibly solicits it. This tendency is illustrated by his term 'implied reader', which provides the title of his first book-length study of reading to appear in English (1974). Like Sarraute's portrait, the Iserian text appeals to the reader through its 'blanks' which he is required to fill in. But here too the reader is denied the right to introduce extraneous material. In *The Act of Reading* Iser explains: 'The structured blanks of the text stimulate the process of ideation to be performed by the reader *on terms set by the text* [. . .] The blanks leave open the connections between perspectives in the text, and so spur the reader into coordinating these perspectives' (1978: 169; my emphasis). In addition, Iser, like Sarraute, strongly suggests that the blanks are not even places of pure emptiness, but paradoxically already contain in an unformulated way the truth which the reader should intuit through them. While they are not filled with a material reality in the way the gaps in the surface of reality and of its artistic representation were for Sarraute's narrator, they are still supported by an underlying textual structure, the formulated text's 'unformulated double' (p. 226). This structure regulates the

---

[9] See esp. Stanley Fish (1981): 'Why No One's Afraid of Wolfgang Iser', a review of *The Act of Reading* (Iser 1978); also Iser's response, 'Talk Like Whales' (1981). Other discussions of Iser's theory can be found in Ray 1977: *passim*; 1984: 33–40, 50–9; Holub 1984: 82–106; Freund 1987: 134–51.

connections between segments without articulating them, and so determines the intended imaginary object they outline (pp. 196–7). In fact, Iser ultimately equates the textual blank with this unseen structure: more than just 'the empty space between segments', it is itself 'the unformulated framework of these interacting segments [which] enables the reader to produce a determinate relationship between them' (p. 198). Just as the appeal by Sarraute's incomplete painting was for recognition of its unformulated truth by one who would share its perspective on reality, so the blanks in the Iserian text invite no new perspective but fill themselves in, directing as well as inducing 'the reader's constitutive activity' (p. 202).

In this way, although Iser claims that the reader (here of *Tom Jones*) 'is bound to insert his own ideas into the process of communication', it is clear that he also sees these ideas as produced by the text before being returned to it in 'a constant "feedback" of "information" already received' (p. 67). The reader's response has its source in the text, just as the Sarrautean 'note timide [. . .] hésitante et grêle' was produced by the work which then reabsorbed it: 'Cette réponse timide qu'il avait fait sourdre de moi, pénétrait en lui etc.' (*PI* 81). Thus in Iser's own words, the reader's 'affective' role (as opposed to the text's 'verbal' one) in the act of reading is simply 'the fulfillment of that which has been *prestructured* by the language of the text' (1978: 21; my emphasis).

What is interesting about the affinity between Sarraute and Iser is that, if they both end up on the same side, their aims initially seem opposed, for whereas Sarraute clearly tries to neutralize the reader's difference, Iser in fact wants to assert the importance of what the reader brings to the text. Yet his attempt to establish for the reader a constructive role in creating the work (he claims that the text–reader interaction is governed by a 'mixture of determinacy and indeterminacy', p. 24, and that the reader's acts of comprehension, 'though set in motion by the text, defy total control by the text itself', p. 108) relapses again and again into a theory of reading as the obedient adherence to a set of textual instructions. Ultimately, the constructive activity of Iser's reader is directed towards the same brand of fusion Sarraute desires and—at least in her earlier fiction—represents (although always as an identity which pre-exists the reading process rather than being produced by it): the Iserian reader is enabled 'gradually to take over the author's unfamiliar view of the world *on the terms laid down by the author*' (p. 97; my emphasis).

If Iser ends up subscribing to the same ideal of reading that Sarraute desires (with the difference that for him it is the *reality* of reading), it is because his project to include the reader's activity in any definition of literature is shadowed by the same anxiety her fiction displays regarding the threat an entirely independent reader must pose to authorial intention. For Iser too, it is because the reader is other that the text must be given authority over him: 'Although the reader must participate in the assembly of meaning by realizing the structure inherent in the text, it must not be forgotten that he stands outside the text. His position must therefore be manipulated by the text if his viewpoint is to be properly guided' (p. 152). Like Sarraute, Iser is aware that the text–reader dialogue is marked by mutual alienation; and he too sees this as an exacerbation of the nature of all communication.[10]

In this light, Iser's constant slide from the reader to the text's 'prestructuring' of how it should be read seems to be an attempt, in the language of theory, to limit the possibilities of interpretation it originally seemed to be opening up, just as Sarraute's equation of ideal reader and authorial *alter ego* does in her novels. Formulating the text's meaning, for Iser, 'draws the reader into the text but also away from his own habitual disposition' (p. 218). The text–reader dialogue thus differs from spoken dialogue in that it overcomes the difficulties of communication not through transforming the projections of *both* parties, but through the sole transformation of the reader: 'As the blank gives rise to the reader's projections, but the text itself cannot change, it follows that a successful relationship between text and reader can only come about through changes in the reader's projections' (p. 167). It is, in addition, a permanent transformation: the text does not simply suspend the reader's

---

[10] Iser owes his view of dialogue as inherently alienated largely to R. D. Laing's account of the inability of each partner in dialogue to experience the way the other experiences him: '*Your experience of me is invisible to me and my experience of you is invisible to you.* I cannot experience your experience. You cannot experience my experience. We are both invisible men. All men are invisible to one another. Experience is man's invisibility to man' (R. D. Laing: *The Politics of Experience* (Harmondsworth, 1968), 16; cited in Iser 1978: 165). Elsewhere Laing discusses how this inaccessibility of the other's perspective leads us to imagine his view of us and to act accordingly: 'I may not actually be able to see myself as others see me, but I am constantly supposing them to be seeing me in particular ways, and I am constantly acting in the light of the actual or supposed attitudes, opinions, needs, and so on the other has in respect of me' (R. D. Laing, H. Phillipson, and A. R. Lee, *Interpersonal Perception: A Theory and a Method of Research* (New York, 1966), 4; cited in Iser 1978: 165). This is precisely the predicament of Sarraute's characters.

disposition for the duration of his reading, but actually alters his consciousness permanently. In reading, 'past experiences become marginal and [the reader] is able to react spontaneously; consequently, his spontaneity—evoked and formulated by the text— penetrates into consciousness' (p. 158). Thus the text creates in its reader 'a new and real consciousness [. . .] Each text constitutes its own reader' (p. 157). It is hardly surprising that the main strategy Iser indicates, through which fictional works can 'fix' their readers' position (a strategy which suggests, against his theory, that the act of reading is not in itself enough to dissipate the reader's dangerous otherness), is that privileged by Sarraute: the use of a fictitious reader to which the real reader must adapt, 'if the meaning he assembles is to be conditioned by the text and not by his own disposition' (p. 153).

Iser's perception of the way the text acts on the reader prevents him from even entertaining the possibility that the reader might transform the text (by skipping certain parts and rereading others, by reading against the intended order, by reading literally instead of figuratively or vice versa, by interpreting ambiguous language in ways not intended by the author, etc.).[11] This immutability of the text, and its simultaneous ability to transform the reader, in fact contradicts Iser's assertion that the text–reader relationship is not marked by the dualism of subject and object. He claims that in the act of reading, 'text and reader no longer confront each other as object and subject, but instead the "division" takes place within the reader himself. In thinking the thoughts of another, his own individuality temporarily recedes into the background, since it is supplanted by these alien thoughts, which now become the theme on which his attention is focussed' (1974: 293; cp. 1978: 155).[12] But

[11] This raises a point made by Stanley Fish in his critique of *The Act of Reading*, namely that even the 'determinate' text, that which the reader must engage with, only exists as such by means of an act of interpretation. That is, if (as Iser argues in his rejoinder to Fish) 'the words of a text are given, the interpretation of the words is determinate, and the gaps between given elements and/or interpretations are the indeterminacies' (1981: 83), these distinctions are only perceived as a result of a reader's interpretation. For Fish, 'the distinction between the determinate and the indeterminate [. . .] will not hold [. . .] There is no distinction between what the text gives and what the reader supplies; he supplies *everything*' (1981: 6–7). I shall discuss this position more closely in the next section.

[12] In *The Act of Reading*, Iser also explains how 'as text and reader [. . .] merge into a single situation, the division between subject and object no longer applies, and it therefore follows that meaning is no longer an object to be defined, but is an effect to be experienced' (1978: 9–10). Ironically, he illustrates this fact with Henry James's 'The Figure in the Carpet', to

the reader's passivity and his transformation by the text suggest that Iser's theory merely reverses these positions, making the reader into an object acted on by the text as subject. The paradox, whereby theories of reading which argue the absence of such a dualism (whether by claiming that texts create their readers or that readers create the texts they read) are none the less unable to do without it, is of great importance to any discussion of reading. In the closing section of this chapter I shall attempt to explain why this dualism is indispensable and what implications it has for the way we read Sarraute. Now, though, I would like to look briefly at the source of Iser's view of reading as suspending the subject-object dualism (a view of course also central to Sarraute's conception of reading), the work of his fellow-phenomenologist Georges Poulet.

Poulet differs from Iser in the openness (and enthusiasm) with which he defines the text–reader interaction as the possession of the reader by the ideas presented in the text which invade his consciousness. Iser indeed emphasizes this difference when he claims to give the reader's conscious 'orientations' a more active role in the reading process than Poulet does (Iser 1978: 155). While the activity of the Iserian reader is questionable, given that he 'leave[s] behind that which has hitherto made him what he is' and 'forget[s] [him]self' (p. 156), Poulet takes the reader's passivity to a theoretical extreme. He openly deprives him of any constitutive role, and celebrates his total submission to the power of a text personified as a consciousness greater than the words which comprise it:

I am someone who happens to have as objects of his own thought, thoughts which are part of a book I am reading, and which are therefore the cogitations of another [. . .] Since every thought must have a subject to think it, this *thought* which is alien to me and yet in me, must also have in me a *subject* which is alien to me [. . .] As soon as something is presented as *thought*, there has to be a thinking subject with whom, at least for the time being, I identify, forgetting myself, alienated from myself [. . .] Now it is important to note that this possession of myself by another takes place not only on the level of objective thought, that is with regard to images, sensations, ideas which reading affords me, but also on the level of my very subjectivity. (1980: 44–5)

which, by seeing it as giving an account of meaning as effect, he in fact attributes an objective meaning. By reading the text as a statement of his own theory, Iser himself commits the sin of 'explaining' literature, although for him 'explanations [. . .] dull the effect, for they relate the given text to a given frame of reference, thus flattening out the new reality brought into being by the fictional text' (p. 10).

Poulet's view of reading is even more emphatically close to that dreamt of by Sarraute than was Iser's, not only in terms of his humanization of the text as a dominant consciousness, but also because this conscious text seems to communicate with the reading consciousness on a level where what is involved is identity itself. He asserts that 'the extraordinary fact in the case of a book is the falling away of the barriers between you and it. You are inside it; it is inside you; there is no longer either outside or inside' (p. 42). These words could be a gloss on the reader's apostrophe to the text at the end of *Les Fruits d'or*: 'Nous sommes si proches maintenant, vous êtes tellement une partie de moi, qu'il me semble que si vous cessiez d'exister, ce serait comme une part de moi-même qui deviendrait du tissu mort' (*FO* 157). Poulet also shares the humility of Sarraute's ideal reader ('Car enfin, qui suis-je? Qu'ai-je fait?': *FO* 154) when he marvels that the book being read, humanized into 'the consciousness of another, no different from the one I automatically assume in every human being I encounter', is open and welcoming (Poulet 1980: 42). The textual consciousness 'lets me look deep inside itself, and even allows me, with unheard-of license, to think what it thinks and feel what it feels'. The reader's humility means that, as with Sarraute, reading for Poulet is an exercise in self-surrender: 'As soon as I replace my direct perception of reality by the words of a book, I deliver myself, bound hand and foot, to the omnipotence of fiction [. . .] I become the prey of language. There is no escaping this takeover' (p. 43). And here too, the submission of the reader to the text, his transformation into the double of its consciousness, has overtones of violence: the work, 'not satisfied [. . .] with defining the content of my consciousness, takes hold of it, appropriates it, and makes of it that *I* which, from one end of my reading to the other, presides over the unfolding of the work, of the single work which I am reading' (p. 47; cp. *TTP* 79).

There is, however, a prescriptive quality to Poulet's discourse, which seems to acknowledge the possibility that this submissive response might not be guaranteed as an inevitable element of reading. Like Sarraute and Iser, Poulet is not just describing what happens when we read; he is establishing a programme for how we *should* read: 'When I read as I *ought*—that is without mental reservation, without any desire to preserve my independence of judgment, and with the total commitment required of any reader—my comprehension becomes intuitive and any feeling proposed to me is immediately assumed by me' (p. 45; my emphasis).

Poulet's anthropomorphic view of the text's 'subjective principle' (p. 46) as a consciousness to which the reader's mind is required to play host in a suspension of its own life, is complemented by a highly metaphorical evocation of the work as a living human body: 'Such is the characteristic condition of every work which I summon back into existence by placing my own consciousness at its disposal [. . .] So long as it is animated by this vital inbreathing inspired by the act of reading, a work of literature becomes at the expense of the reader whose own life it suspends a sort of human being' (p. 47). While the similarity to Sarraute's ideal text–reader relationship is again striking here, in terms both of the text's personification and of its disempowerment of the reader in the kind of human relationship of domination and submission which her fiction explores so powerfully, there is one subtle yet significant point of difference. The Sarrautean text, as we saw at the beginning of Chapter 1, relies on readers to recognize what it has left unspoken; in this way they allow it to remain in that state of unfinishedness which makes of it something 'living'. But this life is not *produced* by the act of reading, rather it is simply *supported* by it. The Sarrautean artwork is not dependent on its readers to summon it into existence in the way Poulet's text is; it is an organic being and so, even if forgotten, will remain alive. Thus when the reader of 'Les Fruits d'Or' wonders 'ce que vous deviendrez plus tard, sans moi . . . où vous allez aborder? où échouer?' (*FO* 157), he can reassure himself by thinking of those books which 'longtemps repoussés de partout, reviennent tout à coup, après bien des années, s'installer aux tables des cafés, se pavaner dans les salons' (p. 158). For Sarraute, the true artwork is already alive *before* the reader comes to it, and so it lives on after its reading. By contrast, the inauthentic text, composed of literary commonplaces rather than of language 'exudé' by an unnameable referent (*EVM* 166), is, as we saw in *Entre la vie et la mort*, dead even when it is being read. If for Poulet the text only breathes when the reader breathes life into it, for Sarraute the reader merely provides recognition of the text which breathes independently of him, using him as a mirror not only to provide the reflection of its authorial subject but also to testify to, though not produce, its life: 'Vous mon double, mon témoin . . . là, penchez-vous avec moi . . . ensemble regardons . . . est-ce que cela se dégage, se dépose . . . comme sur les miroirs qu'on approche de la bouche des mourants . . . une fine buée?' (*EVM* 174). It is because Sarraute sees the text as receiving life from its author rather than from the reader who is present as a more or less trustworthy witness of its expressive power (the less trustworthy the more he identifies with the reading public) that the act of reading could become ever more marginalized in her recent work.

Whichever side the metaphorical life-giving power is situated on for Poulet and Sarraute, its presence in their conceptions of the text–reader relationship leads to a marked de-emphasizing of the work of linguistic interpretation involved in reading. Chapters 3 and 4 have noted the way Sarraute's metaphors of the body as source of literary language seek to present the linguistic relationship formed through reading as a merging of selves prior to language. Poulet too isolates the textual subject from the language which constitutes it, though for him it transcends language rather than returning prior to it; it is pure mind rather than pure body:

When reading a literary work there is a moment when it seems to me that the subject *present* in this work disengages itself from all that surrounds it, and stands alone [. . .] All subjective activity present in a literary work is not entirely explained by its relationship with forms and objects within the work. There is in the work a mental activity profoundly engaged in objective forms; and there is, at another level, forsaking all forms, a subject which reveals itself to itself (and to me) in its transcendence relative to all which is reflected in it. At this point, no object can any longer express it; no structure can any longer define it; it is exposed in its ineffability and in its fundamental indeterminacy. (1980: 48–9)

This perception of the humanized text leads him to recommend to critics an approach which, astonishingly, ignores its objective linguistic form: 'It seems then that criticism, in order to accompany the mind in this effort of detachment from itself, needs to annihilate, or at least momentarily to forget, the objective elements of the work, and to elevate itself to the apprehension of a subjectivity without objectivity' (p. 49).

The view of the textual subject as either pure mind or pure body, and relating on one or other level to a passively conforming reader,[13] thus involves ignoring the materiality of language which gives the text (and its subject) objective existence. Yet Poulet himself acknowledges that what gives the reader access to the text, or rather

---

[13] For Poulet, 'the consciousness inherent in the work is active and potent [. . .] I myself, although conscious of whatever it may be conscious of, play a much more humble role content to record passively all that is going on in me' (p. 47).

gives the text access to the reader's mind, is the fact that both share the same language. Moreover, he seems to recognize at one point that the reader's language is not just an instrument which he employs to decipher the text's linguistic objectivity, but a constitutive element of his consciousness:

As soon as I replace my direct perception of reality by the words of a book, I deliver myself, bound hand and foot, to the omnipotence of fiction [. . .] Language surrounds me with its unreality [. . .] *This interior universe constituted by language does not seem radically opposed to the me who thinks it.* Doubtless what I glimpse through the words are mental forms not divested of an appearance of objectivity. But *they do not seem to be of another nature than my mind which thinks them* [. . .] In short, since *everything has become part of my mind thanks to the intervention of language*, the opposition between the subject and its objects has been considerably attenuated. (1980: 43; Poulet's underlining, my italics)

The sense of oneness with the subjective principle of the text is thus a linguistic unity, an area of overlap between the symbolic lexicon of the reader and that of the text. Reader and text meet in the language they share. Poulet does not follow up the consequences of the intimacy he identifies between consciousness and words, specifically its suggestion that the mind functions in terms of language. This would invalidate the claim that the textual subject transcends the linguistic form of the text, for it would entail recognizing that both the author's act of creation and the reader's perception of the text's subjectivity are governed by their language. Poulet sees the mind's translation of words into 'mental objects' (p. 43) as moving beyond language. Yet if it is the constitutive presence of language in the reader's mind which permits these objects to enter it in the first place, this language will remain the filter through which everything—even the transcendent textual subject which 'forsak[es] all forms' (p. 48)—is understood. Poulet's 'transcendence of mind', like Sarraute's sensory and physical truth, is a product of the shared language of text and reader which enables their dialogue in different historical and social contexts; it is therefore hard to see how it could ever be perceived by critics as a 'subjectivity without objectivity' (p. 49). The rest of this chapter will argue that the linguistic nature of the text–reader relationship is what causes it to appear as a dualism even to its participants. In this context it is interesting that in the passage just quoted, Poulet himself acknowledges that the subject-object opposition is not actually dissolved but just 'considerably attenuated' by this linguistic relationship.

The problems that the linguistic nature of text–reader relations raises for Poulet's (and by extension Sarraute's) conception of reading are illustrated at a different level of the act of literary communication, in the difficulties surrounding the notion of the narratee, a concept developed by Gerald Prince and Mary Ann Piwowarczyk. The narratee is the implied recipient of the narrator's discourse; it differs from the reader addressed by the text to the same degree as the narrator differs from the author. Leaving aside the differences between narratee and addressed reader (which will clearly be reduced to the degree that the narrator's voice approaches that of the author), it is obvious that they have in common the status of being the addressees of a linguistic communication, and so are assumed to share the same mental apparatus necessary to understand it.[14] William Ray, reviewing the work of Prince (1973), Piwowarczyk (1976), and Iser (1974), sums up the very minimum or 'degree-zero' requirement for the narratee. It is an addressee who, while knowing the narrator's language and the conventions of storytelling, being able to reason, and possessing a perfect memory, yet 'lacks any identity or particularizing characteristics', 'has no knowledge of social conventions, moral systems or values', and 'no temporal extension—no past, present or future, no existence outside of the text' (1977: 20; see Prince 1973: 180–2). As an addressee who lacks all personal identity and all extratextual existence, it has a lot in common with Poulet's reader who places his consciousness at the disposal of the work and whose own life is suspended by it (Poulet 1980: 47).[15]

[14] For William Ray, the reader is the text's ultimate narratee, the one it does not thematize by overtly acknowledging its existence. If it does—as in *L'Usage de la parole*—the narratee is turned into a character: once 'particularizing determinative references to the narratee are introduced into the narration, a radical reformulation occurs: from recipient of the message, the narratee becomes its content. And his ground shifts from his function within the narrative act as apprehending receiver, to a location within the structure of the message content itself. From co-subject, he falls to the status of object' (Ray 1977: 23). In this event, the narratee-turned-character's function as addressee is taken over by a new 'meta-narratee' who, as long as it remains unthematized, holds the position of the reader. While a theoretical difference subsists between them, 'this distinction blurs within the confines of critical praxis' (p. 25), for the meta-narratee's reading 'remains perfectly congruent with that of the reader' (p. 24).

[15] It is equally close to Sarraute's ideal reader, esp. as described by Françoise Dupuy-Sullivan who sees the final, good reader of *Les Fruits d'or* as embodying a 'retrait momentané dans la lecture d'un système temporel, linguistique et social' (1990: 45). Despite the contradiction of an experience of language taking place outside the linguistic system, Dupuy-Sullivan seems to accept this as a possible, though transitory, state of reading: 'L'erreur serait [. . .] de croire en une possibilité quelconque de permanence de ce moment de lecture'.

Yet as Ray points out, the concept of the degree-zero narratee is riven by internal contradictions; these same contradictions will also apply to the concept of a reader who, like it, is given only as much conscious existence as will enable him to assent passively to the truth of the text. The problem with Prince's degree-zero narratee is that some of the aspects specifically denied it (namely temporal extension and a sense of causality) are inherent to its main quality, mastery of the language of the text. 'For beyond the mere possession of a static nominative instrument, language confers and implies the ability to conceptualize, make abstractions, differentiate between entities, and assign causes (names) to perceived effects' (Ray 1977: 21). These basic abilities in turn ground the individuation of the narratee as a concrete personality, and so prevent its suspension of all differentiating features in the service of the textual subject. It is only by ignoring the way possessing (or in a more poststructuralist perspective, being possessed by) language is inseparable from the constitution of identity that narratee theory can see narration as progressively investing a narratee who understands everything but knows nothing with the same knowledge as the narrator (and thus as creating a double of the addressing voice, just like that desired by Sarraute). The inadequacy of this model of narrator-narratee relations results from a view of communication as the simple transmission of a coded message from sender to receiver, with coding and decoding regarded as exactly symmetrical. It is a view which fails to take into account the particular linguistic apparatus into which the addressee receives the text, and the way this complicates the whole process. (The fact that Sarraute's own perception of language as a code underlies the impossibility of the dialogue to which her heroes and texts aspire will be discussed in the Conclusion, in the context of *Ici*.)

Ray considers Iser's theory of the implied reader as offering 'a more post-lapsarian paradigm' (p. 31) for the reception of a textual message than does Prince's narratee and the code-based view of communication on which it depends. This is of course because the notion of a *reader* deals with the text as written, and so acknowledges that mediate quality of linguistic communication which writing emphasizes; the narratee, by contrast, as an embodiment of listening, represents a conception of language founded on spoken discourse and the illusion of mutual presence it promotes. The fact that Iser's implied reader 'finds its basis in the conventions of literary production and consumption' which 'accept as a given the radical separation between producer and consumer [. . .] imposed by the text' (Ray 1977: 26) locates it within a mode of communication whose structural alienation openly enacts something Iser sees as inherent to dialogue (see n. 10).

Accepting that the text's 'consumption' takes place in the absence of its 'producer' means a new emphasis on the role the reader's personal experiences play in his reception of the text. Iser acknowledges that the reader's prior knowledge of the world is vital to the function of the novel (the literary genre on which his theory concentrates and which is written specifically to be read); this function is 'to uncover a new dimension of human existence, [and] this can only present itself to the conscious mind of the reader against a background made recognizable by allusions and references which will thus provide a sufficient amount of familiarity' (Iser 1974: 182; cited in Ray 1977: 28). For this reason, Ray sees Iser's theory as showing how the reader makes the text's language relate to his world.[16]

Thus if the narratee is like a blank page onto which the text can write itself, the Iserian reader is presented (though, as we have seen, far from unequivocally) as integrating the text he reads into the text of his own life. Yet for Ray, neither perspective—neither the originally innocent and unindividuated narratee who acquires by the end of the narration a command of the narrated content congruent with the narrator's, nor the implied reader who 'appropriat[es the text's] knowledge in a gesture of self-discovery' (p. 31)—gives the whole story of response to a text. Even if the 'postlapsarian' implied reader takes into account the implications of the fact that readers have language (that is, that they also have a specific social and cultural experience which constitutes their identity), it is still inadequate as a model of linguistic understanding. Language, Ray argues, both refers *and* creates, so that as well as evoking the personal knowledge to which the reader refers it, it also aims to give him new knowledge. This 'bivalency' (p. 32) of language, as both

---

[16] Ray is clearly not concerned by the degree to which, as I have argued, Iser still sees the reader's construction of the text and relation of it to his own life as controlled by that text. If the reader's 'persistent referentialization of the new objectivities' helps assure 'his self-discovery in the proclaimed intent of the text' and 'denies the narration its right to constitute a world unrelated to his' (p. 31), the relationship he insists on between those worlds is still, as far as Iser is concerned, constructed on the text's terms.

referential and creative, means that conceptualizations of reading as either the total appropriation of the text by the reader or that of the reader by the text which posits him, ignore a large part of what is really going on by focusing on only one aspect of the text's language.

The rest of this chapter will deal with the problems associated with identifying either the text or the reader as sole repository of literary meaning, problems which arise from the attempt to define one independently of the other and of the language from which both derive their identity while also being united by it.[17] To see the text as either transmitting a determinate content to a reader it creates, or as being entirely 'naturalized' by its reader, is to be blind to what Ray calls 'that excess of language which [those views] do not comprehend' (p. 31). However, I shall suggest, in line with my discussion of dialogue (specifically but not solely that of text and reader) throughout this study, that this instinct to see either text or reader as an autonomous entity, in spite of the imbrication of each in the other and in the language which constitutes them, may be an unavoidable moment in representations of the reading process. Once either one is claimed to exist 'in itself', to see it then as creating the other rather than encountering it in the language which creates both of them is to see dialogue from the point of view of one or other interlocutor alone. It is thus to manifest the monological limits of consciousness, limits which the conception of dialogue that my readings of Sarraute have helped to develop both acknowledges and overcomes.

Thus representations of reading which argue for textual determinacy or indeterminacy, for language as creative or referential, for interpretative authority as wielded by either text or reader, subscribe to one or other version of this monologism where the other is an object one creates rather than a subject one encounters. This perception of reading as a non-dialogue, and the way, I would argue, it can be transcended by an awareness of the relative position of all (socio-historically situated) subjects within language, is obviously relevant both to Sarraute's representation of reading and to any reader's engagement with her work and discussion of that

---

[17] As David Shepherd puts it in his discussion of Bakhtin's attitude to the question of reading: 'The dialogic act of reading is disruptive of the seemingly fixed positions of text and reader; these positions cannot come through the dialogic encounter unchanged because they do not pre-exist it' (Shepherd 1989: 99).

dialogue. Before dealing with the way reading as a dialogue transcends these limited views of textual or readerly omnipotence, I wish to look more closely at the second school, that which gives the reader interpretative authority over an entirely indeterminate text, and whose approach to literature is clearly condemned by Sarraute. In *Les Fruits d'or*, the view that 'une œuvre d'art n'est jamais une valeur sûre' (*FO* 118) betrays the integrity of the work by sanctioning a host of mutually contradictory readings: 'Clair. Sombre. Perçant. Confiant. Souriant. Humain. Impitoyable. Sec. Moite. Glacé. Brûlant [. . .] Les Fruits d'Or, c'est tout cela' (*FO* 88). If Sarraute's ideal reader, silent before the text or with just enough language to articulate his submission to its truth, finds a clear theoretical echo in that area of reader-response criticism which privileges the text as source of meaning, her 'bad' conventional reader has much in common with the opposite tendency in theories of reading. This tendency is most often associated not (as Ray sees it) with Iser whose reader appropriates only what the text allows him to, but with Stanley Fish and his theory of 'interpretive [sic] communities'.

2. *Theories of the conventional reader*

For Sarraute, once the reader asserts his independence from the writer and no longer roots his interpretation of the text in authorial intention, he becomes condemned to read through a filter of convention. For Stanley Fish, this filter of convention is not an avoidable evil but is integral to the act of reading; the strategies of interpretation which make up our linguistic understanding shape our perception of the text from the start, denying the possibility of access to any expressive truth of that text. I argued in relation to *Entre la vie et la mort* that Sarraute in fact comes close to acknowledging that the way language is used in our environment inevitably influences how we read. Once the double in that novel was asked to read the text of its *alter ego*, it lost its unity with it as well as its ability to empathize with the sentiments its writing expressed, becoming instead totally dependent on the conventions of literary language for the terms of its interpretation. In so far as this development illustrates both a desire to make the reader into a second self and the way the activity of reading makes this desire unrealizable, it seems reluctantly to anticipate Ray's criticism of the concept of the narratee-as-double.

Neither the narratee, nor Sarraute's or Poulet's ideal reader, can be provided with language and yet be deprived of particularizing social and cultural features, for these are embedded in the individual's language and so govern his interpretative abilities.

Fish's collection of essays *Is There a Text in This Class?* (1980) charts the development of his thinking about reading from an initial, rather Iserian standpoint, where the emphasis on reading was really on the way texts dictate how they are to be read, to the refusal to accord any authority whatsoever to the text. I shall focus here on the final phase of this development, Fish's 'escape from the text/reader dichotomy in the monistic concept of "interpretive communities" [. . .] the always already given systems and institutions of interpretive authority that engender both readers and texts' (Freund 1987: 91). However, the extent to which he does in fact abandon the dualistic approach of his earlier work will remain an issue. Fish himself later criticized his early position (articulated in the 1970 essay 'Literature in the Reader: Affective Stylistics'), seeing it as 'equivocating between a reference to the action of the text *on* a reader and the actions performed *by* a reader as he negotiates (and, in some sense, actualizes) the text' (1980: 3). This equivocation allowed him 'to retain the text as a stable entity at the same time that I was dislodging it as the privileged container of meaning'. The residual subordination of reader to text accounts for the echoes of the depersonalization of Poulet's reader or Prince's narratee in Fish's early attempt to become an informed reader, an attempt which involved 'suppressing, insofar as that is possible [. . .] what is personal and idiosyncratic and 1970ish in my response' (p. 49).

Fish's solution to the way his early position persisted in attributing control of the reading experience to the text, is to claim that the formal features of the text which structure its reading are themselves imposed on it by the reader's perceptual powers. These features are *read into* the texts rather than found in them: 'Rather than intention and its formal realization producing interpretation (the "normal" picture), interpretation creates intention and its formal realization by creating the conditions in which it becomes possible to pick them out' (p. 163). He illustrates this view by explaining how, in a previous critical reading of *Lycidas*:

I 'saw' what my interpretive principles permitted or directed me to see, and then I turned around and attributed what I had 'seen' to a text and an intention. What my principles direct me to 'see' are readers performing acts; the points at which

I find (or to be more precise, declare) those acts to have been performed become (by a sleight of hand) demarcations *in* the text; those demarcations are then available for the designation 'formal features', and as formal features they can be (illegitimately) assigned the responsibility for producing the interpretation which in fact produced them. (p. 163)

Thus for Fish, 'the choice is never between objectivity and interpretation but between an interpretation that is unacknowledged as such and an interpretation that is at least aware of itself' (p. 167). There is no such thing as pure perception: 'Interpretive strategies are not put into execution after reading [. . .] They are the shape of reading [. . .] They give texts their shape, making them rather than, as it is usually assumed, arising from them' (p. 168).

In the end, however, it is not even the reader himself who is responsible for the meanings he infers. Instead, the particular community of linguistic subjects to which we belong establishes the principles by which we interpret texts: 'Meanings are the property neither of fixed and stable texts nor of free and independent readers but of interpretive communities that are responsible both for the shape of a reader's activities and for the texts those activities produce' (p. 322). Just as for Lacan it is only from within the Symbolic that we think we perceive the Real, in Fish's view of reading, what we perceive as a 'brute fact' (e.g. a line of verse as a unit, with a clear ending) is in fact 'a convention' (p. 166), determined by our 'interpretive community'.

Yet Fish's interpretive communities are not just another articulation of a widely held poststructuralist notion of understanding as mediated through the general symbolic apparatus which speakers of a language automatically share. Where he goes beyond this notion is by giving these communities a localized, specific status. It is not just the fact of speaking a language which determines one's interpretative activity, but also being a member of a specific community which holds certain community assumptions (for example about what counts as literature). If these communities are more narrowly defined, they none the less determine the individual just as much as the Lacanian Symbolic does: the strategies which proceed from 'the interpretive community of which [one] is a member [. . .] at once enable and limit the operations of [one's] consciousness' (p. 14).

Fish seems to be aware of the gross limitations which this argument places on the concept of consciousness, for he is ultimately obliged to give his institutionalized readers some possibility of moving from one community to another, and of understanding not only, as he repeatedly argues, what is permitted by their own interpretative strategies, but also what other communities permit. Disagreement exists, and since, on Fish's definition, it cannot take place within a single interpretive community, it must result from a collision between different communities. Yet the fact that these disagreements 'can be debated in a principled way' (p. 15) implies that some common denominator must exist between the different communities, and thus that there is for Fish a more fundamental but unacknowledged level of understanding than the community-specific interpretative strategies which, he claims, 'enable and limit' conscious processes. If understanding takes place only when words are 'read or heard within the same system of intelligibility from which they issue' (p. 316), the fact that we can understand the interpretations with which we disagree must mean that we share with our opponents a 'system of intelligibility' not reducible to our separate, internally consensual, interpretive communities and their strategies, and on the basis of which these are constructed.[18] (This point also arose in relation to Jauss's 'horizons of expectations': the different horizons of different social and historical communities—including multiple coexisting ones (see n. 8)—are formed on a foundation of similarity which permits the evolution of later horizons out of earlier ones, and by extension the accessibility of past horizons to readers in the present.)

One of the mechanisms by which, according to Fish, we can come to see things from the perspective of an interpretive community other than our own, and so increase our understanding, is particularly enlightening in this respect. Analogy, he suggests, can establish 'a new and wider basis for agreement' between opposing communities (p. 315). Thus a student whose teacher misunderstands her question 'Is there a text in this class?' as referring to the existence of a course syllabus rather than to the objective validity of a basic literary concept, can make her sense known by 'find[ing] a

---

[18] Robert Scholes describes as 'truly astonishing' Fish's conclusion that he has explained not only why disagreements exist but why they can be debated 'in a principled way': 'This conclusion is astonishing because principled debate is precisely what Fish's theory cannot describe [. . .] If every different interpretation is the product of a different community, making different assumptions and perceiving a different text, how could one possibly debate or settle such differences?' (Scholes 1985: 155–6).

category of [the teacher's] own understanding which might serve as an analogue to the understanding he does not yet share' (p. 315). But if understanding can be expanded through establishing resemblances in this way, it seems that it is a function not primarily of social beliefs but of more basic symbolic operations (similarity, according to Roman Jakobson (1956: 76), is one of the two basic semantic lines along which discourse is developed, contiguity being the other; these are the axes of metaphor and metonymy which for Lacan structure the subject's entry into and existence in the Symbolic order). The porous nature of Fish's interpretive communities suggests that these are only arbitrary divisions of the totality of the activity of interpretation, and depend on a wider notion of community within which shared symbolic operations like the identification of similarities make communication possible (and that includes the communication with texts). It seems that a basic ability to interpret, which means possessing a shared lexicon and the ability to relate different symbolic structures within that to one another, precedes and grounds the particular kinds of interpretation practised by different individuals in different times and places. Fish in fact acknowledges this when he says that though 'interpretive strategies are not natural or universal, but *learned*', they are made possible by 'the ability to interpret [which] is not acquired; it is constitutive of being human' (1980: 172; my emphasis).

How does this dilution of the notion of discrete interpretive communities into a generalized activity of interpretation affect relations between readers and texts? For Fish, the fact that interpretation (whether general or community-specific) is basic to consciousness means that the subject-object dualism where the reader faces an independent object (the text) misrepresents the reality of reading:

The opposition between objectivity and subjectivity is a false one because neither exists in the pure form that would give the opposition its point [. . .] We do *not* have free-standing readers in a relationship of perceptual adequacy or inadequacy to an equally free-standing text. Rather, we have readers whose consciousnesses are constituted by a set of conventional notions which when put into operation constitute in turn a conventional, and conventionally seen, object. (1980: 332)

Because the reader creates the text he reads from within 'the communal or conventional categories of thought that enable [the self's] operations (of thinking, seeing, reading)' (p. 335), the meaning he confers on it is neither objective nor subjective: it is not objective, because it is the product of a point of view; yet it is not subjective either, because that point of view is socially or institutionally constructed. However, the Fishian reader invariably *posits* the text as an object, in a move which recalls Sarraute's representation of the way public relations to texts or others are characterized by objectification (a gesture which is also an unintended feature of her representation of the ideal relationship to the other or to a text). Where Fish differs from Sarraute is in his refusal to attribute any activity to the 'real' text as other in this relationship.

Yet the way Fish's discrete 'interpretive communities' rest on a general interpretative activity which unites speakers of a language and so makes communication between communities possible, in fact restores the possibility of some degree of communication within reading too. This becomes clear when we consider that the communication made possible across interpretive communities is between humans who, in so far as they are conscious, are *textual* beings, for they are constantly producing interpretations (the interpretative act is 'performed at so deep a level that it is indistinguishable from consciousness itself': Fish 1980: 272). Taken together, these two points—the fact that individuals appear both to one another and to themselves as texts, and the fact that they are able to communicate beyond each one's imposition on the other of what his interpretative strategies allow him to see—suggest that the engagement with the subjects who address us in the texts we 'literally' read (rather than reading 'textual humans' face to face) should also allow some input from them. Within the terms of Fish's own theory, then, the possibility of some kind of exchange between the reader and the literary text returns. It takes place not, as Sarraute would have it, through a humanization of the text, but through our awareness of the textuality of humans and the fact that while this complicates dialogue, it does not preclude it.

If reading is seen in terms of the kind of process by which one establishes common ground with another individual, through 'principled debate' with the textual interpretation of the world he embodies, then an ideal Sarrautean fusion of a reader with a text would involve the total coincidence of the interpretative strategies used by each to interpret reality. This is exactly what is described in the portrait scene of *Portrait d'un inconnu* (where, as in 'A très bientôt' (see Ch. 4, pp. 168–72), the fusion depends on the symbolic structure it desires to precede). Though such complete identity of two different interpretative perspectives is impossible, it can be assumed that areas of overlap exist. In Fish's theory this is what gives rise to an interpretive community; in the case of reading, one example would be the likelihood that a reader's perception of lines of poetry as units of meaning which have endings (a perception seen by Fish in 'Interpreting the *Variorum*' as imposing a form on the text: 1980: 165–6) is also shared by many poets and so *is* inscribed in the poem in a way not dealt with by his theory.

The point of this is not to claim that reading as a dialogue must be a matter of consensus and can take place only within one of Fish's specialized interpretive communities where agreement is a foregone conclusion. It is simply to demonstrate that ultimately both reader and text are constituted (with points of overlap but also of irreducible difference) within the same macrocosmic 'interpretive community'. This community is formed by the fact that conscious beings perceive reality, including themselves, in terms of symbols, and articulate what they perceive in their variously individualized versions of a shared language which, as William Ray points out, exceeds the reader's referentialization of its message as much as that message's determination of its addressee. The problems which beset all dialogue and which have been constantly to the fore of this study remain, even if they are articulated not in terms of absolute barriers between different interpretive communities, but in terms of the different positions which can be taken up within a shared community of subjects of language.

One of the problems which beset dialogue at the level of structure, before even particular social and historical differences come into play, is the fact that, as Fish points out, readers impose an identity on the text they confront (just as speakers and writers project one onto their interlocutors). But Fish does not allow for the way texts can resist this imposed image and even lead to its correction, giving rise to a form of two-way communication on shared linguistic ground. Thus the reader may be persuaded beyond his initial interpretation, in a reading which, with its revisionary dimension, fits the description in the last chapter of dialogue in general, and reading in particular, as constantly hampered by yet proceeding despite the way each partner constantly deals with his projected image of the other rather than with the other in his reality. The Fishian reader who decides that Milton's *Lycidas* is a pastoral and reads it accordingly certainly imposes an image on the text he confronts. He can impose the same image on other texts, for example deciding that George Eliot's *Adam Bede* is also a pastoral in the style of Milton, and reading it as such (see Fish 1980: 168–9). But texts can resist the identities decided for them by the Fishian reader, and so lead him to revise them. That this is the case is clear from the many texts which would not lend themselves to being defined as pastorals and which, through their resistance to such definitions, would change the reader's way of reading them. The to-ing and fro-ing between text and reader which, I argued at the end of the last chapter, keeps the act of reading from being a purely solipsistic engagement by each party with its image of the other, is ignored by Fish's theory.[19]

If both reader and text are located within the same general symbolic community, the fact that the objectivity of the text is the reader's construction rather than a reality independent of him loses its monistic implications. The subject–object dualism does not really collapse into an all-creating subjectivity, because while the text as object is only the creation of the reader's interpretative (thus linguistic) activity, the same can be said for his own identity as a subject, for it is equally constructed in terms of the language he possesses (or which possesses him). If the reader is incapable of gaining access to the 'real' text as a discrete object, he is also incapable of gaining access to his own 'real' self other than through the same filter of interpretative strategies through which he relates to the text. So if the real object disappears from the reader–text encounter, to be replaced by what interpretative conventions allow the reader to construe as the object of his reading, so does the reading subject in his true selfhood, similarly replaced by what those same interpretative conventions make of him. Interpretation is the source not only of 'texts, facts, authors and intentions' (Fish 1980: 16), but also of the reading subject who creates these, for, as Fish himself is aware (and as Sarraute simultaneously recognizes and strives to overcome), 'the self is constituted, no less than the texts it constitutes in turn, by

---

[19] Elizabeth Freund notes how 'Fish's subject, imprisoned in communal norms of interpretation and coerced by their authority, has no means of engaging with the more recalcitrant features of texts, with their rhetoricity, with the infinite regress of figuration, with doubt, uncertainty, or irony, with the strangeness and "otherness" of poetry or language. He can only appropriate them blindly as the already available terms for naturalizing meaning' (Freund 1987: 110).

conventional ways of thinking' (p. 11).[20] 'Reader' and 'text' appear
as products of a (vast) set of interpretative possibilities rather than as
phenomena existing independently of interpretation.

The fact that the reader's interpretative activity defines him as
much as it does the text undermines Fish's vision (and Sarraute's
nightmare) of an all-powerful reader imposing identical interpretative grids on every text he reads, and allows us to see some exchange
as taking place between them. This exchange is not, admittedly,
between 'real' entities, but between entities which possess the symbolic integrity of products of interpretation. The language of the
text, and which the reader shares, reaffirms, as he reads it, his own
status as subject as much as it does that of the textual subject to
which he attributes it. It thus restores a dualism which is no less
perceptible for being conventional. So while it may be impossible to
make an absolute distinction between the text and its realization in
the reader's mind, practical distinctions will be made all the time.
The nature of reading makes these unavoidable: as an experience of
language it entails the reaffirmation of the integrity of each consciousness taking part, that articulated in the text and that of the
reader who, attributing the language he reads to an enunciating
subject, will define his own subjectivity as recipient of the address in
relation to that subject. The language of the text, in so far as it conceptualizes and defines as well as running through all those who
possess it, will reinforce the reader's sense of his own identity as an
autonomous subject, distinct from the enunciating voice of the text
(which becomes the object of his attention).

This distinction between the participants in the reading process
is taken to an extreme in writing like Sarraute's which constantly
refers to the roles of writer and reader as separate even while trying

---

[20] The idea that the reading self as well as the text is an interpretation is argued, via
Charles Sanders Peirce, by Walter Benn Michaels (1980: 185–200). Michaels recalls Peirce's
famous claim that we can only know the self as an inference or thought, and that, as all our
thoughts are signs, this means that we can only know the self as a sign. Thus for Peirce (so
Michaels), the contemporary claim by champions of a 'subjective paradigm' of reading
(notably David Bleich) that our minds are 'more accessible to us than anything else' (p. 199),
would be unacceptable. Instead 'our minds are accessible to us in *exactly the same way* that
everything else is. The self, like the world, is a text', not only an interpreter but an interpretation. Where Peirce's/Michael's view of the self as located in a community of interpretation
or system of signs differs from that of Fish is in the reciprocity this is held to create in the
text–reader relationship: 'The rhetoric of the community of interpretation emphasizes the
role readers play in constituting texts, while the rhetoric of the self as sign in a system of signs
emphasizes the role texts play in constituting consciousness' (p. 199).

to unite them; but it is an effect of all language, even at the most basic level of pronouns (which also create to some extent those to whom they refer; see Ch. 4 n. 20). The more self-conscious the conscious activity in the experience of the text becomes, either as the text's presentation of itself as something to be read (we can think of the readings of 'Les Fruits d'Or' in *Les Fruits d'or*), or as the reader's reflection on his own activity as he reads (a self-consciousness that culminates in theories of reading), the more explicit the self-definition by each partner will be. Yet, as we saw Sarraute's works illustrate if not acknowledge in the last two chapters, the symptoms of self-consciousness merely magnify properties inherent in consciousness, without being qualitatively different from them.

3. Reading and the recreation of identity

It seems then that reading, because it takes place in a language which defines and distinguishes those who participate in it as source and as recipient of the message, will always give rise to a dualism where a falsely coherent textual other is established and opposed to an equally illusory reading self. It is thus impossible in linguistic practice to see the act of reading in the monistic terms in which Fish proclaims it. If the constant recreation of subject and object in reading[21] seems in one sense to be a loss, for the engagement with the text as an object is founded on an illusion, it is almost certainly a more substantial gain. For even if the perceived text is an effect of the possibilities of interpretation which construct us too (also illusorily) as readers, the fact that it and we are equally constructed means that we can engage with it as an other; it can respond to us, as a subject rather than an object of reading, and offer some resistance to our way of looking at the world (and at it). Seeing the text as constructed not by us but by what constructs us too enables a practical distinction to be made between what are none the less the products of a single universe of symbols, a distinction which allows for some reciprocal transformation within that universe, and beyond the definition by each of the other which is an indisputable feature of dialogue.

[21] This recreation recalls Lacan's description of everyday dialogue as an interaction not of true selves whose linguistically structured unconscious would make present the whole Symbolic order, but of the artificial constructs of *moi* and *moi autre* (Lacan 1978: 286).

The theorization of reading, I have said, simply makes more explicit the constant separation of text and reader entailed by the linguistic nature of the act of reading. Jonathan Culler (1982) points out the constant relapse into dualism on the level of studies of reading,[22] but attributes it specifically to the attempt to talk *about* the experience of reading texts, and to the fact that this attempt invariably contains an element of narration. Yet he does see this narrative element in turn as resulting from the fact that the experience of reading is itself problematic, for ' "experience" always has this divided, duplicitous character: it has always already occurred and yet is still to be produced—an indispensable point of reference, yet never simply there' (1982: 63). The gap which causes problems for accounts of the reading process is thus not between an experience of reading and the act of talking about it; it is *within* the notion of an experience of reading which those accounts posit as singular: 'To read is to operate with the hypothesis of a reader, and there is always a gap or division within reading' (p. 67; cp. p. 82). Analyses of reading, Culler argues, resolve these internal divisions by incorporating them into a dualistic narrative. Thus in terms of our discussion of reading so far, we can say that while the narrative element in accounts of reading is the mode in which the text–reader dualism is articulated (a text acts on a reader or vice versa), this dualism is an effect of the way readers, in the very *act* of reading, conform to an image or 'hypothesis of a reader' (so showing self-definition to be an effect not just of self-conscious but of unreflective conscious reading). Furthermore, this construction, in reading, of an image of one's role as a reader, is based for Culler too on the nature of identity in general as something one constructs rather than experiences unproblematically (he takes the example of 'reading as a woman' as involving the creation of the feminine identity it calls on: p. 64).

---

[22] His sensitivity to this phenomenon may be due to having participated in it himself in an earlier essay, 'Literary Competence' (1975: 113–30). There, while claiming that the self is constituted by interpersonal conventions and thus that a poem 'has meaning only with respect to a system of conventions which the reader has assimilated' (p. 116), he none the less evokes an autonomous self capable of becoming aware of his own guiding assumptions and so of acceding 'painfully or joyfully [. . .] to an expansion of self' (p. 130). Jane Tompkins explicitly compares his hesitation here 'between a structuralist rejection of self as an organizing principle and a liberal humanism that defines moral and intellectual growth in terms of self-awareness and self-development' (1980a: p. xviii) to the way Fish's presentation, in 'Interpreting the *Variorum*', of his own growth as a critic implies an idea of the self as independent and responsible, in direct opposition to his theoretical view of that self as the product of public interpretative conventions (p. xxiii).

I would add simply that what grounds this construction of an identity in the first place is the conceptualizing, defining nature of the language which constitutes us; this is why reading, as an encounter with the language of the text, stimulates the reaffirmation of one's particular reader-identity.

The elementary level at which language defines its users casts doubt on a distinction Culler makes between this dualism as informing accounts of specific readings, and what he sees as the monism of abstract theoretical writing (about the act of reading in general). Theoretical discourse too operates in terms of a language which individuates its users—its own source and addressee, as well as those implied by any experience of language it posits. The way abstract theory, though it may *assert* a monistic view of the reading experience, cannot do without the concepts of individuated readers and texts which I see the linguistic nature of that experience as making unavoidable, is nicely illustrated by Stanley Fish (a prime example of theoretical monism for Culler). Fish's language lets his theoretical claims down in an especially striking way in a remark he makes when he points out a previous instance of such linguistic dualism in his own work. He had described *Coriolanus* as 'a play about speech-acts', and so contradicted his theoretical belief in the inaccessibility of the text as such, independent of its appearance in terms of some interpretative system. But even as he indicates and condemns this past involuntary relapse into binary thinking, he is unable to avoid re-establishing the play and its reader as separate concepts: 'It is with speech-act theory in mind that *I approached the play* in the first place' (Fish 1980: 200; my emphasis). However much he may problematize the text–reader opposition, it cannot be entirely evacuated from his language, or by extension from the theory formed out of that language.

Indeed, it is not only the tenacity of dualistic thinking about reading that Fish's writing illustrates. His presentation of his theory is a prime example of the narrativity to which such dualism, in Culler's account, gives rise. The 'narrativization' of the reading process is taken to an extreme of self-consciousness in *Is There a Text in This Class?*, for Fish so organizes this collection of essays and comments on those essays that through a reading of his own writings he can tell the story of his development as a reader of other works. The collection narrates one reader's engagements with his own texts (themselves accounts of engagements with others), and thereby tells the story of his evolution from a formalist view of reading to the dissolution of text and reader into interpretive communities. As Elizabeth Freund notes, the book's 'intensely self-conscious rhetorical disposition [. . .] invests the collection as a whole with the dramatic air and shape of a reader's *Bildungsroman*' (1987: 105).

I shall conclude by looking at the implications which these hypotheses on the nature of reading and the kind of relationship it institutes between readers and texts have for the activity of reading Sarraute. How does the practice of reading, as it emerges from this presentation of some of the insights and limitations of reader-response criticism, relate to the ideal of reading as aspired to and apparently finally abandoned by Sarraute? More importantly, what response does it allow readers of her work to the submissive role her valorization of different modes of reading recommends to them?

Given the textual constitution of the reader as well as of the work he can thereby engage with, we can say that the fusion of reader and text aspired to by Sarraute (as by Poulet) does in fact exist, but it is located within language rather than prior to it. When Sarraute suggests that the failure to achieve the kind of prelinguistic fusion she desires is the fault of readers who fall back on generally linguistic and specifically literary conventions in order to interpret the text, we can both acknowledge the validity of this perception of reading as proceeding according to established conventions, and also apply her identification of those conventions to the text itself. In this way, we subsume both parties into a larger symbolic body which embraces their different socio-historical horizons and allows them to find common ground. Yet the nature of this symbolic body in which text and reader have their being, the way in which, as a set of signs and concepts, it gives the illusion of coherence and self-identity to everything it names, means that the language of the text, beyond being a meeting-place, is also a place where the illusory integrity of text and reader is constantly re-established. Thinking about reading, and specifically about reading work like Sarraute's where the text–reader dialogue is a recurring theme, should then include an awareness of both the inevitability and the conceptual instability of each party's assertion of its distinctness from the other in that act.

Both *Enfance* and *Tu ne t'aimes pas* illustrated how language, if it makes absolute distinctions between self and other impossible, is also the site of the subject's constant self-redefinition: in both texts, the 'centrifugal' movement towards the disintegration of the authorial subject was undermined by an inverse centripetal consolidation of the self. This assertion of the self's integrity is also more generally evident in the self-conscious (and thus doubly self-defining) nature of Sarraute's writing. Constantly aware of its status as a text to be read,[23] it inevitably makes impossible the fusion to which it aspires in the very act of appealing for it to a reader whose sense of his own individuality it simultaneously affirms. Yet, as writing, it necessarily remains blind to the way it perpetuates the distinction between text and reader; thus Sarraute's novels, through their ever more emphatic representation of the reader as prey to convention, give the problem of textual communication a fictional setting which identifies the failure to achieve the merging of reader and text as due solely to misreading.

If Sarraute's fictional representations of reading dissimulate the way the texts being read must participate in that linguistic self-definition which makes fusion with the reader impossible and which she attributes exclusively to a failure of reading, the language of her own representing text cannot conceal its subjection to the rules of symbolization. We have seen how Sarraute's authorial discourse, deeply sensitive to all that is conventional in language, asserts its own truth-claim by anchoring itself in the body. Yet this claim to 'viscerality', read in the light of her own representation of inauthentic discourse, shows itself to be governed by the same dependency on the metonymic and metaphoric identification and elaboration of signs (here to establish the body which guarantees truth) that marks the inauthenticity of others' language. To read Sarraute's representing discourse in the light of the discourses it represents is a move her novels actually encourage, for right from *Portrait d'un inconnu* onward, the act of writing the text we are reading is ever more explicitly evoked within the story it tells, to the point of

---

[23] We are reminded of Jean-Yves Tadié's observation of the 'theoretical' dimension of Nathalie Sarraute's fictional writing, and vice versa (see Ch. 1 n. 6). This dual character again undermines Culler's distinction between theory and story, in particular his claim that theory (unlike narrative) articulates a monistic view of reading. One reason for the impossibility of making a clear distinction between theory and narrative is that the temporality to which the latter gives concrete form in the shape of a story is constructed on the basis of the temporality of all discourse and not just that which is specifically narrative. Thus 'theoretical' language will be no more able than the language of fiction to overcome the conceptual separation of the reader and text it names.

overturning it in *L'Usage de la parole*. Sarraute of course intends us to perceive the contrast between these discourses, yet the fact that underlying similarities are also evident merely illustrates the way her written text exceeds its founding intention.

This alienation of authorial intention in the text is of course responsible for the reappearance in Sarraute's own writing of something else to which her explorations of the difficulties of dialogue are highly sensitive—namely the way speakers define not only themselves as they speak, but also those *to whom* they speak. This definition is compounded by the way the appeal in address for an uninfluenced but affirmative response coexists with an attempt to *produce* that response by projecting in the address itself the affirmation one desires from the (defined) other (for a memorable fictional portrayal of such projection and its disappointment see *Les Fruits d'or*, 76). Sarraute's authorial discourse tries to obtain its reader's assent in advance by figuring the response of an ideal reader within itself. Yet just as we can read her claim to expressive truth in the light of her simultaneous representation of second-hand and conventional language, we can also see the way the characteristics of her fictional exchanges, which are struggles for control of the other, are manifest too in her own prescriptions for reading. By reading, in this way, Sarraute's whole text as marked to some extent by mechanisms which she highlights in the discourses of her characters, we provide not the prescribed response (which we read as part of the text), but a real, dialogic response to it. For by recognizing that what her discourse articulates as expressive truth is determined by what the conventions of language let us formulate, rather than by an immediately sensed reality which demands to be given shape in language, we evoke the whole Symbolic order and so play the role of the Other. We thus unmask the illusory authenticity every speaker's discourse holds for him and which Sarraute can see through so well in others' words but, like all speakers, less well in her own.[24]

---

[24] This is the position of response the Lacanian analyst takes up toward the analysand's discourse. If the response is to avoid strengthening the analysand's self-objectification, then, Lacan tells analysts, 'ce n'est pas de lui que vous avez à lui parler [. . .] Si c'est à lui que vous avez à parler, c'est littéralement d'autre chose, c'est-à-dire d'une chose autre que ce dont il s'agit quand il parle de lui, et qui est la chose qui vous parle, chose qui, quoi qu'il dise, lui resterait à jamais inaccessible, si d'être une parole qui s'adresse à vous elle ne pouvait évoquer en vous sa réponse, et si, d'en avoir entendu le message sous cette forme inversée, vous ne pouviez, à le lui retourner, lui donner la double satisfaction de l'avoir reconnu et de lui en faire reconnaître la vérité' (1966: 419–20).

If this conception of reading Sarraute seems to put the reader in a position of absolute power with regard to her text, two final points need to be made which will undo this impression. First, if the real reader can see the way the ideal reader is not, as he is presented, the embodiment of a 'true' way of reading, but simply a construct within the larger symbolic structure which is the text, he is nevertheless unable to read his own constructed nature, and the larger Symbolic universe in which his limited consciousness, which similarly appears to him to be his true self, is contained. If he cannot consciously experience the linguistic forces which have formed his conscious self, he can at least be aware that the text's demonstration of this situation extends to his own engagement with the text as well. That is, the discursive universe of the fictional text, with the addressing subject and ideal addressee it defines and embraces, can figure for him the way in which the conscious opposition of the real text's authorial voice and its reader conceals their status as symbolic entities constructed out of the language which they share and which exceeds them.

Thus Sarraute's texts, if not Sarraute's intentions as author, demonstrate how language, and specifically the language which constitutes the text, both embraces author and reader, so permitting the transfer of the text into the reader's mind, yet also reinforces the illusory subjective integrity of each, that sense of self which has built into it for its subject the inability to see through it. The way language both transcends and defines the parties in dialogue explains not only how one can identify in the utterance a speaker-intention for whose establishment the recipient is not solely responsible (thus I have inferred Sarraute's desire to articulate the truth of the tropism, as well as the strategies by which she tries to ensure that this articulation is received as expressed). It also accounts for the way that, despite this degree of communication, the partners in dialogue will always, as conscious, maintain a distinctness from each other which makes it impossible to guarantee the accuracy of what is inferred as the intended message (hence the speaker's attempt to ensure the correct interpretation), as well as allowing the recipient to identify an utterance-meaning beyond what the speaker may have intended.

The final point concerns the status of Sarraute's texts, whose role in demonstrating to the reader the limits of his own subjective autonomy seems suddenly to have transformed them from being the passive object of scrutiny to in fact dictating how we read not only them but also ourselves. Jonathan Culler, in a survey of deconstructive literary criticism, has claimed that one of its most problematic aspects is 'the identification of what texts say about language, texts, articulation, order and power as truths about language, texts, articulation, order and power' (1982: 279). This belief in the truth of the text is of course ultimately only a belief in the truth of what one reads as being in the text, but the fact of attributing this to the discourse which one receives rather than to that which one produces bears witness, even in the kind of criticism which might be said to be least respectful of the idea of meaning, and certainly of authorial meaning, to a certain priority of the text over our readings of it. Robert Scholes sees this priority (in the sense of authority) as a consequence of the temporal priority of the text's writing over its reading, for 'the reader's choices in "making" meaning are [. . .] severely limited by the writer's previous choices of what marks to put on the page' (1985: 154).[25] It is clear that despite this priority there remains considerable leeway for variations of interpretation, but it also appears that, however much the interpretation may deviate from what the author intended to be understood and assented to, in some way readers still feel a desire to attribute the authority for their conclusions to the text to whose address they are responding.

What consequences does this twist in the understanding of the text–reader dialogue have for the issue with which this study opened, namely the capacity of irony to overcome the limitations of expression through a shared constitution of meaning over the head of the utterance whose inadequacy is thus simultaneously acknowledged and transcended? After outlining the—generally overlooked—dialogic element in irony (its cooperative dimension), I established a distinction between verbal irony as articulating, through a language which is overtly false to the intended sense, an attitude already established in the speaker and which requires only

---

[25] He demonstrates this with a criticism of Stanley Fish's example, in 'How to recognise a poem when you see one' (1980: 322–37), of the way a class studying 17th-cent. religious poetry construed as a poem a list of writers on linguistics left on the blackboard from a previous class. One of the names was that of Richard Ohmann, which Fish misspelt with one 'n' and which students read as the exclamation 'Oh man'. For Scholes, the fact that had the name been spelt properly this interpretation was less likely to have been offered, simply proves that 'texts have a certain reality. A change in a letter or a mark of punctuation can force us to perceive them differently, read them differently, and interpret them differently' (Scholes 1985: 161).

READING IN THEORY AND PRACTICE 219

the addressee's recognition of it, and epistemological irony, where despite the inadequacy of language something is created through the equal participation of both interlocutors. I claimed in Chapter 2 that Sarraute's two-tier view of language, as largely deadened through conventional use but with enclaves of authentic expression not explored by other writers, in fact generates a kind of dialogue with the reader which has much more in common with verbal irony than with epistemological irony. Her belief in the expressive power of language, and her mistrust of the reader who must be deprived by the text of any space for independent activity,[26] makes this aspect of her writing particularly explicit.

However, Chapter 3 recognized the fact that in so far as Sarraute's attempts to control the reader are a reaction to that alienation from one's addressee which particularly characterizes written texts with an anonymous public audience but which is to some degree a feature of all utterances, those strategies draw attention to an important feature of dialogue in general. That is the way each speaker will attempt to ensure, across the distance of linguistic communication, his addressee's correct reception of his intended meaning. This element of persuasion inherent in address, taken to an extreme when the kind of reception desired becomes articulated as an explicit part of the message itself (as with Sarraute's representation of her ideal reader), leads one to question perceptions of dialogue which see it as involving the unrestricted cooperation of autonomous subjects. Instead, as I have suggested, it proceeds more haltingly through the alternating attempts by each participant to acquire the other's assent to his proposition. Thus the overt attempt by Sarraute to direct the response of her readers ultimately leads one to question the whole notion of a dialogic, epistemological irony where language would be transcended in a moment of creative cooperation. Her strategies of control, a reaction to the intensely alienated nature of the kind of dialogue a text written for an unknown public initiates, suggest that in a more attenuated form something similar may be going on in all linguistic exchanges.

The discussion just now of the way readers acknowledge the truth of texts apparently puts the final nail in the coffin of the notion

[26] 'Beaucoup d'auteurs modernes renvoient à du non-dit; et cet énorme non-dit, où le lecteur est libre de mettre ce qu'il veut, il l'emplit souvent de sentiments d'une grande banalité, comme ceux qu'on lui a appris à connaître. Cette sorte de collaboration-là avec le lecteur chez moi n'existe pas: rien n'est sous-entendu [. . .]' (1985c: 13; see also 1956: 76).

of dialogue as an ideal moment of shared reflection free from domination or submission, for the temporal priority of the written text (as, less emphatically, of the spoken utterance) seems to bring with it a recognition of its authority by the reader, one not consonant with a role of equal creativity for him. This introduces a new dimension into the idea of the text as establishing power over its addressee, for it suggests that readers may collaborate in this assignment of authority to what they read. The degree to which the text–reader dialogue enacts the power structure of verbal irony, with the text already knowing the meaning to be interpreted, may in fact be partly the work of the reader.

However, this should not be seen as a straightforward 'victory' for the text over a reader who submits to it without resistance. The text whose authority the reader acknowledges is always the result of his interpretation, and is not reducible to the intentions of the author-ial subject. If the reader does then submit to the text, it is in a free act which is not simply passive, and it is to the text as he has 'written' it in his reading. The text this reading defers to is thus the product of the reader's definition (but also of the way the resistance his defini-tion encounters during his reading helps to shape it). Yet if his definition is to have credence before its own public (including him-self), it must be justified, and so the construed meaning is claimed to be located in the words on the page, in a gesture of surrender by the reader on which his authority in the face of his own addressees paradoxically depends. Thus if, as I said in Chapter 4, talking about texts cannot avoid turning them into mastered objects, the ultimate assertion of mastery seems, strangely, to be the claim that the mean-ing one's reading has appropriated *was* dictated by the work after all. Reading, finally, seems to involve not only the reader's establish-ment of an identity for the more or less compliant text he responds to and so realizes, but also his surrender of authority, in an active gesture of submission, to that text which he none the less constituted in a process which also constituted his identity as reader. The com-plexity of the text–reader dialogue, and the conceptual instability of its participants (a text created in a reading which validates itself by giving priority to that text; a reader who, paradoxically, exists only as the interlocutor of the text created by his reading), are such that in the encounter between text and reader it would be foolish to attempt to declare a winner.

CONCLUSION

ICI—FROM LANGUAGE TO SILENCE
AND BACK

Nathalie Sarraute's writing, both as a representation of a fictional world and as an authorial address to a reader, places enormous emphasis on the act of communication, the anxiety and distress caused by its repeated failure, and the tenacity with which, faced with this failure, human beings constantly attempt anew to establish contact. Yet if this consistent focus seems to manifest a belief in dialogue as the completion of one's own limited point of view on the world by that of another, this impression is contradicted by how both the represented dialogues and the Sarrautean address to the reader actually function. While the response of an independent other is certainly sought, it is sought only in so far as it might ideally (if never in reality) be *identical* with the addressor's own outlook. Thus the ideal Sarrautean dialogue is one where response would be entirely affirmative, neutralizing its otherness by doubling the speaker's own perspective.

It is an ideal which remains remarkably constant throughout Sarraute's writing career, even while its unattainability becomes ever more explicitly acknowledged. In section v of *Ici* (1995) it is a fantasized alternative to the reality of non-communication (where the other refuses to accept that the infinite Sarrautean self—here identified simply as 'ici'—really experiences certain feelings). Yet the very terms in which such perfect communication is dreamt of here make its impossibility evident, for it is shown to rest on a view of language which ignores the complex process of interpretation. Instead, for Sarraute, language must ideally be a simple code (though still 'secreted' organically by its referent), capable of transmitting the speaker's idea exactly to the hearer without the slightest alteration:[1]

Ce qui sans lui ne se serait pas montré, des mots ne l'auraient pas enveloppé pour le porter chez lui et l'implanter . . . pour que ça puisse rester chez lui tel que c'était

---

[1] This is fundamentally the same view of language which underlies and invalidates Gerald Prince's notion of the 'degree-zero narratee', so close to Sarraute's ideal reader (see Ch. 5, pp. 198–9).

ici . . . surtout pas de changements, d'embellissements, pas la moindre fantaisie, surtout pas [. . .] S'il avait accepté de le recevoir chez lui, cela aurait pu devenir plus lourd, plus dense . . . D'être recouvert de mots, enserré étroitement par eux l'aurait rendu encore plus stable et sûr, plus résistant, plus durable. (p. 45)

Thus the failure of the attempt at dialogue once again in *Ici* is not only entirely consonant with the evolution of Sarraute's writing as we have traced it up to *Tu ne t'aimes pas*; it also shows itself explicitly to be the inevitable result of a restrictive view of communication which excludes precisely the 'baggage' which the interlocutor brings to the exchange and which contributes to his interpretation of the speaker's words. What Sarraute's ideal dialogue rejects—in the very move which renders it impossible—is what communication theorists Dan Sperber and Deirdre Wilson define as the 'gap between the semantic representations of sentences and the thoughts actually communicated by utterances', a gap 'filled not by [. . .] coding, but by inference' (Sperber and Wilson 1986: 9).[2]

The impossibility of the Sarrautean ideal of identical response, devoid of otherness, is compounded by the fact that if speakers seek from one another only reflection of their own views rather than the experience of encountering a different perspective, then, as her fiction shows, dialogues, if pursued, will invariably turn into power struggles where each participant tries to obtain from the other acquiescence without difference. As long as the desire for sameness remains the impetus to communication, and the unavoidable otherness of the interlocutor is a cause of distress (rather than, for example, being appreciated for what it brings to the self), the only solution seems to be a withdrawal into the guaranteed sameness of the self. (Of course, as *Entre la vie et la mort* showed, this presumed self-identity is itself in fact an illusion, and so withdrawal fails to bring the desired serenity—something which Sarraute's ongoing impulsion to write, and to publish those writings, makes evident.) Only by withdrawing can the subject escape not only from its inability to impose its perspective on others, but also from those

---

[2] Sperber and Wilson, in a detailed critique of the code model of communication (a model which dates back to Aristotle's *De Interpretatione*), have drawn attention to the element of inference which it ignores: 'Verbal communication is a complex form of communication. Linguistic coding and decoding is involved, but the linguistic meaning of an uttered sentence falls short of encoding what the speaker means: it merely helps the audience infer what she means. The output of decoding is correctly treated by the audience as a piece of evidence about the communicator's intentions. In other words, a coding-decoding process is subservient to a Gricean inferential process' (1986: 27).

others' simultaneous attempts to dominate its own internal infinity. Within Sarraute's fiction (a fiction ever more clearly subordinated to the process of writing which creates it), this desire for withdrawal is that 'besoin de fuite . . . nous l'avons tous éprouvé', felt, in *L'Usage de la parole* (p. 85), when two casual acquaintances who are in fact totally indifferent to each other realize that they will have to make conversation. What each wants to flee is that annexation of his internal infinity by the other which will inevitably take place, the 'véritable mue' which occurs when 'cet indéfinissable, ce tout, ce rien, ce vide, ce plein qu'est chacun d'eux soudain rencontre ceci: une forme tracée à grands traits, un schéma grossier, un portrait robot' (p. 85).

On the level of her authorial discourse, Sarraute repeats her characters' scepticism about and withdrawal from dialogue, in her increasingly pessimistic attitude towards her own projected readers.[3] We have seen this pessimism culminate in what seems to be a definitive rejection of intersubjectivity in *Tu ne t'aimes pas*, where the internal universe into which the authorial self escapes manifests itself as a multiplicity of dialoguing voices which release that self from any need to engage with others. *Ici* continues the withdrawal from communication, representing authentic expression of the inner life as profoundly incompatible with intersubjective dialogue. In the eleventh of the text's twenty sections (narratively autonomous yet thematically linked, in a structure reminiscent of *Tropismes* or *L'Usage de la parole*), we see the self accused by its interlocutors of talking as though to itself, of ignoring their presence: 'On a l'impression que vous ne parlez qu'à vous-même . . . que vous oubliez, en tout cas que vous négligez, de tenir compte de notre présence . . .' (*Ici* 102). They berate it for its tendency to interrupt conversations with 'des coq-à-l'âne'—a habit which proves that

---

[3] In *Ici* (as in *Tu ne t'aimes pas* and, most recently, *Ouvrez*), disillusionment with dialogue is mirrored structurally by the absence of any direct concern with the reader. Here reading as an activity is acknowledged, but no longer related at all to the self's discourse. Where a sole reader is shown, it is not of this text (as in *Enfance* or *Entre la vie et la mort*), nor even of a text of the same name (*Les Fruits d'or*), but of an entirely different work which the self too has read. So while he is endowed with all the characteristics of the 'good reader' familiar from *Les Fruits d'or*—a simple amplifier of the text, he refuses to add to it or distort it through interpretation—he is no longer signalled as a possible addressee of Sarraute's own text: '"Il y a des passages . . . j'en ai retenu par cœur . . . celui-ci, tenez . . ." Des mots arrivent, poussés par lui . . . mais a-t-il besoin de les pousser? ils avancent de leur propre mouvement, sa voix, ses intonations ne font que respectueusement les aider . . .' (*Ici* 56).

what it has to say has no connection to those to whom it articulates
the thoughts of its self-sufficient inner world, disrupting the 'legit-
imate' exchanges going on around it:[4]

Il en vient sans cesse de partout . . . un mouvement incessant . . . le défilé silencieux
d'âmes en peine . . . privées des mots qui seuls pourraient leur permettre de
prendre corps, de faire irruption et de rompre brusquement le fil de la conversation qui en toute légitimité, en toute sécurité ici au centre se déroule [. . .]
   Mais voilà qu'il se produit dans l'enchaînement des propos un léger arrêt . . . on
dirait qu'il y a entre les chaînons comme une solution de continuité où ce hors-de-
propos-là pourrait bien aller s'insérer . . . il n'y tient plus, il faut qu'il sorte, des mots
lui viennent [. . .] (pp. 102–3)

The fact that the self is 'really' present not where it appears to
others to be (in a social conversation) but on its own internal scene,
attributes to it once more a plane of intellectual activity inaccessible
to the one-dimensional others with whom it interacts (cp. *TTP* 105,
and *O passim*). Yet again, the mode in which the Sarrautean self
engages in dialogue is structurally closer to verbal than to epistemological irony:[5] ' "C'est drôle, vous ne trouvez pas, cette impression
qu'on a parfois de se dédoubler, de fonctionner sur deux plans à la
fois . . . Vous ne trouvez pas?" Non. Leur silence le montre: ils ne
trouvent pas' (*Ici* 106).

What is new in *Ici*, however, is the fact that what the self focuses
on when it withdraws from intersubjective dialogue to its 'other
scene' is not, as one might expect from earlier works, the tropistic
activity it senses going on around it. Instead, in this text, the withdrawal from communication takes a further, still more dramatic
step towards a withdrawal from language altogether, even from the
authentic expression epitomized in the articulation of the tropism.
No longer just opposing 'living' to 'dead' language, the infinite self
to its conceptualized effigy, with the purveyors of the latter world-
view (readers included) being the object of the infinite self's
authorial irony, *Ici* sets up an opposition between language of any
kind and silence. After a section (XIV) in which the whole pursuit of
the tropistic truth behind others' actions has its value cast into
doubt, given the depressing vista of selfish and aggressive human

---

[4] Just as the fragment from Pascal which is so admired in the final section is composed of
words 'adressés à personne' (p. 195).
[5] See Ch. 3, pp. 127–8.

motivations which it invariably reveals,[6] the authorial voice of *Ici* refuses (in s. xv) to give language even to its own entirely private and (therefore) positive experience of peace and serenity. Though words are sensed on the horizon of experience, words sanctioned as worthy, living bearers of the tropism through the organic metaphors so familiar in Sarraute ('On dirait que d'ici une tiédeur se répand très loin qui réchauffe, fait germer, éclore . . . des paroles vont en jaillir et venir se déposer ici dans ce terreau': p. 154), they are repelled by a self which instead embraces silence:

Mais non, il ne faut pas, surtout pas, pas maintenant, que tout cela reste encore très loin [. . .]

Que rien là-bas ne bouge, ne mûrisse, n'éjecte et projette jusqu'ici . . . ici doit rester pur de toute parole [. . .]
Que rien ne puisse si peu que ce soit entamer cette plénitude, troubler tant soit peu cette sérénité . . .
Juste encore pour cette fois . . . (pp. 155–6)

Language seems no longer to provide an adequate arena for the life-and-death struggle for authenticity. Even a single word would destroy the pure abstraction of the ineffable self ('aucun espace à traverser, rien vers quoi se diriger, rien à atteindre, rien à rejoindre': p. 153) and make of it 'un espace bien délimité, durci, aplani, bien nivelé et balisé parcouru d'autoroutes, de voies ferrées où les paroles circulent' (p. 154). Authenticity is no longer to be found within language; it is in the silence which results when language is abandoned that perfection is to be found, a perfection which now even the words of the self's own internal dialogue threaten to destroy:

Et voici dans cette immobilité parfaite, dans ce silence . . . il semblait qu'il ne pouvait y avoir ici aucune présence . . . brusquement ces mots: 'Comment il s'appelle déjà, cet arbre?' . . .
Mais ce n'est rien, une brève intrusion, une menace de destruction qui sera repoussée en une seconde . . . (p. 17)

However, if the life-and-death struggle for authenticity has been displaced from within language to between language and silence, it

---

[6] 'C'était donc cela, cette lumière si prometteuse au bout du labyrinthe . . . Voilà où ont abouti ces laborieux parcours, ces allers et retours, ces efforts pour arriver à se hisser de "Pourquoi?" en "Pourquoi?" [. . .]
A quoi bon persévérer, essayer d'aller plus loin là où ne se dressent à perte de vue que de telles constructions? Y a-t-il la moindre chance d'y rien trouver qui ne soit tout aussi décevant . . .' (p. 148).

would none the less be inaccurate to see silence as the unambiguously positive value, language as the negative (as the fact that Sarraute has chosen to write *Ici*, to extol silence through language, should make clear to us). The 'immobilité parfaite' of silence can very easily become the immobility of death—once that silence ceases to be *chosen* but instead becomes *imposed* through the forgetting of words, especially names (as, above, of the tamarind tree), consciousness itself faces the threat of its own annihilation: 'Et voilà que tout à coup là où il était, où c'était sûr qu'il se trouverait, cette béance, ce trou . . . "Un trou de mémoire" comme on dit négligemment, insouciamment [. . .] Mais ici ce qu'il a laissé derrière lui, cette ouverture, cette rupture disjoint, disloque, fait chanceler . . .' (p. 11). One may choose to forsake language and privilege instead non-linguistic lived experience, but to have language forsake us when we find we need it to name our world is to be confronted with the sense of our own inevitable extinction, that sense of death as the 'envers inséparable' of life that Sarraute's Chekhov discovered on his deathbed in 'Ich sterbe' (*UP* 11–18).[7] The loss of *objects* has always been associated in Sarraute with the 'angoisse de la mort', as Sartre pointed out in his 1947 preface to *Portrait d'un inconnu* (*PI* 12); the loss of *words* makes of absence and death something internal to the self, already present within the living mind.

Death as intimately present to the self rather than as simply opposed to life complicates retrospectively the whole Sarrautean aesthetic, that aesthetic which holds that writing should allow the human experience it describes to live, to breathe, to circulate like the sap to which she so often compares it (see Sarraute 1972*a*: 34). That aesthetic principle was given its simplest articulation by the critical *alter ego* of *Entre la vie et la mort*: 'Entre nous deux mots suffisent. Aussi grossiers que ceux-là: c'est mort. C'est vivant' (*EVM* 70). Now, however, when not simply the dead, conventional language of the other but more intimately the living, expressive language of the self is removed, death is shown to reside at the heart of existence: 'Ce qui peut n'importe où, à n'importe quel moment s'ouvrir, laisser passer, se répandre ici ces exhalaisons . . . le souffle, l'haleine de l'absence irréparable, de la disparition . . .' (*Ici* 23).

---

[7] 'Depuis des années, des mois, des jours, depuis toujours, c'était là, par-derrière, mon envers inséparable . . . et voici que d'un seul coup, juste avec ces deux mots, dans un arrachement terrible tout entier je me retourne . . . vous le voyez: mon envers est devenu mon endroit. Je suis ce que je devais être. Enfin tout est rentré dans l'ordre: Ich sterbe' (*UP* 16).

The way the loss of language, by bringing death within the self, transcends the attitude to language as either 'dead' or 'living', expressive or arbitrary, either emerging from within the self or imposed on it from without, is emphatically illustrated in the role played by proper names in *Ici*. As conventional labels, names have always been for Sarraute the epitome of writing which kills the tropistic reality of human experience through reductive abstractions: the names Dumontet and Martereau in her first two novels are attached to conventionally delineated fictional characters whose dimensions the novels, through their explorations of tropisms, portray to be inadequate to the complexity of identity. Yet with the displacement of death out of language and into the void left in the self when names like Philippine, the tamarind tree, or Arcimboldo are forgotten (these 'trous de mémoire' are the subjects of the first three sections of *Ici*), such names become positive values. Indeed the name Arcimboldo even becomes a meaningful expression of its referent, for his paintings have infused it with the organic life they embody:

Chacune de ses syllabes s'inscrivait dans la chevelure en grappes de raisin, en feuilles de vigne, en cerises, en fraises, dans la courgette qui émerge entre les deux pommes des joues, dans la bouche, une grenade entrouverte . . . il y avait aussi en lui cette même liberté, cette force d'affirmation, cette audace . . . bold [. . .] et cette lettre qui était nichée en lui, juste en son centre, où on ne s'attendrait pas à la trouver . . . pareille à cette noisette au bas de la joue, à cette mûre . . . Au-dessus de la tête, par-derrière quelque chose flotte dans le brouillard . . . une voûte blanchâtre . . . on dirait une arche [. . .] (p. 24)

To remember the forgotten name of Arcimboldo, far from exposing the mind to a deadening discourse, is temporarily to defeat death. Death can now be relegated to the realm of fiction, a danger to be savoured without any personal threat of extinction, just as when one watches a Western in the cinema:

Arcimboldo! c'est un cri, un hurlement, les spectateurs vont se dresser, les ouvreuses vont accourir [. . .] juste quand le postillon a été touché, il tombe de son siège, tout est perdu, la diligence va stopper, oh non, heureusement il est remplacé, mais les Indiens se rapprochent . . . Arcimboldo . . . il est revenu, il est là de nouveau, c'est bon, très bien, mais il n'est pas possible de s'en occuper . . . un voyageur s'affaisse, une flèche empoisonnée est fichée dans sa poitrine, les chevaux sont à bout, d'un instant à l'autre on sera rattrapés [. . .] mais il est toujours là . . . dans sa présence là-bas quelque chose luit, vacille doucement . . . une promesse secrète, une assurance . . . l'assurance qu'il ne pourra plus disparaître, que rien jamais ne disparaîtra plus. (pp. 26–7)

The return of the lost name to memory is a guarantee of the continued life of the mind: to live is thus to have access to language, including the conventional labels we attach to people and things. Though Sarraute does not go so far as to say that we experience the world within a linguistic context, language does seem to be inseparable from experience, if only as an available resource to be rejected if desired. Yet even the rejection of language must take place through language—even the choice of silence over words in section xv of *Ici*, as an intellectual act is carried out within the language of the text. This is the difference between choosing to forsake language and being forsaken by it: the former still locates one within language whereas the latter is death.

Just as the claim to leave language behind never escapes language, the claim to withdraw from communication, once articulated, remains an act of communication—as we as readers of *Ici* can testify.[8] Though Sarraute by now seems entirely untouched by the issue of the reception of her text, its writing and publication none the less address it to a community of readers and thus place it in a situation of dialogue which is no less real for not being anticipated or acknowledged within the text. Indeed *Ici* itself gives us an example of the intrinsically dialogic nature of all utterances, in its closing meditation on the famous fragment 206 from Pascal's *Pensées*, 'Le silence éternel de ces espaces infinis m'effraie' (see Pascal 1953: 428). Though these words are 'adressés à personne' (p. 195), as the words of a 'semblable' (p. 198)[9] they arouse a response in the self: 'A leur approche tout se ranime, se met à vibrer . . .' (p. 194). Moreover, this response, in its extended metaphoric elaboration and its evocation of personal memories (the feeling of eternity created by repetition of the days of the week, an experience already described in *Enfance*, 43–4), contradicts its own account of itself as that minimal reception

---

[8] Interestingly, even the withdrawal from social conversation, while embraced by the solitary self, carries overtones of death—the 'hors-de-propos' which assail the self in s. xi confront it with ideas of mortality. The mind first wanders to a lost document which leaves behind a void: 'Un bout de néant s'ouvre par où quelque chose s'échappe . . . comme le signe avant-coureur de la disparition définitive, de l'anéantissement' (p. 104). A little later, a misunderstanding which already featured in *Entre la vie et la mort* and in *'disent les imbéciles'* (*EVM* 143–4; *DI* 70–1) is revived to disrupt once again the comfortable circuit of public conversation, and this time with an explicit articulation of the idea of death, when the detached self hears 'les Maures' as 'les morts' (pp. 108–9).

[9] The double is still the ideal interlocutor to whom the self, having abandoned the quest for an identical addressee, and seeming close to abandoning expression altogether, now listens rather than speaks.

('decoding') without interpretative addition which is desired by all Sarrautean utterances: 'Et tout ici porté par ces mots, adhérant entièrement à eux, se dilate, s'étire, s'étend, s'élève . . .' (p. 195). The contemplation of Pascal's fragment offers a closing paradigm of the oscillation between silence and language throughout *Ici*. Section xx begins in admiration of the poetic power of these words which evoke the internal infinity of 'ici' as much as the external infinity of the cosmos.[10] Yet the void which their poetry evokes, and at first seems to transcend, finally overwhelms them:

Ils étendent à perte de vue sur ces ténèbres informes une écharpe d'un tissu étincelant, solidement tressé, un chemin qui a l'éclat, la dureté souple de l'acier . . . Porté par ces mots, le long de ces mots ébloui, étourdi, on s'avance . . . 'Le silence éternel de ces espaces infinis' . . .

Mais qu'ont-ils donc, ces mots? Que leur est-il arrivé? L'écharpe étincelante s'est déchirée, effilochée . . . le brillant chemin d'acier a craquelé, ses débris se sont éparpillés . . .

On dirait que ce que ces mots avaient maîtrisé, dompté, ce à quoi ils avaient communiqué leur splendeur, leur rigueur élégante, soudain, par une violente, brutale poussée les a fendus, disloqués [. . .]

'M'effraie' . . . le signe. La preuve.

C'est donc certain. C'est ainsi. Et on y est arrivé. On s'y trouve. On est où il n'y a plus rien. Nulle part. Rien. Rien. Rien. Jamais. A jamais. A-ja-mais. Rien. (pp. 197–8)

Silence would seem to be the only logical stance to adopt before an infinite and indifferent universe which promises our annihilation and will be utterly unaffected by it: 'Quelque chose est là . . . à peine visible, très sombre, informe, illimité . . . si on voulait l'atteindre, si on s'en approchait, on serait aspiré, entraîné . . . un fétu tourbillonnant, absorbé, dissous . . .' (pp. 196–7).[11] Yet no sooner has the self

[10] Sarraute was sensitive to the poetry of this *Pensée* as far back as the 1940s—her first critical essay, 'Paul Valéry et l'enfant d'éléphant' (1947), offers as a closing example of what she sees as Valéry's arrogance, his comments on the same fragment in his 'Variation sur une *Pensée*' (see Valéry 1957: 458–73).

[11] Pascal's inevitable poetic failure in the face of an infinity he successfully evokes seems especially relevant to Sarraute's particular literary project of writing the tropism. Her urge to unearth microscopic tropistic movements—an activity which she repeatedly describes as her 'recherches'—confronts Pascal's 'effroi' before what he calls in fragment 72 ('Disproportion de l'homme') the 'abîme nouveau' revealed by the microscope. The reflections of *Ici* emphatically echo his claim in that famous fragment that man, faced with 'ces deux abîmes de l'infini et du néant', 'sera plus disposé à les contempler en *silence* qu'à les *rechercher* avec présomption' (Pascal 1953: 350; my emphasis). While Sarraute frequently uses the image of the microscope

confronted this void and the vanity of expression in the face of it,
than out of its emptiness hurtles language itself, like a meteorite, in
an association of ideas, sounds, and entire words which shows the
irrepressibility of language within the self, and in a resurgence of
linguistic memory which defies oblivion to turn the *angoisse* of
forgetting into the joy of unexpected remembrance:

> Arcimboldo! c'est lui . . . Un bolide, tombé ici tout d'un coup, Dieu sait comment,
> Dieu sait d'où . . . Arcimboldo tout entier. Arcimboldo au grand complet. L'Arci
> . . . énorme, démesuré . . . et le bold audacieux et le 'o' insolent, arrogant qui le
> redresse encore plus haut, le cambre, le cabre . . . (p. 199)

As contemplation of silence and the cosmic void is itself inevitably
linguistic, the cosmos spontaneously suggests the word 'bolide'
which in turn retrieves the lost name 'Arcimboldo'; and this,
through a complex of semantic and phonetic associations, calls up a
whole string of other words: '*au*dacieux', 'ins*o*lent', 'ar*ro*gant', 'ca*m*-
*br*er', 'cabrer'. Language may be bound to fail when pitched against
the entire universe,[12] but it also defines the mental universe in which
we move, providing the lens through which we perceive even its own
failure, its 'envers inséparable' which is silence (and which, as its
binary opposite, is still located within a semiotic structure), as well
as the inevitable death which that silence prefigures.

Linguistic expression thus ultimately defeats the lure of silence in
Ici, and defies even the ultimate challenge of death. Language is still
expression rather than dialogic address: like the name Arcimboldo
which presents itself not as a question but as an emphatic statement
('Arcimboldo, l'assurance même. L'affirmation. Le défi': p. 199), the
text of *Ici* no longer seeks a response from its reader, that response of
submission which Sarraute's earlier texts regularly solicited. Here,
as at *Tu ne t'aimes pas*, 79, the authorial self, rather than vainly hoping for such a response to its own words instead presents itself as
responding in this way to the word which invades it: 'Arcimboldo.
Tout ici est à lui. Ici est l'espace dont il a besoin pour prendre ses

---

to describe the way her writing aims to magnify the imperceptible tropism, she does acknowledge that it is problematic in that it gives an erroneous impression of language as simply an
instrument applied to the sensation rather than giving it an existence (see *OC* 1921 n. 1).

[12] We recall Sarraute's only partly tongue-in-cheek description of writers devoted (as she
has always been) to revealing aspects of reality outside the known universe of conventional
literary subjects as 'des individus isolés, inadaptés, solitaires, morbidement accrochés à leur
enfance et repliés sur eux-mêmes, cultivant un goût plus ou moins conscient pour une certaine forme d'échec' (*ES* 149–50).

aises . . . répandre aussi loin qu'il le voudra ses ondes . . .' (p. 199).
The authorial voice thus takes the place of the kind of reader it can
never find for its own text, one who would be nothing more than
that text as uttered by its author, a space in which it can be ampli-
fied. Yet in the same way as Pascal's words evoked a multiplicity of
memories and images, the response to the name Arcimboldo is in
fact much more creative than is claimed, arousing in the self echoes
of other words and objects associated with the painter's name either
through sound or as features of his work. Thus Sarraute's 'reading'
of the name Arcimboldo creates a new text from it, in a process of
interpretation which not only decodes the word but also filters it
through a complex of individual associations; and this new linguistic construct, while it may not acknowledge its status as a text to be
read, or be overtly addressed to a reader, is none the less made available for us in turn to interpret.

Given Sarraute's increasing pessimism with regard to dialogue and
reading, her ever more explicit identification of the self as its own
ideal interlocutor, and, most recently, her representation of speech
as more an affirmation of life and defiance of death than a means of
communication with anyone outside the self, how much can we
learn from her about how dialogue works? I have argued in this
study that the very ways in which she resists the otherness of the
reader while embodying in so much of her work that 'terrible desire
to establish contact' (*ES* 37) which her fiction describes, may tell us
something about complexities and tensions inherent in dialogue
generally. The way the Sarrautean double and model reader is
solicited in order to confirm a point of view which the self has
already established shows how that self considers its own discourse
as able to constitute a meaning on its own, rather than depending
on the dialogic intervention of another to make it meaningful. Yet
Sarraute's conviction that her literary discourse can express a
personal truth even if its language is common property simply
reflects that subjective investment every speaker is bound to have in
his utterance. If the subject's very identity is determined by his
language, he will necessarily be unable to see beyond its limits;
because he experiences the world through the filter of language,
he will perceive some necessary link between that experience
and the language in which, however inadequately, he tries to
articulate it.

Sarraute's more recent and dramatic withdrawal from dialogue altogether to an explicitly solitary contemplation of experience in *Ici* is thus more than just a logical development from the desire for dialogue with a double rather than with an other. It reflects too the way in which all speech, while it is dialogical in that it refers outward to a listener (even if that listener is not acknowledged, or is an imaginary *alter ego*), *also* refers back to a lived experience.[13] What *Ici* does is choose overtly the contemplation of experience over communication—yet this is of course a false opposition and so a false choice, for such contemplation, as linguistic, is of necessity implicated in dialogue even as it articulates a refusal of dialogue.[14]

Language use in fact implicates the speaker in dialogue in two ways. Even where no interlocutor is envisaged, no response anticipated, the self's solitary reflections will, as Bakhtin has taught us, still be diluted by other voices—voices which have already spoken the words used to articulate those reflections and whose inflections the present speaker unconsciously preserves. It is at the moment of reception (even by the self as it listens to itself) that discourse reveals the way it exceeds the singular expressive intention animating it. We can identify in what we hear or read traces of previous inflections which have marked the common stock of words out of which the individual's discourse—and identity—is assembled.[15] Thus every utterance is in the first instance the dialogic product of an

[13] See Paul Ricoeur (1976: 16) on discourse as a dialectic of event and meaning, where the meaning of an experience which 'as experienced, as lived, remains private' is made public, 'expressed and communicated', in 'the happening of dialogue'.

[14] Interestingly, the linguistic character of the mind even when it is not engaged in inter-subjective communication is in fact made explicit in *Ouvrez* (which appeared too recently for extended discussion here). Not only the public persona but also the private self is composed of words. As the *prière d'insérer* explains, those 'capables de recevoir convenablement des visi-teurs' remain on one side of a *paroi*, while behind it languish the 'exclus', by definition the vehicles of truth ('Chez nous, les vérités, même celles qui sont le moins bonnes à dire circu-lent librement': *O* 16). Disenchantment with public dialogue continues here—when the *paroi* is lowered to enable spontaneous expression, it is to liberate a 'gros mot' launched in reaction to the other's racist views (pp. 43–4). Otherwise the cries of 'Ouvrez' from the words of sin-cerity and truth go largely ignored. The title exemplifies the ambiguity of Sarraute's later works which make themselves present to a readership they no longer acknowledge. Although the request to 'Open up!' is explicitly *not* addressed to us, the fact that we are given privileged access to what is happening behind the *paroi* means that by virtue of opening the book (an unwitting intrusion, on one level) we are invited behind the scenes and the self does 'open up' to us.

[15] For Sarraute, too, the individual 'n'est qu'un assemblage fortuit, plus ou moins heureux, d'éléments provenant d'un même fond commun' (*ES* 40), though for her these common elements are of course prelinguistic tropisms.

interaction of other discourses which establish its ties to that totality of language within which it has constituted itself. Secondly, the very existence and interaction of these discourses itself only becomes evident in the further dialogic reception of the utterance.

Throughout this study I have argued that reading relativizes the expressive intention of the written text by engaging with it as a linguistic construct rather than as the unique expression of an experience; a basic feature of the text as a construct is that it bears the traces of other prior constructs which the reader can recognize. This mode of engagement does not make the reader all-powerful with regard to that text. As a subject of language, his own perspective is just as limited as the author's, and so just as much relativized in the linguistic encounter with the text as the text is in its reading. The language of the text, in other words, in its position as both other to the reader and, as such, a representative of what grounds his (linguistic) identity, is bound to challenge the limits of that identity, providing the reader with something which is both new to him and part of him.

This 'other' dimension of the text's language which the reader both understands and is enriched by includes those traces of social and historical contexts outside his own and traversed by that language up to the moment of reading, traces which since Bakhtin are widely acknowledged to be an integral part of the text. We saw in Chapter 5 (pp. 187–8) Jauss's conception of how the shaping force of the historical and social acts of writing and reading through which the text passes, simultaneously makes that text accessible to us and expands our own horizons. Jauss's affinity to Bakhtin has been noted by David Shepherd (1989); indeed he argues that Bakhtin not only anticipates Jauss's view of the text but maintains it with greater consistency, permitting no suggestion of a determinate text separate from the contextual forces which shape it to creep into his thinking.[16] These pre-existing contexts are bound to bear upon the

---

[16] Bakhtin's conception of the text as the ever-changing product of the contexts through which its language passes from the moment of writing is clearly closely related to Jauss's theory of 'horizons of expectations' (see Ch. 5, pp. 187–8). Shepherd indeed presents Bakhtin as not only anticipating much of Jauss's thinking on reception but as pursuing more insistently ideas whose potential in Jauss's work 'remains sadly unrealised' (Shepherd 1989: 103). Specifically, Jauss repeatedly reinstates the text as a determinate entity and so 'puts himself in a position where he is unable to follow through the full implications of his notion of the dialogic character of texts'; emphasizing the socially formative function of literature (see Ch. 5 n. 6), he 'loses sight of the fact that the concept of literature is also socially *formed*, that its social and historical reception is, as Bakhtin points out, one of its key constitutive moments' (p. 103).

reader's new, present contextualization of that text, just as comparable forces influenced the author's mode of expression. The power
to define the text's meaning thus lies neither with the author nor
with the reader alone: 'A text continues to bear the marks of its past
historical engagements which, as well as being open to recontextualisation, must also place some limit on the nature and degree of
that recontextualisation. Determinate meaning exists to the extent
that the production of meaning is contextual' (Shepherd 1989: 98).
The past and present contexts of the text's language ensure that
reading a text and assigning a meaning to it is a dialogic activity: 'If
the meanings of the text are indissociable from the reader's active
understanding, then that understanding in its turn must strictly
speaking be equally indissociable from the encounter with the text,
must be precisely context-specific' (p. 99).

   This impossibility of isolating the reader's understanding from
the text's meaning, and from the wider linguistic context of the acts
of writing and reading, seems finally to dismiss the fear which prevails in Sarraute (as well as in Iser or Poulet, whose descriptions of
reading have a markedly prescriptive quality) that her readers will
betray the texts they read by deriving from them meanings which
are somehow inadmissible. The meanings readers attribute to texts
have their source in the words on the page, but only as these words
exist in their innumerable social and historical contexts. If the
meanings construed differ from one reader to another, as well as
from author to reader, it is because different users of language will
actualize different dialogic contexts for those words from the totality available. But no language user can assert the right to define his
(unconscious) choice of contexts for words as the only one permis-
sible. And that includes the writer, whose definition of the meaning
of her words in advance of their reading, while understandable and
indeed in some form or other probably unavoidable, cannot stand,
for those words' communicative power depends precisely on their
already being part of the 'stock commun' (*UP* 89) humans share. This
communality, moreover, is what guarantees some degree of consensus in terms of interpretation, for the public use of words means that
their contextual meanings are also largely (though not entirely)
public and shared. Thus for a writer to fear that her readers will
make off with her text and impose aberrant interpretations on it is
to misconstrue her own relationship to her text, and more generally
the subject's relationship to language. Yet it is to misconstrue it in a

way which that very relationship to language makes unavoidable: shaped by language, we reach spontaneously for words to articulate who we are and what we feel, words which, although we merely borrow them from the wider linguistic community which has formed us, we are bound, as subjects of language, to consider as our own.

BIBLIOGRAPHY

References to Nathalie Sarraute's fictional works (including her plays) use the abbreviations listed at the beginning of the book. All other references (to critical works as well as to Sarraute's essays and interviews) use the author-date system. Where consecutive quotations have the same reference, it is generally given for the first quotation alone.

While Sarraute's *Œuvres complètes* have recently been published in the Bibliothèque de la Pléiade series, paperback editions remain the most easily accessible. For this reason, references are to the 'Folio' editions of her works, with the exception of *Tropismes* (Minuit), *Ouvrez* (Gallimard, coll. 'Blanche'), and the plays (also Gallimard, coll. 'Blanche').

WRITINGS BY NATHALIE SARRAUTE

Collected works

Œuvres complètes, ed. J.-Y. Tadié and others (Paris: Gallimard, Bibliothèque de la Pléiade, 1996).

Prose works

Tropismes, 2nd revised edn. (Paris: Minuit, 1957; originally published by Denoël, Paris, 1939).
Portrait d'un inconnu, 2nd edn. (Paris: Gallimard, 1956; coll. Folio, 1977; originally published by Robert Marin, Paris, 1948).
Martereau (Paris: Gallimard, 1953; coll. Folio, 1972).
Le Planétarium (Paris: Gallimard, 1959; coll. Folio, 1972).
Les Fruits d'or (Paris: Gallimard, 1963; coll. Folio, 1973).
Entre la vie et la mort (Paris: Gallimard, 1968; coll. Folio, 1973).
Vous les entendez? (Paris: Gallimard, 1972; coll. Folio, 1976).
'disent les imbéciles' (Paris: Gallimard, 1976; coll. Folio, 1978).
L'Usage de la parole (Paris: Gallimard, 1980; coll. Folio, 1983).
Enfance (Paris: Gallimard, 1983; coll. Folio, 1985).
Tu ne t'aimes pas (Paris: Gallimard, 1989; coll. Folio, 1991).
Ici (Paris: Gallimard, 1995; coll. Folio, 1997).
Ouvrez (Paris: Gallimard, coll. Blanche, 1997).

Tape-recorded versions exist of the following prose works

Tropismes and *L'Usage de la parole* (extracts), read by Nathalie Sarraute and Madeleine Renaud (Paris: des femmes, coll. écrire, entendre, 1981).

Enfance, read by Nathalie Sarraute (Paris: Audivis, 1986).

Entre la vie et la mort, read by Nathalie Sarraute (Paris: des femmes, coll. écrire, entendre, 1987).

L'Usage de la parole, read by Nathalie Sarraute (Paris: des femmes, coll. écrire, entendre, 1988).

Tu ne t'aimes pas, read by Nathalie Sarraute (Paris: des femmes, coll. écrire, entendre, 1990).

Ici, read by Nathalie Sarraute (Paris: des femmes, coll. écrire, entendre, 1995).

Dramatic works

Théâtre: Elle est là, C'est beau, Isma, Le Mensonge, Le Silence (Paris: Gallimard, coll. Blanche, 1978).

Pour un oui ou pour un non (Paris: Gallimard, coll. Blanche, 1982).

Exhibition catalogue

Nathalie Sarraute: portrait d'un écrivain, ed. A. Angrémy and N. Giret (Paris: Bibliothèque Nationale de France, 1995).

Essays and interviews

Sarraute, Nathalie (1947). 'Paul Valéry et l'enfant d'éléphant', *Les Temps modernes*, 16: 610–37 (repr. in *'Paul Valéry et l'enfant d'éléphant'—'Flaubert le précurseur'*, Paris: Gallimard, 1986).

—— (1956). *L'Ère du soupçon*. Paris: Gallimard (coll. Folio/Essais, 1987).

—— (1959*a*). 'Le Roman est en train de réfléchir sur lui-même', interview with Anne Villelaur, *Lettres françaises*, 764 (12 Mar.): 1, 4–5.

—— (1959*b*). 'Nathalie Sarraute nous parle du *Planétarium*', interview with Geneviève Serreau, *Les Lettres nouvelles*, 9 (29 Apr.): 28–30.

—— (1961*a*). 'Rebels in a World of Platitudes', in (no ed.) *The Writer's Dilemma*, (essays first published in *The Times Literary Supplement* under the heading 'Limits of Control'). London: Oxford University Press, 35–41.

—— (1961*b*). 'Virginia Woolf ou la visionnaire du "maintentant"', *Lettres françaises*, 882 (29 June): 1, 3.

—— (1961*c*). 'Le Roman jugé par Nathalie Sarraute', interview with André Bourin, *Les Nouvelles littéraires*, 1764 (22 June): 7; 1765 (29 June): 8.

—— (1962). 'La Littérature, aujourd'hui—II', *Tel Quel*, 9: 48–53.

—— (1963). 'Nouveau Roman et réalité', *Revue de l'Institut de Sociologie*, 36/2: 431–41.

—— (1964). 'Les Deux Réalités', *Esprit*, 32/7: 72–5.

—— (1965). 'Flaubert, le précurseur', *Preuves*, 168: 3–11 (repr. in *'Paul Valéry et l'enfant d'éléphant'—'Flaubert, le précurseur'*, Paris: Gallimard, 1986).

—— (1967*a*). 'Entretien avec Nathalie Sarraute à propos du *Mensonge* et du *Silence*', interview with Nicole Zand, *Le Monde* (18 Jan.): 18.

Sarraute, Nathalie (1967*b*). 'Interview avec Nathalie Sarraute', interview with Bettina Knapp, *Kentucky Romance Quarterly*, 14/3: 283–95.

—— (1968). 'Nathalie Sarraute et les secrets de la création', interview with Geneviève Serreau, *La Quinzaine littéraire*, 50 (1 May): 3–4.

—— (1970). 'Où en est l'avant-garde?', *La Quinzaine littéraire*, 102 (16 Sept.): 10–12.

—— (1972*a*). 'Ce que je cherche à faire' followed by 'Discussion', in J. Ricardou and F. van Rossum-Guyon (eds.), *Nouveau Roman: Hier, aujourd'hui*, ii. Paris: Union Générale d'Éditions (coll. 10/18), 25–57.

—— (1972*b*). 'Nathalie Sarraute a réponse à tous', interview with Bernard Pivot etc., *Le Figaro littéraire*, 1342 (4 Feb.): 13–15.

—— (1972*c*). 'Drames microscopiques', interview with Guy Le Clec'h, *Les Nouvelles littéraires*, 2318 (28 Feb.): 4–5.

—— (1973). 'Nathalie Sarraute', interview with Germaine Brée, *Contemporary Literature*, 14/2: 137–46.

—— (1974). 'Nathalie Sarraute: A contre-courant du théâtre traditionnel, à contre-courant du théâtre d'avant-garde', interview with Simone Benmussa, *Combat* (14 Mar.): 13.

—— (1975). 'Le Gant retourné', *Cahiers Renaud Barrault*, 89: 70–9 (repr. in *Digraphe*, 32 ('Aujourd'hui Nathalie Sarraute'), 1984: 51–7).

—— (1976*a*). 'Nathalie Sarraute: Sartre s'est trompé à mon sujet', interview with Jean-Louis Ézine, *Les Nouvelles littéraires*, 2552 (30 Sept.): 5.

—— (1976*b*). 'Colloque avec Nathalie Sarraute, 22 avril 1976', interview with Gretchen Rous Besser, *French Review*, 50/2: 284–9.

—— (1978). 'Nathalie Sarraute: Mon théâtre continue mes romans', interview with Lucette Finas, *La Quinzaine littéraire*, 292 (16 Dec.): 4–5.

—— (1979). 'Comment j'ai écrit certains de mes livres', interview with Lucette Finas, *Études littéraires*, 12: 393–401.

—— (1981). 'Nathalie Sarraute', interview with Jean-Louis Ézine, J.-L. Ézine, *Les Écrivains sur la sellette*. Paris: Seuil, 34–9.

—— (1983*a*). 'Nathalie Sarraute', interview with P. Boncenne, *Lire*, 94 (June): 87–92.

—— (1983*b*). 'Portrait de Nathalie', interview with Viviane Forrester, *Magazine littéraire*, 196 (June: 'Nathalie Sarraute'): 18–21.

—— (1984*a*). 'Le Bonheur de l'homme', *Digraphe*, 32 ('Aujourd'hui Nathalie Sarraute'): 58–62.

—— (1984*b*). 'Quand j'écris, je ne suis ni homme ni femme ni chien', interview with Sonia Rykiel, *Les Nouvelles*, 2917 (9 Feb.): 39–41.

—— (1984*c*). 'Nathalie Sarraute Talks About her Life and Works', interview with F. Donnelly and A. Howells, *Romance Studies*, 4: 8–16.

—— (1984*d*). 'Conversation avec Nathalie Sarraute', interview with Serge Fauchereau and Jean Ristat, *Digraphe*, 32 ('Aujourd'hui Nathalie Sarraute'): 9–18.

—— (1984*e*). 'Portrait d'une inconnue: Conversation biographique', interview with Marc Saporta, *L'Arc*, 95 ('Nathalie Sarraute'): 5–23.

—— (1985*a*). 'Conversation with Nathalie Sarraute', interview with Alfred Cismaru, *Telescope*, 4/2: 17–24.

—— (1985*b*). 'Propos sur la technique du roman', interview with Alison Finch and David Kelley, *French Studies*, 39/3: 305–15.

—— (1985*c*). ' "Qu'est-ce qu'il y a, qu'est-ce qui s'est passé? Mais rien": Entretiens avec Nathalie Sarraute', interview with Carmen Licari, *Francofonia*, 9: 3–16.

—— (1986*a*). Untitled lecture from a colloquium on the *Nouveau Roman* at New York University (1982), in Lois Oppenheim (ed.), *Three Decades of the French New Novel*. Urbana, Ill.: University of Illinois Press, 119–31.

—— (1986*b*). 'The New Novel—Past, Present, Future: A Roundtable', with Tom Bishop, François Jost, Robert Pinget, Alain Robbe-Grillet, Michel Rybalka, Claude Simon, Monique Wittig, in Lois Oppenheim (ed.), *Three Decades of the French New Novel*. Urbana, Ill.: University of Illinois Press, 179–94.

—— (1987*a*). *Nathalie Sarraute: Qui êtes-vous?* ed. S. Benmussa. Lyons: La Manufacture. (Includes the essay 'Le Langage dans l'art du roman', pp. 183–202.)

—— (1987*b*). 'Interview de Nathalie Sarraute', interview with Grant E. Kaiser, *Roman 20/50*, 4: 117–27.

—— (1989*a*). 'Intérieur Sarraute', interview with Marianne Alphant, *Libération* (28 Sept.): 21–3.

—— (1989*b*). 'Amare Nathalie', interview with Gabriella Bosco, *La Stampa* (18 Nov.): 15.

—— (1990). 'Dialogue avec Nathalie Sarraute autour de Jean-Paul Sartre', interview with Françoise Dupuy-Sullivan, *Romance Quarterly*, 37/2: 187–92.

—— (1992). 'Leur Jardin secret', interview with Françoise Asso, *La Quinzaine littéraire*, 606 (1 Aug.): 29–30.

—— (1993*a*). 'Un Entretien avec Nathalie Sarraute', interview with Michèle Pardina, *Le Monde* (26 Feb.): 25, 29.

—— (1993*b*). 'Pour Nathalie Sarraute', programme produced by Kaye Mortley and broadcast on France-Culture (18 July).

—— (1994). 'Rencontre: Nathalie Sarraute', interview with Isabelle Huppert, *Cahiers du cinéma*, 477 (Mar. 1994): 7–14.

—— (1996). 'Le Déambulatoire: Entretien avec Nathalie Sarraute', interview with Monique Wittig, *L'Esprit créateur*, 36/2 ('Nathalie Sarraute ou le texte du for intérieur'): 3–8.

CRITICAL WRITINGS ON SARRAUTE

Adert, Laurent (1996). *Les Mots des autres: Lieu commun et création romanesque dans les œuvres de Gustave Flaubert, Nathalie Sarraute et Robert Pinget*. Villeneuve d'Ascq (Nord): Presses universitaires du Septentrion (coll. Objet).

Alazet, Bernard (1990). '*Entre la vie et la mort*: Le Tragique en éclats', *Revue des sciences humaines*, 217 ('Nathalie Sarraute'): 39–48.

Allemand, André (1980). *L'Œuvre romanesque de Nathalie Sarraute*. Neuchâtel: Baconnière.

Arendt, Hannah (1986). '*Les Fruits d'or*: Nathalie Sarraute' (trans. Claude Habib), *Cahiers du G.R.I.F.*, 33 ('Hannah Arendt'): 17–28. (Originally published in New York Review of Books, 5 Mar. 1964: 5–6.)

Asso, Françoise (1995). *Nathalie Sarraute: Une écriture de l'effraction*. Paris: Presses Universitaires de France.

—— (1996). 'La Forme du dialogue', *L'Esprit créateur*, 36/2 ('Nathalie Sarraute ou le texte du for intérieur'): 9–20.

Barbour, Sarah (1993). *Nathalie Sarraute and the Feminist Reader: Identities in Process*. Lewisburg, Pa.: Bucknell University Press; London and Toronto: Associated University Presses.

Bell, Sheila (1981). *Nathalie Sarraute: A Bibliography*. London: Grant & Cutler.

—— (1983). 'The Figure of the Reader in *L'Usage de la parole*', *Romance Studies*, 2: 53–68.

—— (1988). '*Portrait d'un inconnu*' and '*Vous les entendez?*' London: Grant & Cutler.

—— (1996). 'Endings in Autobiography: The Example of *Enfance*', *L'Esprit créateur*, 36/2 ('Nathalie Sarraute ou le texte du for intérieur'): 21–36.

Benmussa, Simone (1984). 'Les Paroles vives', *L'Arc*, 95 ('Nathalie Sarraute'): 76–82.

Besser, Gretchen Rous (1979). *Nathalie Sarraute*. Boston, Mass.: Twayne's World Author Series.

—— (1985). 'Sarraute on Childhood—Her Own', *French Literature Series*, 12 ('Autobiography in French Literature'): 154–61.

Bianciotti, Hector (1984). 'Nathalie Sarraute', *Digraphe*, 32 ('Aujourd'hui Nathalie Sarraute'): 65–8.

Boué, Rachel (1997): *Nathalie Sarraute: La Sensation en quête de parole*. Paris: L'Harmattan.

Brée, Germaine (1986). 'Autogynography', *The Southern Review*, 22/2: 223–30.

—— (1989). 'Experimental Novels? Yes, but Perhaps "Otherwise": Nathalie Sarraute, Monique Wittig', in Ellen G. Friedman and Miriam Fuchs (eds.), *Breaking the Sequence: Women's Experimental Fiction*. Princeton: Princeton University Press, 267–83.

—— (1996). 'Le "For intérieur" et la traversée du siècle', *L'Esprit créateur*, 36/2 ('Nathalie Sarraute ou le texte du for intérieur'): 37–43.

Britton, Celia (1973). 'Language as Text and Language as Theme: An Analysis of the Novels of Nathalie Sarraute' (unpublished doctoral thesis, University of Essex).

—— (1982). 'The Self and Language in the Novels of Nathalie Sarraute', *Modern Language Review*, 77/3: 577–84.

—— (1983). 'Reported Speech and *sous-conversation*: Forms of Intersubjectivity in Nathalie Sarraute's Novels', *Romance Studies*, 2: 69–79.

—— (1992). *The Nouveau Roman: Fiction, Theory and Politics*. Basingstoke and London: The Macmillan Press.

Brulotte, Gaëtan (1984). 'Tropismes et sous-conversation', *L'Arc*, 95 ('Nathalie Sarraute'): 39–54.

Calin, Françoise (1976). *La Vie retrouvée: Étude de l'œuvre romanesque de Nathalie Sarraute*. Paris: Minard.

Charras, Marie-Claude (1982). 'Nathalie Sarraute: Aux portes de la conscience', *Saggi e ricerche di letteratura francese*, 21: 63–83.

Clayton, Alan (1989). *Nathalie Sarraute ou le tremblement de l'écriture*. Paris: Lettres Modernes (Archives des lettres modernes, 238).

—— (1990). 'Coucou . . . attrapez-moi', *Revue des sciences humaines*, 217 ('Nathalie Sarraute'): 9–22.

Cranaki, Mimica, and Belaval, Yvon (1965). *Nathalie Sarraute*. Paris: Gallimard.

Davin, Antonia (1981). 'Nathalie Sarraute's *"disent les imbéciles"*: The Critic's Dilemma', in *New Zealand Journal of French Studies*, 2/1: 56–79.

Dupuy-Sullivan, Françoise (1990). 'Le Lecteur et ses lectures dans *Les Fruits d'or* (Nathalie Sarraute)', *Australian Journal of French Studies*, 27/1: 39–46.

Eakin, Paul John (1990). 'The Referential Aesthetic of Autobiography', *Studies in the Literary Imagination*, 23/2 ('The Vexingly Unverifiable: Truth in Autobiography'): 129–44.

Eigenmann, Eric (1988). 'Sarraute: The Use of Speech', *Yale French Studies* ('After the Age of Suspicion: The French Novel Today', ed. Charles A. Porter): 7–10.

Eliez-Ruegg, Elisabeth (1972). *La Conscience d'autrui et la conscience des objets dans l'œuvre de Nathalie Sarraute*. Berne: Peter Lang.

Finas, Lucette (1978). 'Des corps en eau trouble: Nathalie Sarraute—de *Tropismes* à *Fruits d'or*', in *Le Bruit d'Iris*. Paris: Digraphe Flammarion, 235–50. (Originally published in *Tel Quel*, 20 (1965): 68–77.)

—— (1997). 'Ouvrons!', *La Quinzaine littéraire*, 725 (16 Oct.): 5–6.

Flambard-Weisbart, Véronique (1990). 'Nathalie Sarraute and the Thought from the Outside', *Paroles gelées*, 8: 1–9.

Fleming, John A. (1969). 'The Imagery of Tropism in the Novels of Nathalie Sarraute', in W. M. Frohock (ed.), *Image and Theme*. Cambridge, Mass.: Harvard University Press.

Gosselin, Monique (1991). '*Enfance* de Nathalie Sarraute: Les Mots de la mère', *Revue des sciences humaines*, 222: 121–42.

Goulet, Alain (1989). 'Le Jeu des tropismes sarrautiens', *Estudios franceses* (University of Salamanca, Faculty of Philology), 5: 85–96.

Gratton, Johnnie (1995*a*). 'Autobiography and Fragmentation: The Case of Nathalie Sarraute's *Enfance*', *Nottingham French Studies*, 34/2: 31–40.

—— (1995*b*). 'Towards Narrativity: Nathalie Sarraute's *Enfance*', *Forum for Modern Language Studies*, 31/4: 300–11.

Greene, Robert W. (1983). 'Nathalie Sarraute's *L'Usage de la parole*, or Re(en)trop(iz)ing *Tropismes*', *Novel: A Forum on Fiction*, 16/3: 197–214.

Hanson, Susan A. (1984). 'The Subject and its Simulacra: Nathalie Sarraute's *Portrait d'un inconnu*', *Nuova corrente: Rivista de letteratura*, 31/93–4: 237–62.

Heath, Stephen (1972). *The Nouveau Roman: A Study in the Practice of Writing*. London: Elek.

Hewitt, Leah D. (1983). 'Nathalie Sarraute's *Les Fruits d'or*: Literary Apples of Critical Discord', *Modern Language Studies*, 13/3: 104–11.

—— (1990). *Autobiographical Tightropes*. Lincoln, Nebr., and London: University of Nebraska Press.

Jefferson, Ann (1975). 'Aspects of the Poetics of Fiction: The Novels of Nathalie Sarraute' (unpublished doctoral thesis, University of Oxford).

—— (1977). 'What's in a Name? From Surname to Pronoun in the Novels of Nathalie Sarraute', *PTL: A Journal for Descriptive Poetics and Theory of Literature*, 2: 203–20.

—— (1978). 'Imagery versus Description: The Problematics of Representation in the Novels of Nathalie Sarraute', *Modern Language Review*, 73/3: 513–24.

—— (1980). *The Nouveau Roman and the Poetics of Fiction*. Cambridge: Cambridge University Press.

—— (1990). 'Autobiography as Intertext: Barthes, Sarraute, Robbe-Grillet', in Michael Worton and Judith Still (eds.), *Intertextuality: Theories and Practices*. Manchester and New York: Manchester University Press, 108–29.

—— (1992). 'Materialism and the Mind: Nathalie Sarraute', *Romance Studies*, 20: 31–43.

—— (1996). 'Nathalie Sarraute: Criticism and the "Terrible Desire to Establish Contact"', in *L'Esprit créateur*, 36/2 ('Nathalie Sarraute ou le texte du for intérieur'): 44–62.

Le Gall, Jean (1987). 'Le Thème de l'eau dans *Enfance* de Nathalie Sarraute', *Cahiers du C.E.R.F. XXe*, *3* ('Trois femmes romancières: Duras, Sarraute, Yourcenar'): 23–36.

Lejeune, Philippe (1990). 'Paroles d'enfance', *Revue des sciences humaines*, 217 ('Nathalie Sarraute'): 23–38.

Licari, Carmen (1991). 'L'Usage du dialogue dans le roman de Nathalie Sarraute *Tu ne t'aimes pas*', in S. Stati, F. Hundsnurscher, E. Weigand (eds.), *Dialoganalyse III: Referate der 3. Arbeitstagung, Bologna 1990*. Tübingen: Niemeyer (Beiträge zur Dialogforschung, 1–2), 131–39.

Linsen, Erhart (1981). *Subjekt-Objektbeziehungen bei Balzac, Flaubert und Sarraute unter besonderer Berücksichtigung der Sprachproblematik*. Frankfurt and Berne: Peter Lang (Saarbrücker Arbeiten der Romanistik, 1).

Micha, René (1966). *Nathalie Sarraute*. Paris: Éditions universitaires (Classiques du XXe siècle).

Minogue, Valerie (1981). *Nathalie Sarraute and the War of the Words*. Edinburgh: Edinburgh University Press.

—— (1982). 'Realism and the *Nouveau Roman*', *Romance Studies*, 1: 77–94.

—— (1983). 'Nathalie Sarraute: "L'Usage de la parole"', *Romance Studies*, 2: 35–52.

—— (1986). 'Fragments of a Childhood: Nathalie Sarraute's *Enfance*', *Romance Studies*, 9: 71–83.

—— (1987*a*). 'Ironie et réalité dans les romans de Nathalie Sarraute', *Cahiers du C.E.R.F. XXe*, 3 ('Trois femmes romancières: Duras, Sarraute, Yourcenar'): 7–22.

—— (1987*b*). 'Sticks and Stones: The Weaponry of Words in *Vous les entendez?*', in D. G. Coleman and G. Jondorf (eds.), *Words of Power: Essays in Honour of Alison Fairlie*. Glasgow: Glasgow University Press, 243–65.

—— (1988). 'Nathalie Sarraute's *Enfance*: From Experience of Language to the Language of Experience', in Robert Gibson (ed.), *Studies in French Fiction in Honour of Vivienne Mylne*. London: Grant & Cutler, 209–24.

—— (1990). 'Le Cheval de Troie: À propos de *Tu ne t'aimes pas*', *Revue des sciences humaines*, 217 ('Nathalie Sarraute'): 151–61.

—— (1995). 'Voices, Virtualities and Ventriloquism: Nathalie Sarraute's *Pour un oui ou pour un non*', *French Studies*, 49/2: 164–77.

—— (1996). 'Nathalie Sarraute, Anti-Terrorist: A Reading of *"disent les imbéciles"*', *L'Esprit créateur*, 36/2 ('Nathalie Sarraute ou le texte du for intérieur'): 75–88.

Minor, Anne (1959). 'Nathalie Sarraute: *Tropismes*, *Portrait d'un inconnu*, *Martereau*', *The French Review*, 33: 107–15.

Morot-Sir, Édouard (1981). 'L'Art des pronoms et le nommé dans l'œuvre de Nathalie Sarraute', *Romanic Review*, 72: 204–14.

Mylne, Vivienne (1994). *Le Dialogue dans le roman français de Sorel à Sarraute*. Paris: Universitas, and Oxford: Voltaire Foundation.

Nadeau, Maurice (1980). 'Nathalie Sarraute et le pouvoir du mot', *La Quinzaine littéraire*, 321 (16–31 Mar.): 7.

—— (1984). 'L'Évolution du roman', *Digraphe*, 32 ('Aujourd'hui Nathalie Sarraute'): 92–7.

Nelson, R. J. (1981). 'Territorial Psychology in Nathalie Sarraute's *Les Fruits d'or*', *Symposium*, 35: 307–24.

Newman, A. S. (1976). *Une Poésie des discours: Essai sur les romans de Nathalie Sarraute*. Geneva: Droz.

—— (1996). 'Le Sentiment de culpabilité: Domaine tropismique par excellence?', *L'Esprit créateur*, 36/2 ('Nathalie Sarraute ou le texte du for intérieur'): 89–102.

O'Callaghan, Raylene (1988). 'Voices in Sarraute's *Enfance*', *New Zealand Journal of French Studies*, 9/1: 83–94.

—— (1989). 'Reading Nathalie Sarraute's *Enfance*: Reflections on Critical Validity', *Romanic Review*, 80/3: 445–61.

Orr, Mary (1994). 'The Space of Satire: *Le Planétarium* by Nathalie Sarraute', *Forum for Modern Language Studies*, 30/4: 365–73.

Phillips, John C. (1991). 'La Métaphore, la mère et le conte de fées: A Study of Movements and Displacements in the Work of Nathalie Sarraute' (unpublished doctoral thesis, University of London: Birkbeck College).

Phillips, John C. (1994). *Nathalie Sarraute: Metaphor, Fairy-Tale, and the Feminine of the Text*. New York: Peter Lang.

Picard, Hans Rudolf (1982). 'Die Rolle der direkten Rede und des Dialogs in Romanen der "sous-conversation"' in R. Lachmann (ed.), *Dialogizität*. Munich: Wilhelm Fink, 131–40.

Pierrot, Jean (1990). *Nathalie Sarraute*. Paris: Corti.

Pingaud, Bernard (1963). 'Le Personnage dans l'œuvre de Nathalie Sarraute', *Preuves*, 154: 19–34.

Prince, Gerald (1987). 'Réécriture et fiction dans *"disent les imbéciles"'*, *Neophilologus*, 71: 531–5.

Racevskis, Karlis (1977). 'Irony as a Creative and Critical Force in Three Novels of Nathalie Sarraute', *The French Review*, 51/1: 37–44.

Raffy, Sabine (1988). *Sarraute romancière: Espaces intimes*. New York, Berne, Frankfurt: Peter Lang.

Raillard, Georges (1971). 'Nathalie Sarraute et la violence du texte', *Littérature*, 2: 89–102.

Ricardou, Jean (1967). *Problèmes du nouveau roman*. Paris: Seuil.

—— (1971). *Pour une théorie du nouveau roman*. Paris: Seuil.

—— (1973). *Le Nouveau Roman*. Paris: Seuil (coll. 'Écrivains de toujours').

Rousseau, François-Olivier (1983). 'Une enfance', *Magazine littéraire*, 196 (June: 'Nathalie Sarraute'): 25–6.

Rykner, Arnaud (1988). *Théâtres du Nouveau Roman: Sarraute, Pinget, Duras*. Paris: Corti.

—— (1991). *Nathalie Sarraute*. Paris: Seuil.

—— (1992). 'Narcisse et les mots-miroirs (Sartre, Leiris, Sarraute autobiographes)', *Romanic Review*, 83/1: 81–93.

Savigneau, Josyane (1997). 'Chez Sarraute, les mots se marrent', *Le Monde* (17 Oct.), p. i.

Sheringham, Michael (1989). '*Ego redux*? Strategies in New French Autobiography', *Dalhousie French Studies*, 17: 27–36.

—— (1993). *French Autobiography: Devices and Desires*. Oxford: Clarendon Press.

Smyth, Edmund J. (1986). 'Sarraute's *Enfance* and the Rhetoric of the "Ressenti"', *French Studies Bulletin*, 18: 11–13.

Tadié, Jean-Yves (1984). 'Un traité du roman', *L'Arc*, 95 ('Nathalie Sarraute'): 55–9.

Temple, Ruth Z. (1968). *Nathalie Sarraute*. New York: Columbia University Press ('Columbia Essays on Modern Writers', no. 33).

Tison Braun, Micheline (1971). *Nathalie Sarraute ou la recherche de l'authenticité*. Paris: Gallimard.

Van Roey-Roux, Françoise (1984). '*Enfance* de Nathalie Sarraute ou de la fiction à l'autobiographie', *Études littéraires*, 17/2: 273–82.

Vercier, Bruno (1985). '(Nouveau) Roman et autobiographie: *Enfance* de Nathalie Sarraute', *French Literature Series*, 12 ('Autobiography in French Literature'): 162–70.

Went-Daoust, Yvette (1987). '*Enfance* de Nathalie Sarraute ou le pouvoir de la parole', *Les Lettres romanes*, 41/4: 337–50.

Wittig, Monique (1984). 'Le Lieu de l'action', *Digraphe*, 32 ('Aujourd'hui Nathalie Sarraute'): 69–75.

—— (1996). 'Avatars', *L'Esprit créateur*, 36/2 ('Nathalie Sarraute ou le texte du for intérieur'): 109–16.

Wunderli-Müller, Christine B. (1970). *Le Thème du masque et les banalités dans l'œuvre de Nathalie Sarraute*. Zurich: Juris Druck.

Zeltner, Gerda (1962). 'Nathalie Sarraute et l'impossible réalisme', *Mercure de France*, 1188: 593–608.

—— (1984). 'Quelques Remarques sur l'"art dramatique" de Nathalie Sarraute', *Digraphe*, 32 ('Aujourd'hui Nathalie Sarraute'): 102–7.

GENERAL CRITICAL WORKS

Allemann, Beda (1956). *Ironie und Dichtung*. Pfullingen: Neske.

Assoun, Paul Laurent (1980). 'L'Ironie comme rhétorique de l'inconscient', in (no ed.) *L'Ironie*. Paris: Marketing, 157–65.

Bakhtin, Mikhail M. (1968). 'L'Énoncé dans le roman', *Langages*, 12: 126–32.

—— (1981). *The Dialogic Imagination*, ed. M. Holquist (trans. C. Emerson and M. Holquist). Austin, Tex: University of Texas Press.

—— (1984*a*). *Problems of Dostoevsky's Poetics*, ed. and trans. C. Emerson. Manchester: Manchester University Press.

—— (1984*b*). *Rabelais and his World*, trans. H. Iswolsky. Bloomington, Ind.: Indiana University Press.

Bally, Charles (1912). 'Le Style indirect libre en français moderne', *Germanisch-Romanische Monatsschrift*, 4: 549–56, 597–606.

Banfield, Ann (1973). 'Narrative Style and the Grammar of Direct and Indirect Speech', *Foundations of Language*, 10: 1–39.

Barthes, Roland (1970). *S/Z*. Paris: Seuil.

—— (1973). *Le Plaisir du texte*. Paris: Seuil.

Behler, Ernst (1972). *Klassische Ironie, romantische Ironie, tragische Ironie*. Darmstadt: Wissenschaftliche Buchgesellschaft.

Benjamin, Walter (1974). 'Der Begriff der Kunstkritik in der deutschen Romantik', in *Gesammelte Schriften*, i, ed. R. Tiedemann and H. Schweppenhäuser. Frankfurt am Main: Suhrkamp, 7–122.

Benveniste, Émile (1966). *Problèmes de linguistique générale*, i. Paris: Gallimard.

—— (1970). 'L'Appareil formel de l'énonciation', *Langages*, 17 ('L'Énonciation'): 12–18.

Berrendonner, Alain (1981). *Éléments de pragmatique linguistique*. Paris: Minuit.

Bishop, Lloyd (1989). *Romantic Irony in French Literature from Diderot to Beckett*. Nashville, Tex.: Vanderbilt University Press.

Bleich, David (1980). 'Epistemological Assumptions in the Study of Response', in J. P. Tompkins (ed.), *Reader-Response Criticism: From Formalism to Post-Structuralism*. Baltimore, Md., and London: Johns Hopkins University Press, 134–63. (Originally published as ch. 9 of *Subjective Criticism*, Baltimore, Md.: Johns Hopkins University Press, 1978.)

Booth, Wayne C. (1961). *The Rhetoric of Fiction*. Chicago, Ill.: University of Chicago Press.

—— (1974). *A Rhetoric of Irony*. Chicago, Ill.: University of Chicago Press.

—— (1983). 'The Empire of Irony', *Georgia Review*, 37/4: 719–37.

Bové, Paul A. (1982). 'Irony and the Ironic Imagination', *Contemporary Literature*, 23/2: 244–53.

Bowie, Malcolm (1987). *Freud, Proust, and Lacan: Theory as Fiction*. Cambridge: Cambridge University Press.

—— (1991). *Lacan*. London: Fontana Press.

Brooks, Peter (1984). *Reading for the Plot: Design and Intention in Narrative*. Oxford: Clarendon Press.

Burton, Deirdre (1980). *Dialogue and Discourse: A Sociolinguistic Approach to Modern Drama Dialogue and Naturally Occurring Conversation*. London, Boston, Henley: Routledge & Kegan Paul.

Carroll, David (1981). *The Subject in Question: The Languages of Theory and the Strategies of Fiction*. Chicago, Ill.: University of Chicago Press.

Cerquiglini, Bernard (1984). 'Le Style indirect libre et la modernité', *Langages*, 73: 7–16.

Chambers, Ross (1984). *Story and Situation: Narrative Seduction and the Power of Fiction*. Minneapolis: University of Minnesota Press.

Chatman, Seymour (1978). *Story and Discourse: Narrative Structure in Fiction and Film*. Ithaca, NY, and London: Cornell University Press.

Clark, S. H. (1990). *Paul Ricoeur*. London: Routledge.

Cohn, Dorrit (1978). *Transparent Minds: Narrative Modes for Presenting Consciousness in Fiction*. Princeton, NJ: Princeton University Press.

Compagnon, Antoine (1979). *La Seconde Main: Ou le Travail de la citation*. Paris: Seuil.

Culler, Jonathan (1975). *Structuralist Poetics: Structuralism, Linguistics, and the Study of Literature*. Ithaca, NY: Cornell University Press, and London: Routledge & Kegan Paul.

—— (1981). *The Pursuit of Signs: Semiotics, Literature, Deconstruction*. Ithaca, NY: Cornell University Press, and London: Routledge & Kegan Paul.

—— (1982). *On Deconstruction: Theory and Criticism After Structuralism*. Ithaca, NY: Cornell University Press, and London: Routledge & Kegan Paul.

Dällenbach, Lucien (1977). *Le Récit spéculaire: essai sur la mise en abyme*. Paris: Seuil.

Davis, Robert Con (1983*a*). 'Introduction: Lacan and Narration', *MLN* 98/5 ('Lacan and Narration: The Psychoanalytic Difference in Narrative Theory'): 848–59.

—— (1983*b*). 'Lacan, Poe, and Narrative Repression', *MLN* 98/5 ('Lacan and

Narration: The Psychoanalytic Difference in Narrative Theory'): 983–1005.

de Man, Paul (1979). *Allegories of Reading: Figural Language in Rousseau, Nietzsche, Rilke and Proust*. New Haven, Conn., and London: Yale University Press.

—— (1983). *Blindness and Insight: Essays in the Rhetoric of Contemporary Criticism* (2nd revised edn.). London: Methuen. (Originally published New York: Oxford University Press, 1971.)

Derrida, Jacques (1967*a*). *L'Écriture et la différence*. Paris: Seuil.

—— (1967*b*). *De la grammatologie*. Paris: Minuit.

—— (1971). 'La Mythologie blanche', *Poétique*, 2: 1–52.

—— (1972). 'Signature, événement, contexte', *Marges de la philosophie*. Paris: Minuit, 365–93.

—— (1975). 'Le Facteur de la vérité', *Poétique*, 21: 96–147.

—— (1977). 'Limited Inc.', *Glyph*, 2: 162–254.

Dillon, George I., and Kirchhoff, Frederick (1976). 'On the Form and Function of Free Indirect Style', *PTL: A Journal for Descriptive Poetics and Theory of Literature*, 1: 431–40.

Dor, Joël (1985). *Introduction à la lecture de Lacan, i. L'Inconscient structuré comme un langage*. Paris: Denoël.

Eco, Umberto (1979). *The Role of the Reader: Explorations in the Semiotics of Texts*. Bloomington, Ind., and London: Indiana University Press.

Enright, D. J. (1986). *The Alluring Problem: An Essay on Irony*. Oxford: Oxford University Press.

Felman, Shoshana (1977). 'To Open the Question', *Yale French Studies*, 55–6 ('Literature and Psychoanalysis: The Question of Reading: Otherwise'): 5–10.

—— (1983). 'Beyond Oedipus: The Specimen Story of Psychoanalysis', *MLN* 98/5 ('Lacan and Narration: The Psychoanalytic Difference in Narrative Theory'): 1021–53.

—— (1987). *Jacques Lacan and the Adventure of Insight: Psychoanalysis in Contemporary Culture*. Cambridge, Mass., and London: Harvard University Press.

Fish, Stanley (1980). *Is There a Text in This Class? The Authority of Interpretive Communities*. Cambridge, Mass., and London: Harvard University Press.

—— (1981). 'Why No-one's Afraid of Wolfgang Iser', *Diacritics*, 11/1: 2–13.

Freud, Sigmund (1953–74). *The Standard Edition of the Complete Psychological Works*, i–xxiv, ed. and trans. J. Strachey. London: The Hogarth Press and The Institute of Psycho-Analysis.

Freund, Elizabeth (1987). *The Return of the Reader: Reader-Response Criticism*. London and New York: Methuen.

Furst, Lilian R. (1985). 'Irony and the Spirit of the Age', in W. Balakian *et al.* (eds.), *Proceedings of the Tenth Congress of the International Comparative Literature Association*, i. New York: Garland Press, 94–8.

Genette, Gérard (1972*a*). 'Avatars du cratylisme', *Poétique*, 11: 367–94.

—— (1972*b*). *Figures III*. Paris: Seuil.

Genette, Gérard (1991). *Fiction et diction*. Paris: Seuil.

Grisé, Catherine (1990). 'Ironie dramatique ou ironie cognitive', *Neophilologus*, 74/3: 353–60.

Guellouz, Suzanne (1992). *Le Dialogue*. Paris: Presses Universitaires de France.

Guespin, Louis (1984). 'Introduction', *Langages*, 74 ('Dialogue et interaction verbale'): 5–14.

Hamon, Philippe (1982). 'Analyser l'ironie', *Michigan Romance Studies*, 2 ('Discours et pouvoir'): 165–75.

Handwerk, Gary (1985). *Irony and Ethics in Narrative: From Schlegel to Lacan*. New Haven, Conn., and London: Yale University Press.

Holdcroft, David (1983). 'Irony as a Trope, and Irony as Discourse', *Poetics Today*, 4/3 ('The Ironic Discourse'): 493–511.

Holland, Norman N. (1980). 'Unity Identity Text Self', in J. P. Tompkins (ed.), *Reader-Response Criticism: From Formalism to Post-Structuralism*. Baltimore, Md., and London: Johns Hopkins University Press, 118–33. (Originally published in *PMLA* 90/5 (1975): 813–22.)

Holquist, Michael (1990). *Dialogism*. London and New York: Routledge.

Holub, Robert C. (1984). *Reception Theory: A Critical Introduction*. London and New York: Methuen.

Hörisch, Jochen (1976). *Die fröhliche Wissenschaft der Poesie*. Frankfurt am Main: Suhrkamp.

Hutcheon, Linda (1978). 'Ironie et parodie: Stratégie et structure', *Poétique*, 36 ('Ironie'): 467–77.

——— (1981). 'Ironie, satire, parodie: Une approche pragmatique de l'ironie', *Poétique*, 46: 140–55.

Iser, Wolfgang (1974). *The Implied Reader: Patterns of Communication in Prose Fiction from Bunyan to Beckett*. Baltimore, Md., and London: Johns Hopkins University Press. (Originally published as *Der implizierte Leser: Kommunikationsformen des Romans von Bunyan bis Beckett*, Munich: W. Fink, 1972.)

——— (1978). *The Act of Reading: A Theory of Aesthetic Response*. Baltimore, Md.: Johns Hopkins University Press, and London: Routledge & Kegan Paul. (Originally published as *Der Akt des Lesens: Theorie ästhetischer Wirkung*, Munich: W. Fink, 1976.)

——— (1980). 'Interaction Between Text and Reader', in S. R. Suleiman and I. Crosman (eds.), *The Reader in the Text: Essays on Audience and Interpretation*. Princeton, and Guildford: Princeton University Press, 106–19.

——— (1981). 'Talk Like Whales: A Reply to Stanley Fish', *Diacritics*, 11/3: 82–7.

Jakobson, Roman (1956). 'Two Aspects of Language and Two Types of Aphasic Disturbances', in R. Jakobson and M. Halle, *Fundamentals of Language*. The Hague: Mouton & Co., 53–82.

Jameson, Frederic (1977). 'Imaginary and Symbolic in Lacan: Marxism, Psychoanalytic Criticism, and the Problem of the Subject', *Yale French Studies*, 55–6

('Literature and Psychoanalysis: The Question of Reading: Otherwise'): 338–95.

Jankélévitch, Vladimir (1964). *L'Ironie*. Paris: Flammarion.

Jauss, Hans Robert (1982). *Toward an Aesthetic of Reception*, trans. Timothy Bahti, with an Introduction by Paul de Man. Brighton: Harvester.

Jefferson, Ann (1983). 'Balzac and the *Nouveau Roman*: Problems of Reading', *Romance Studies*, 2: 166–80.

—— (1986). 'Beyond Contract: The Reader of Autobiography and Stendhal's *Vie de Henry Brulard*', *Romance Studies*, 9: 53–69.

—— (1989). 'Bodymatters: Self and Other in Bakhtin, Sartre and Barthes', in K. Hirschkop and D. Shepherd (eds.), *Bakhtin and Cultural Theory*. Manchester: Manchester University Press, 152–77.

Johnson, Barbara (1977). 'The Frame of Reference: Poe, Lacan, Derrida', *Yale French Studies*, 55–6 ('Literature and Psychoanalysis: The Question of Reading: Otherwise'): 457–505.

—— (1980). 'The Critical Difference: BartheS/BalZac', in *The Critical Difference: Essays in the Contemporary Rhetoric of Reading*. Baltimore, Md., and London: Johns Hopkins University Press, 3–12.

Kearney, Richard (1984). *Dialogues with Contemporary Continental Thinkers*. Manchester: Manchester University Press.

Kerbrat-Orecchioni, Catherine (1978). 'Problèmes de l'ironie', in C. Kerbrat-Orecchioni *et al.* (eds.), *L'Ironie*. Lyons: Presses Universitaires de Lyon (Travaux du Centre de Recherches linguistiques et sémiologiques de Lyon), 10–46.

—— (1980). 'L'Ironie comme trope', *Poétique*, 41: 108–27.

Kierkegaard, Søren (1989). *The Concept of Irony, with Continual Reference to Socrates*. Princeton: Princeton University Press.

Kloepfer, Rolf (1980). 'Dynamic Structures in Narrative Literature: The Dialogic Principle', *Poetics Today*, 1/4 ('Narratology II: The Fictional Text and the Reader'): 115–34.

Koelb, Clayton (1988). *Inventions of Reading: Rhetoric and the Literary Imagination*. Ithaca, NY, and London: Cornell University Press.

Kristeva, Julia (1969). *Sèméiotikè: Recherches pour une sémanalyse*. Paris: Seuil.

Kundera, Milan (1988). *The Art of the Novel*. New York, Cambridge, Philadelphia: Harper & Row.

Lacan, Jacques (1966). *Écrits*. Paris: Seuil.

—— (1973). *Le Séminaire XI: Les Quatre Concepts fondamentaux de la psychanalyse*, ed. J.-A. Miller. Paris: Seuil.

—— (1975). *Le Séminaire I: Les Écrits techniques de Freud*, ed. J.-A. Miller. Paris: Seuil.

—— (1978). *Le Séminaire II: Le Moi dans la théorie de Freud et dans la technique de la psychanalyse*, ed. J.-A. Miller. Paris: Seuil.

—— (1981). *Le Séminaire III: Les Psychoses*, ed. J.-A. Miller. Paris: Seuil.

Lacoue-Labarthe, Philippe, and Nancy, Jean-Luc (1978). *L'Absolu littéraire: Théorie de la littérature du romantisme allemand*. Paris: Seuil.

Lang, Candace D. (1988). *Irony/Humor: Critical Paradigms*. Baltimore, Md., and London: Johns Hopkins University Press.

Lemaire, Anika (1977). *Jacques Lacan* (4th revised edn.). Brussels: Mardaga. (Originally published Brussels: Denart, 1970.)

Lodge, David (1977). *The Modes of Modern Writing: Metaphor, Metonymy and the Typology of Modern Literature*. Ithaca, NY: Cornell University Press.

McHale, Brian (1978). 'Free Indirect Discourse: A Survey of Recent Accounts', *PTL: A Journal for Descriptive Poetics and Theory of Literature*, 3: 249–87.

—— (1987). *Postmodernist Fiction*. New York: Methuen.

Maclean, Ian (1985). 'Un Dialogue de sourds? Some Implications of the Austin-Searle-Derrida Debate', *Paragraph: The Journal of the Modern Critical Theory Group*, 5: 1–26.

Madou, Jean-Pol (1987). 'Ironie socratique, ironie romanesque, ironie poétique', *French Literature Series*, 14: 62–73.

Mehlman, Jeffrey (1972a). 'The "Floating Signifier": From Lévi-Strauss to Lacan', *Yale French Studies*, 48 ('French Freud: Structural Studies in Psychoanalysis'): 10–37.

—— (1972b). 'Introduction and Notes to J. Lacan, "Seminar on the Purloined Letter" ' trans. J. Mehlman, *Yale French Studies*, 48 ('French Freud: Structural Studies in Psychoanalysis'): 38–72.

Michaels, Walter Benn (1980). 'The Interpreter's Self: Peirce on the Cartesian Subject', in J. P. Tompkins (ed.), *Reader-Response Criticism: From Formalism to Post-Structuralism*. Baltimore, Md., and London: Johns Hopkins University Press, 185–200. (Originally published in *Georgia Review*, 31 (1977): 383–402.)

Muecke, Douglas C. (1969). *The Compass of Irony*. London: Methuen.

—— (1978). 'Analyses de l'ironie', *Poétique*, 36 ('Ironie'): 478–94.

—— (1982). *Irony and the Ironic* (2nd edn.). London: Methuen ('Critical Idiom').

—— (1983). 'Images of Irony', *Poetics Today*, 4/3 ('The Ironic Discourse'): 399–413.

Ong, Walter J. (1977). *Interfaces of the Word: Studies in the Evolution of Consciousness and Culture*. Ithaca, NY, and London: Cornell University Press.

Pascal, Blaise (1953). *Pensées et opuscules*, ed. Léon Brunschvicg. Paris: Hachette (coll. Classiques).

Pascal, Roy (1977). *The Dual Voice*. Manchester: Manchester University Press.

Piwowarczyk, Mary-Ann (1976). 'The Narratee and the Situation of Enunciation: A Reconsideration of Prince's Theory', *Genre*, 9: 161–77.

Poulet, Georges (1980). 'Criticism and the Experience of Interiority', in J. P. Tompkins (ed.), *Reader-Response Criticism: From Formalism to Post-Structuralism*. Baltimore, Md., and London: Johns Hopkins University Press, 41–9. (Originally published as 'Phenomenology of Reading', *New Literary History*, 1/1 (1969): 53–68.)

Prendergast, Christopher (1986). *The Order of Mimesis: Balzac, Stendhal, Nerval, Flaubert*. Cambridge: Cambridge University Press.

Prince, Gerald (1973). 'Introduction à l'étude du narrataire', *Poétique*, 14: 178–96.

Proust, Marcel (1987). *Du côté de chez Swann*, ed. B. Brun and A. Herschberg-Pierrot. Paris: GF Flammarion.

Ramazani, Vaheed K. (1989). 'Lacan/Flaubert: Towards a Psychopoetics of Irony', *Romanic Review*, 80/4: 548–59.

Ray, William (1977). 'Recognizing Recognition: The Intra-Textual and Extra-Textual Critical Persona', *Diacritics*, 7/4: 20–33.

—— (1984). *Literary Meaning: From Phenomenology to Deconstruction*. Oxford: Blackwell.

Reid, Ian (1990). 'What is a Textual Exchange?', *AUMLA* 74 ('Narrative Issues'): 10–24.

Ricoeur, Paul (1965). *De l'interprétation*. Paris: Seuil (coll. L'Ordre philosophique).

—— (1976). *Interpretation Theory: Discourse and the Surplus of Meaning*. Fort Worth, Tex.: The Texas Christian University Press.

—— (1979). 'The Metaphorical Process as Cognition, Imagination, and Feeling', in S. Sacks (ed.), *On Metaphor*. Chicago, Ill., and London: University of Chicago Press, 141–57. (Originally published in *Critical Inquiry*, 5/1 (1978): 143–59.)

—— (1981). 'Narrative Time', in W. J. T. Mitchell (ed.), *On Narrative*. Chicago, Ill. and London: University of Chicago Press, 165–86.

—— (1983–5). *Temps et récit*, i–iii. Paris: Seuil.

—— (1984). 'Paul Ricoeur', interview with Richard Kearney, in R. Kearney, *Dialogues With Contemporary Continental Thinkers*. Manchester: Manchester University Press, 15–45.

—— (1991). 'L'Identité narrative', *Revue des sciences humaines*, 221: 35–47.

Rimmon-Kenan, Shlomith (1980). 'The Paradoxical Status of Repetition', *Poetics Today*, 1/4 ('Narratology II: The Fictional Text and the Reader'): 151–9.

Robbe-Grillet, Alain (1963). *Pour un Nouveau Roman*. Paris: Minuit.

Rougé, Bertrand (1988a). 'L'Ironie, ou la double représentation', *Lendemains*, 13/50: 34–40.

—— (1988b). 'Le "Premier Étonnement", ou l'ironie comme re-présentation de l'origine (du langage)', in (no ed.) *Représentations de l'origine: Littérature, histoire, civilisation*. Saint-Denis and Paris: Université de la Réunion and Didier-Érudition, 111–31.

Saussure, Ferdinand de (1972). *Cours de linguistique générale*, ed. T. de Mauro. Paris: Payot.

Schafer, Roy (1981). 'Narration in the Psychoanalytic Dialogue', in W. J. T. Mitchell (ed.), *On Narrative*. Chicago, Ill., and London: University of Chicago Press, 25–49.

Schlegel, Friedrich (1958–). *Kritische Friedrich-Schlegel-Ausgabe*, ed. E. Behler, J.-J. Anstett, H. Eichner. Munich and Paderborn: Schöningh.

Scholes, Robert (1981). 'Language, Narrative, and Anti-Narrative', in W. J. T. Mitchell (ed.), *On Narrative*. Chicago, Ill., and London: University of Chicago Press, 200–8.

—— (1985). *Textual Power: Literary Theory and the Teaching of English*. New Haven, Conn., and London: Yale University Press.

252

BIBLIOGRAPHY

Scholes, Robert (1989). *Protocols of Reading*. New Haven, Conn., and London: Yale University Press.

Searle, John R. (1977). 'Reiterating the Differences: A Reply to Derrida', *Glyph*, 1: 198–208.

—— (1979). 'Metaphor', in A. Ortony (ed.), *Metaphor and Thought*. Cambridge: Cambridge University Press, 92–123.

Shepherd, David (1989). 'Bakhtin and the Reader', in K. Hirschkop and D. Shepherd (eds.), *Bakhtin and Cultural Theory*. Manchester: Manchester University Press, 91–108.

Smith, Barbara Herrnstein (1978). *On the Margins of Discourse: The Relation of Literature to Language*. Chicago, Ill., and London: University of Chicago Press.

—— (1981). 'Narrative Versions, Narrative Theories', in W. J. T. Mitchell (ed.), *On Narrative*. Chicago, Ill., and London: University of Chicago Press, 209–32.

Smith, Keren (1990). 'Dialogue as a Basis for Novelistic Structure: A Reexamination of "Polyphony" and "Intertextuality" in Dostoevsky and Robbe-Grillet', *AUMLA* 74 ('Narrative Issues'): 124–35.

Sperber, Dan, and Wilson, Deirdre (1978). 'Les Ironies comme mentions', *Poétique*, 36 ('Ironie'): 399–412.

—— (1981). 'Irony and the Use-Mention Distinction', in P. Cole (ed.), *Radical Pragmatics*. New York: Academic Press, 295–318.

—— (1986). *Relevance: Communication and Cognition*. Oxford: Blackwell.

Strohschneider-Kors, Ingrid (1960). *Die romantische Ironie in Theorie und Gestaltung*. Tübingen: Niemeyer.

Suleiman, Susan Rubin (1980a). 'Redundancy and the "Readable" Text', *Poetics Today*, 1/3 ('Narratology I: Poetics of Fiction'): 119–42.

—— (1980b). 'Introduction: Varieties of Audience-Oriented Criticism', in S. Suleiman and I. Crosman (eds.), *The Reader in the Text: Essays on Audience and Interpretation*. Princeton and Guildford: Princeton University Press, 3–45.

Todorov, Tzvetan (1970). 'Problèmes de l'énonciation', *Langages*, 17 ('L'Énonciation'): 3–11.

Tompkins, Jane P. (1980a). 'An Introduction to Reader-Response Criticism', in J. P. Tompkins (ed.), *Reader-Response Criticism: From Formalism to Post-Structuralism*. Baltimore, Md., and London: Johns Hopkins University Press, pp. ix–xxvi.

—— (1980b). 'The Reader in History: The Changing Shape of Literary Response', in J. P. Tompkins (ed.), *Reader-Response Criticism: From Formalism to Post-Structuralism*. Baltimore, Md., and London: Johns Hopkins University Press, 201–32.

Valéry, Paul (1957). *Œuvres*. Paris: Gallimard (Bibliothèque de la Pléiade).

Voloshinov, V. N. (1973). *Marxism and the Philosophy of Language*, trans. L. Matejka and I. R. Titunik. New York: Seminar Press. (Originally published as *Marksizm i Filosofija Jazyka*, Leningrad, 1930.)

Walser, Martin (1981). *Selbstbewußtsein und Ironie*. Frankfurt am Main: Suhrkamp.

Wilde, Alan (1981). *Horizons of Assent: Modernism, Postmodernism, and the Ironic Imagination*. Baltimore, Md.: Johns Hopkins University Press.

Wright, Elizabeth (1984). *Psychoanalytic Criticism: Theory in Practice*. London and New York: Methuen.

Yell, Susan (1990). 'Control and Conflict: Dialogue in Prose Fiction', *AUMLA* 74 ('Narrative Issues'): 136–53.

Ziedler, Heide (1983). 'Postromantic Irony in Postmodernist Times', in M. Couturier (ed.), *Representation and Performance in Postmodern Fiction*. Montpellier: Delta, 85–98.

INDEX